Early Doors

My Life and the Theatre

Philip Burton   (Alan Grossman.)

Early Doors
My Life and the Theatre

by *Philip Burton*

---

with a Preface by Agnes de Mille

The Dial Press, Inc. New York 1969

To R. and E. with love

Contents

Preface by Agnes de Mille

I first came to know Philip Burton during the acrimonious and quarrelsome negotiations between the Society of Stage Directors and Choreographers of New York and the League of New York Theaters. I had heard of him as Richard Burton's father. He had come into the production of *Camelot* at a moment of dire peril when the entire creative staff became ill, took to their hotel beds, and issued ringing orders that nothing whatever was to be done while they lay flat. He kept the show in a heartening state of status quo while there seemed to be universal megrims, that is, two of the staff had heart attacks, one grave, and the third bleeding ulcers. The show did not fall apart and for one month no one lost courage, which is a testament to P. Burton's spiritual efficacy. And, indeed, after meeting and conferring with him, Alan Lerner decided to take a good bit of his advice. Under his direction the show was largely reshaped, one hour cut from its running time and several new songs added. It was part of the agreement, however, that Philip Burton was to get no credit whatever.

"Why did you take on such an onerous job?" I asked him later when I knew him.

"Because Richard needed me."

There is no more direct key to his character: If there is need, Burton is there.

There was need at that council table. I have always flattered myself I could handle men in a sort of workmanlike, easily forgettable manner, but here they were giving away or keeping chunks of property, residuals, rights, credits, royalties, working prerogatives, power. My charm thinned. I thought we were talking about justice, and we were. Therefore they yelled. They hollered and yelled until I, the only woman present, begged, "Please don't scream. It unnerves me."

"What?" said a famous producer. "You a theatre woman? unnerved by shouting?"

I was, you know. I'd never been exposed to it before—all kinds of pressure, even brutality, but not oral coercion—not hysteria like this.

Then Philip spoke. "The point is, you see," and his quiet voice, with unequivocal diction, pinpointed our dispute, evaluated it, placed it in context, and offered an exact case to each side. The world lost a judge here. They had to quiet down. He'd shocked them into thinking.

He has persisted in this acetylene logic for eight years at our meetings, quietly, for he never raises his voice, exactly, justly, with prescience and with knowledge to point out, not always the law —we have an excellent counsel for that—but the justice, the feasibility and, perhaps most important of all, the desirability. Burton keeps his cool in an Olympian style. When he gives his opinion you stop and consider, because you know you had better. His opinion is grounded.

He has other admirable qualifications for being our helper. He is precise. Someone says, "About fifteen hundred." "Wait a minute, just a minute there," comes his clipped speech. "I've figured it out by the hour; it comes to one thousand three hundred forty-three dollars and seventy-nine cents, and it's three and a half hours, not four." Trivial? Money-saving, labor-saving, exact. Like a thermometer. If you're going to talk about figures, get them right. If you're going to talk about feelings, get them right too. Can you be precise about feelings? Certainly, says Philip. Why not? They're perfectly recognizable things.

He is precise, but not inflexible when he lectures and teaches.

He promised to give us a speech on Shakespeare after our general annual union meeting in the small, smoky Belasco room of Sardi's Restaurant. We ended business at 12:23 A.M. We'd begun at 9:00 P.M. We were dazed.

"I think you would like to go home," said Philip. "I certainly would." (Cries of "No! No! Speech! Speech! What do you think we came for?") "All right. Fifteen minutes. Not a half-minute more." And he launched himself as off a rocket pad with an exactly (but to the second) fifteen-minute discourse on the playing of Shakespeare. You will find some parts of it in the last chapters of this book. We sat up. We sat forward. We cheered with excitement.

"More, please."

"No, that's it. I'm tired. You're tired. Goodnight."

Well, I enrolled in his classes. I couldn't do the homework because I was choreographing a show among other things and so I couldn't perform, but I could listen. I learned about speech, about sound and rhythm, about tonalities and dynamics, about playwriting, and yes, about choreography, a great deal about choreography. Incidentally, I learned many things about Shakespeare, who repays study.

I saw Philip take the ungifted and the very gifted. He ripped Diana Sands apart, for instance. She could stand it and she could profit by it. She went on to stardom.

He has not mentioned his pupils in this book because he is terribly reluctant to lean on other people's lives, he is fastidious about this to the point of silence, but of course they are noteworthy—Richard Burton, whom he transformed from a brilliant, turbulent, disruptive teenager into one of the greatest theatre men of our age, George Grizzard, Keir Dullea, Maximilian Schell,

Diana Sands, Dina Merrill, Jack Cassidy, Salome Jens, James Daly, Robert Drivas. Ask them how they feel about their teacher and they answer like disciples.

And me—ask me.

He is a craftsman, an expert, a precisionist. In a world given over either to mechanics, or to the vague gastric fantasies of the unsure, this is a welcome service. None of the wonder dims in studying how, in recognizing why. The more he sees, the more he marvels. And all he says to his pupils is: Read! Think! Recognize! The mystery is in the poem, not in your fuzzy eyesight, he says. Oh, how reassuring! How rewarding!

The last chapters of this book are pure gold for anyone concerned with the theatre arts. But throughout the whole there are scattered terse bits of philosophic wisdom he learned under fire on the battlefront, not just about the theatre—about life and about people. They're true, they're economic, and they're unforgettable. The earlier chapters, the progress toward learning, are very touching indeed. Other people we can name have had possibly greater success. But I think none have had more joy, and this blessed happiness in work he has known all along the way. This is a wonderful thing.

Burton is a catalyst. He was an instructor in mathematics. He is no longer. He was a schoolmaster—not now. What drove this young, rather pedantic, reticent schoolteacher to try the theatre of the world, to meet and master the demons, to shape, incite, promote and proselytize?—Not religion, not patriotism, not social reform—but the dreamings and ravings of wild immortal poets. What made him?

Reader, turn the page.

Foreword

On Thursday, March 16, 1967, Mr. William Decker of The Dial Press and I had a very pleasant lunch at Le Marmiton, a Manhattan restaurant where the lunchtime clientele is predominantly male and expense account, the double guarantee of good food. Mr. Decker had read a book review of mine in the *Saturday Review* and thought there might be a book in me. Actors in my Shakespeare classes and people who had heard me lecture had often suggested that I should write a book, but I was always content with the implied compliment and appalled by the prospect of the work involved. I am in large part an actor by instinct and, not to be modest, endowment, and so lecturing comes easily because of the stimulation of the audience, but the lonely task of writing is quite another matter. It took Mr. Decker to persuade me to attempt it.

But what kind of a book should it be? Scholarly? No; too much work resulting in too small an audience; I could not face the tedium of footnotes, cross-references, bibliographies. A book specifically for actors? No; too restricted an audience, and an impoverished one at that. An autobiography? No; too presumptuous. What then? Certainly a book about theatre and drama, but a very personal one, with freedom to follow my memories. A man of the theatre once said of me with amused disparagement, "The trouble with you is that you are stagestruck." This might be said of innumerable young people, but the point of the remark was that I was sixty at the time, and it was true of me, and it still is. I love theatre, as spectator, performer, director, teacher. I get a deep satisfaction from reading plays and am blessed with the kind of theatrical imagination that often makes the performance on the stage of my mind more vivid than that in the playhouse. I enjoy the company of theatre people more than that of any others; I even enjoy their egotisms, their trivial enthusiasms, their absurd values, their childish vanities, which both fascinate and revolt the great majority of worthy people upon whom the world depends.

So what follows will be the theatrical autobiography of a stage-struck man, in which random memories will give rise to divers musings. Most of our memories become shaped and polished by time and telling, and it may well be that some of mine are no longer strictly factual; nor can I vouch for the accuracy of some of the stories I shall recount. I can only hope that in themselves they may provide some entertainment and that the musings they prompt may provide some stimulation. Why not check the accuracy of my memories and stories? Not merely from laziness, but because the form in which I cherish them best serves the point I wish to make: Truth is stranger than fact.

To whom is the book addressed? To all those who have found in the theatre those rich moments of self-revelation which make them aware that they are not alone even in their most secret experiences, those sparkling moments of comedy that give a new impetus to mind and spirit, those profound moments in which the veils that cover the mystery of existence are rent in twain.

Early Doors

My Life and the Theatre

Chapter One

Mountain Ash

How many times have parents, alternately doting and scared, said, "I don't know where he gets it from," as some uninhibited teen-ager gives a lethal imitation of Uncle Harry! The origin of my early and deep absorption with the theatre is such a mystery. Perhaps my father had some artistic leanings. He certainly had instincts of revolt against a settled bourgeois existence. Born of a lower-middle-class family in Staffordshire, he had twice run away to the Army, only to be twice "bought-out." Later he escaped to the Klondike of South Wales in the Coal Rush, where he met my mother whose family had also been drawn to the coalfield, in her case from Somersetshire. They met in the mining town of Mountain Ash, and there they married and there I was born. My father was a powerfully built and gentle man, with a quiet sense of humor and a moustache that came and went and came again. He liked beer, big meals, and my mother and me. My mother had the body of a kitten, the heart of a lion, and the will of a lion tamer.

My father brought with him two unlikely instruments for work in the mines, a clarinet and a violin, from which I believe he extracted more pleasure than he gave. When he became a settled citizen, a feat which my resolute mother accomplished, among the first substantial pieces of furniture in the home was a piano, which he also played for his own pleasure rather than that of the neighbors. And we really had neighbors, for we lived in one of those houses that only stand up because they are joined on to others. I soon learned to read music, with some slight help from my father, but, quite unlike him, I wanted to show off at the piano. Chained audiences in the "front room" were forced to endure such items as Handel's Dead March from *Saul*; I specialized in dirgelike music because the tempo was congenial to my untrained fingers.

The fact that I didn't try to play the violin is indicative of something in me—a reluctance to make a fool of myself during those early stages of agonizing scraping. The same reluctance has always made me timorous of opening my mouth in a foreign language. I would never even try to speak Welsh in my hometown, although I had won prizes in the language at the grammar school, but my acquired Welsh was literary and correct and seemed to have little in common with what I heard in the playground. Strangely enough, I have never had the slightest difficulty in risking making a fool of myself on stage.

My father's violin was the center of an exciting episode in my life. When I was fourteen, my father was killed by a fall of roof in the mine, leaving me to complete my education and look after my mother, who was fifty-nine years old; I had been a late child. This is a book about the theatre and me, and only peripherally about life and me, so I shall not recount yet another story of years of struggle, but the story of the violin has some significance for my present purpose. I was examining it one day, soon after my father was killed, and I noticed a faded label inside. After some contortion I managed to read it. To the best of my memory it said: "Amati fecit in Cremona 1641." I had enough Latin to read it, but all it meant to me was that it was old and might therefore be valuable. I took it to my church choirmaster, a remarkable bachelor who did much for my out-of-school education, in life rather more than in letters. The "Amati" meant something to him, and I gathered that, if it really were genuine, the future that seemed endlessly difficult could suddenly be eased. He decided to take it to London for an evaluation. The result was a trick of the siren Fates, those "juggling fiends . . . That keep the word of promise to our ear, And break it to our hope." The violin was indeed an Amati, but it had an invisible crack in the bridge, which made it of little value. It was worth £25. That, in our state of poverty, was a handsome sum—we were managing to live somehow on a compensation allowance of £6 a month, at that time $30—but with a touch of Byronic romanticism, I refused to sell it. A few years later, while still pinchingly poor, I gave it away to a very promising violin student, who subsequently gave up his musical career to become an Anglican priest. Soon afterwards he married a Plymouth Sister, begot several children, and then complicated all their lives by converting to Roman Catholicism and, willy-nilly, becoming a layman again. Now both he and the violin have passed from my ken. The story of the Amati seems to me to have some relevance to that part of me that finds the theatre irresistible. I have no idea how my father acquired the violin, but the possession of it bespeaks something in him that I am happy to have inherited, and my theatrical munificence in disposing of it I find amusing rather than admirable. It was a performance aimed at the appreciation and approval of a very select audience—myself.

I performed a similarly romantic gesture when I first began to earn my living. This was as a teacher, not yet twenty-one years old, of the most unlikely combination of subjects, mathematics and Latin. I subsequently thought I had been given the job because I was the only applicant who professed sufficient knowledge of both subjects. I was desperately in debt after four years of university. I had won a scholarship to the university at the absurd age of 16—if you have the right kind of intelligence, it's easy to be brilliant in mathematics at that age—but it was sadly inadequate to keep my mother and me in the simple necessities. So when I started to earn, every possible penny went to reduce my debt at the bank, which had been guaranteed by my choirmaster-mentor. I allowed myself no luxuries, which probably accounts for the fact that I never smoked, and I felt myself being obsessed by perpetual thoughts about money, so one Saturday night, having on me a precious ten-shilling note that was to be my pocket money for four weeks, I made the grand gesture by going out and giving it to the first beggar I saw; one side of me applauded, but the other blushed for shame.

Early poverty leaves deep scars that no later grafting of financial security will ever quite efface. I once discussed this with Sean O'Casey and he told me that one of the amusing results of his early poverty—and his was incomparably worse than mine —was that he could never cut the strings on a parcel; however intricate and numerous the knots, he would patiently untie every one. But my reaction to an awareness of the cramping danger was to make a dramatic gesture of freeing myself. The point is that the gesture was, and still is on occasion, dramatic.

I know exactly when I first became aware of the magic of words in the mouth of a master. I think I must have been about ten at the time. What I years later learned was called a diseur came to Mountain Ash. I still, and shall always, remember his name: Fred Duxbury. He was billed as an elocutionist and he recited the whole of Dickens' *A Christmas Carol* from the pulpit of the Wesleyan Chapel, and for one young boy in his audience a new heaven and a new earth were revealed, a very private heaven and a very public earth. How good he really was I cannot tell. Only recently I went to hear a much publicized gentleman give a similar performance of *A Christmas Carol* and was so embarrassed and irritated that I could not but leave at the intermission; and yet there might have been another young boy in his audience whose life was transformed by that performance. I suppose the debatable conclusion to be drawn from this experience is: Better a bad performance for the uninitiated than no performance at all.

I forthwith determined to emulate Mr. Duxbury and set about learning the whole of *A Christmas Carol*. My recollection is that I

4

had no real difficulty with what most people would have considered a gigantic task. Memory is a queer fish. I have never had difficulty in learning words, particularly if I respect them, but I am unable to play anything on the piano from memory. In the school at which I subsequently taught I played the piano for morning assembly at which a hymn was sung and the Lord's Prayer chanted to some music specially composed for us by Sir Walford Davies. I must have played that Lord's Prayer setting many hundreds of times until the original manuscript became limp, tired, and worn. One day it was missing. I managed the opening chord, but could not go on. Fortunately the assembly reacted to that opening chord like Pavlov's dogs, and I discovered that the only function of the piano and me had been to keep them on the leash, and they were chorusing a lusty "Amen" when they should still have been asking deliverance from evil.

As people get older they complain of lapses of memory and attribute them to advancing age. I doubt this. I think we remember most easily what really matters to us, and when our sense of values of what matters changes, so does our memory. Thus at 63 I find my memory for great words as strong as ever, but people's names now quickly elude me, and I'm sure it's because deep down I no longer think it so important to remember them. And words last in my memory only so long as they deserve to. Dickens has long faded, but Shakespeare remains.

Once the ten-year-old boy had committed *A Christmas Carol* to memory, his problem was to find an audience, and here I have no clear recollection, which means that whatever happened I didn't achieve the success I sought. I'm sure my mother nodded to sleep on several occasions, before I had even got to the Ghost of Christmas Past. I have a dim memory of trying it out at a weekly meeting of the Junior Band of Hope, a temperance society where the young were frightened in advance of the terrors of alcohol. The meetings tended to be a bit unruly, so I doubt if I managed to get through the first page before the teacher said, "Very nice, Philip. Now let's all sing a hymn."

5

But from then on, I always wanted to read aloud, and became adept at it. I would seize on any audience, anywhere, willing or unwilling. In later years I even invented a Christmas game that necessitated my reading for hours at a time, day after day, to family and friends. This was in the days of creative leisure, before radio and television. I would choose a "mystery," by Agatha Christie if possible, that none of the company had read; they had to swear most solemnly to this. Then I would put into a hat the names of all possible suspects written on pieces of paper—I, of course, had read the book in advance, which gave me a glorious omniscience throughout the game—and everybody who wanted to would draw a name at sixpence a head; the holder of the murderer's name when it was finally revealed was to collect the pool. It might be some days before the murderer's name was disclosed, because at the end of each reading session, a discussion would break out on the murderous merits of the various suspects, a discussion over which I would preside with a Buddha-like superiority. I gained such skill in this kind of reading that my audience could soon distinguish between the characters without my having to label them, and I took a secret pride in omitting, without their knowledge, such vocal signposts as ". . . Oscar asked with withering sarcasm; to which Mary replied, whimpering piteously. . . ."

Fred Duxbury first made me fall in love with words and the magic spell of storytelling, and I was in the right country for the appreciation of such gifts. If it is true that conversation is the ultimate grace of Irish culture, then oratory is of Welsh culture. Lloyd George could only have come from Wales. The puritanical hand of Methodism lay heavy over the life of nineteenth-century Wales, and so the theatre was the Devil's domain. As a result, many men whose real avocation was the stage turned instead to the pulpit. Great preaching festivals were held at which the stars performed. People would travel miles, in days when travel was difficult, to listen to three great preachers deliver three incredibly long sermons in one day. Nowadays when theatre addicts get together, you hear such things as, "I'll never forget Olivier's cry in

'Oedipus.'" Welsh sermon addicts say, similarly, "I'll never forget Philip Jones on 'Jesus wept.'" But that sentence would be said in Welsh, and now that the puritanical hand has been lifted from Wales, it is heard no more.

Welsh Methodism was always stronger in the rural parts of Wales than in the industrial valleys of the South, where even the language had to fight a desperate battle against the powerful invasion of English, Irish, and Scots, most of whom in the second generation learned to speak English with a Welsh accent but very rarely learned Welsh itself. Only the other day I came across a bilingual New Testament that my father bought when he first came to South Wales. For some time he even attended assiduously the particular church that conducted its services in Welsh, while still being a part of the Church of England. I don't think it did him much good, but I'm certain that very few of the invaders took even that much trouble. They had taken away the Welsh name of the town where I was born, Aberpennar, and had given it an English one from a notable mountain ash tree that stood in front of an inn to which it had also given its name. But the polyglot character of the mining town of Mountain Ash had one great advantage for me. In my boyhood it contained three temples of the Devil—two live theatres, the Workmen's Hall and the Empire, where traveling companies performed, and a cinema, the Palace, and this in a community of never more than fifteen thousand. On the road to desuetude all three became cinemas before I left Mountain Ash, and now, alas, the Workmen's Hall is given over to Bingo every night, and the Empire, after being a skating rink for years, is now owned by the Conservative Club and is being turned into a dance hall for its members! To these base uses has life in a Welsh mining community been brought by prosperity and television. But the Palace, where I thrilled so many years ago to the serialized adventures of Eddie Polo and Maciste, the Mighty, still shows films.

I count myself remarkably fortunate that, without having to travel at all—and in those days the eighteen-mile journey to

7

Cardiff was a rare and heroic adventure—I saw Shakespeare, grand opera, and Gilbert and Sullivan in the Workmen's Hall, and a resident company would take over the Empire for a season each year. When I first met in America that fine actor, Leo G. Carroll, who was to become a very good friend, he asked me where I came from. When I said "Mountain Ash," he surprised and delighted me by saying he knew it because, when he was a young man, he had played there on a tour of some frivolous comedy. It's the resident companies that I remember most vividly, particularly one: Mayne and Scotton. They played the old stock melodramas, such as *Maria Martin, The Dumb Man of Manchester, Conn the Shaughraun,* and on Friday nights, "at somewhat elevated prices to offset the enormous expense of the spectacular costume drama," *The Royal Divorce,* a play about Napoleon and Josephine. Friday, of course, was payday.

The various resident companies that played in the mining towns of South Wales each had its own devoted following, in much the same way that baseball teams do now. One Saturday afternoon as I was traveling in a train with my father to Aberdare, four miles away—even that was a major adventure—two men in the ten-person compartment, in which you were trapped while the train was in motion, got into an almost-to-blows argument about the *Dumb Man of Manchester* as played by two rival actors. The climax of this old melodrama was a court scene in which the Dumb Man had to give evidence about a murder he had witnessed. He gave his evidence entirely in pantomime during which he had to simulate a fall from a height. One actor had done it from a tall ladder, and the other from a chair-upon-a-chair-upon-a-table. The point at issue was which had taken the higher fall. Each aficionado accused the other's idol of using fake furniture. The issue was incapable of resolution, but the boy I was felt it to be important. My father annoyed me by being amused. But then he never saw things straight; once, when we were watching the silent movie of *Madame X,* and the whole audience was wet with tears, he laughed out loud, much to the anger of the weepers and to my embarrassment.

Such championship of actors as was evident in that claustrophobic compartment so long ago has steadily diminished to practical extinction during my lifetime. No actor has any longer sufficient following to weather bad notices on Broadway, and I fear that it is becoming increasingly true in the West End. The play's the thing now wherein to catch the conscience of the audience, or dazzle its eyes, or tickle its ribs. No longer is there widespread delight in the actor's art for its own sake. So many of the great ones of the stage in the past chose to appear in rubbish; the play was nothing so that they might be all. Henry Irving became a slave to his own success in *The Bells,* as did Martin Harvey in *The Only Way,* James O'Neill in *The Count of Monte Cristo,* and Joseph Jefferson in *Rip Van Winkle.* Of course, I have to admit that the decay of this adulation is a sign of the theatre's maturing, and yet a part of me is sad at its passing. And the excitement of partisanship lingers only in the opera, where the voice of the gallery has still some force, although even here it is a weak whimper of what it was. How far we have come from the Astor Place riots of 1849, when nearly twenty people were killed in a clash between the partisans of the rival actors, Charles Macready and Edwin Forrest! Not that one misses the bloodshed, but the enthusiasm that, in excess, prompted it has also gone. In an antiheroic age all men are diminished, and, with a few salutary exceptions, even good actors have become good citizens; all greatness is suspect, even the tinsel greatness of the theatre. Nowadays there is even an antiheroic approach to Shakespeare's great heroes, and our experience is thereby limited. Great plays are only made fully alive by great players. In the absence of such greatness, we identify with the antiheroes, but are not elevated into visionary moments that transcend our mediocrity.

The adulation of movie stars by film fans is a very inferior substitute for that earned by an Irving or a Duse, because it has

9

little, or nothing, to do with the artistic merits of the artist. The life, as revealed or manufactured by the man paid to project and protect the public image of a star, is more important than the performance; the extravagance of the reported life is a matter of such envy that some measure of sharing it is provided by avid adulation.

It seems to me that such wild enthusiasm as was first kindled by the Beatles was, while embarrassingly hysterical and an excuse for uninhibited self-displays, nevertheless of a more wholesome kind. Their appearance and their performance were such as to be emulated as protests against conformity. Once again, even though at a juvenile level, performers had become rogues and vagabonds.

These considerations arose from my boyhood admiration for Fred Mayne and Will Scotton, one the comic and the other the heavy. From Scotton I learned that bad men are more interesting to play than good ones; the Falstaffs of literature are much more memorable than the Lord Chief Justices, the Micawbers more memorable than the Copperfields. But Will Scotton never compromised his villainy; he wanted boos and hisses, not understanding. In our age, we try to excuse the murderer and forget the murdered. In playing classical villains, modern actors want to turn inhuman monsters into misunderstood men. Coleridge's description of Iago as behaving with motiveless malignity is not for them. It is not enough for them that such villains rejoice in evil because of the power it gives them. But Will Scotton's villains had all the strange attraction of the magnetic evildoer who never fools himself and is a liar only to other men.

Strangely enough, my most abiding memory of the Workmen's Hall is not of professional Shakespeare or opera, but of an amateur performance of *The Silver King*, that very skillful melodrama by Henry Arthur Jones. I can still see the handsome and suave villain getting out of a window. Both he and a local doctor who played the hero were for a long time after invested for me with an aura that separated them from other members of the community. I could not understand how they could consent to do anything else when they could act.

Although I learned my acting initially as an amateur, I have never been fair to amateurs, and somehow I never believed I was one. The first full-length play in which I appeared was a Y.M.C.A. production of T. W. Robertson's *Caste*. I managed to get hold of the complete volumes of that prolific writer's work. He is important in the development of the modern theatre for introducing to London audiences over one hundred years ago the box-chamber set with its apparently solid walls in place of wings, and practicable doors and windows instead of painted ones. Of all the many thousands of lines he wrote and I read, only one passage remains with me, an eloquent testimony to my snobbishness toward amateurs. Some character, in defense of amateur actors, says that Shakespeare had shown his respect for them by choosing one for the Fairy Queen to fall in love with, to which the reply was, "Not until he had been turned into an ass." And a word of praise for me from a professional was worth all the complimentary paragraphs of local critics. On one occasion, a community theatre performance of mine stirred up some controversial correspondence in a local paper. There was a professional resident company in the town at the time. They had not been doing too well and the manager was, I'm sure, glad to rent us the theatre for a week. But I was surprised and delighted—the presence of important people in an audience has always stimulated rather than petrified me—when the leading man came to see our production, and then took part in the newspaper controversy by stating in a letter that he would be happy to engage me as a permanent member of his company. I basked in the glow of that letter for years. I did not allow myself even to be momentarily tempted by his offer because I had an aging and ailing widowed mother to look after; conscience has often made me drag my steps.

When I came to America I found that the barrier between amateur and professional was far from fixed, and that certainly the labels were no guarantee of essential differences in the standard of performance, but my innate snobbishness in the matter has taken a long time to die, and still my most withering comment on the conduct or performance of an actor is "amateur."

I certainly must have had my first experience of acting before an audience in Mountain Ash, but all that is still vivid to me is a blush of shame. My first appearance was in "drag." I could not have been more than nine years old at the time. In the boys' elementary school that I attended—its name was Caegarw, meaning "rough field"—I was chosen to appear as Britannia in a patriotic pageant of the Empire. There is still a photograph of this debut extant, but certainly not preserved by me. It shows me pouting, complete with trident, shield, helmet, and long white robe, but the robe was not quite long enough, for it is all too evident that I am wearing some very substantial schoolboy boots. I suppose I was chosen for the role because I was tall for my age, was Saxon fair, and had a complexion of peaches-and-cream smoothness. The ravages of adolescence were soon to obliterate that last qualification. Much though I objected to the sex of Britannia, I'm certain that I reveled in her position and power and had my first intoxicating moment of stage glory when my schoolfellows, in motley hues of garb and face, laid the treasures of the colonies at my ill-shod feet and made their awkward obeisances.

I was a bright boy, much too bright for my own happiness, and was placed first in the competitive examination for the scandalously few places in the local high school. Only a month ago I received a cutting from the local paper describing some event at which one of my old teachers was being honored. Old, indeed! It must have been a diamond occasion, at least. I was amazed and reassured to find that he was still alive and, to judge from his photograph and reported remarks, still very recognizable. His name, inevitably, was Jones. He was quoted as saying that he was my first producer; had he been American, he would have said "director." This remark has dredged from its buried depths only the haziest recollection of a one-act play performed in the school gymnasium at a house party. I wonder why Mr. Jones remembered it. Was I good, or just difficult?

With my predilections, I should have been an eager and successful English student, but young adolescents are very much at the mercy of their teachers, and my teachers of English were disgracefully bad (I hasten to add that the Mr. Jones of the last paragraph taught geography). There was one lady teacher of formidable presence, terrifying discipline, and an incipient moustache, who turned literature into a daily toil of loathsome tasks. I have never yet recovered from her teaching of Sir Walter Scott. I have always promised myself that, in fairness to the reputation of that romantic knight, I must read him again, but I am fairly sure that he will remain on the long list of my unfulfilled reading promises. It was seeing him in the theatre that alone rescued Shakespeare from her baneful influence; even so, it was many years before I could find virtue in As You Like It, which had been rent for me to distasteful bits by her footnote dissection of the text. It was a delightful performance by Fabia Drake at Stratford-on-Avon that years later enabled me to appreciate and enjoy the radiance of the play.

My most successful high school teacher was completely untrained and had never been to a university. He taught mathematics with a brilliant instinct because he loved it as he did chess. I have frequently defined teaching as the art of communicating enthusiasm, and whenever I use the phrase I think of Ted Richards, that memorable teacher. The first essential for any good teaching is that the teacher must love his subject. The lady who murdered Walter Scott for me was a highly trained teacher, but for her it was merely a respectable way of making a living and involved the ramming of tedious books prescribed from above into unreceptive and rebellious minds.

I am a good teacher, but, like Ted Richards, completely untrained. The Headmaster who first employed me as a teacher—I never taught in another high school—was a delightful character who made his own rules as he went along and managed by devious and mysterious ways to avoid red-tape entanglement. He told me once that when choosing a teacher he never questioned him about his qualifications, but only about his subject. "If he could interest me, he stood a chance of interesting his pupils." I must have interested him, but the only recollection I have of our initial interview is that I called him "Mr. Bull," which I subsequently learned was his nickname; his name was Lewis. It speaks well of him that he appointed me, but, as I mentioned before, I don't think there were many applicants; I never saw another.

It is only human to set small value on those things that come most easily to us, as teaching to me. I never meant to be a teacher but I always seem to end up being one. I originally became a teacher because the need to earn money was desperate and the job I was really hoping for was hanging fire. The job, which came through a day too late, was educational assistant to Zwingli Willis, the general secretary of the Y.M.C.A. in Great Britain. Later he was knighted, and never man deserved it more. When I joined the staff of the British Broadcasting Corporation it was as a producer-writer-director, but within two years I was Chief Instructor of the Training Department. I was first persuaded to stay in the United States to head the script department of a newly formed film company. The venture came to naught and now I find myself the president and director of a theatre school, the American Musical and Dramatic Academy.

The death of my father when I was fourteen, and our resulting poverty, made it essential that I should be put through the educational machine as expeditiously as possible, and the result was absurd. I jumped from a second-year to a fourth-year class, and then did the two years' Higher Certificate course in one year. Before I was seventeen I had won a university scholarship and went to the university to do second-year work. I was just absorbing knowledge to parade it again for examination purposes. My real education had little to do with my schooling.

A very big early influence toward my theatre addiction was the Church. There I met the choirmaster I have already spoken about.

For a time he was also my Sunday school teacher, a truly great one. He brought the Bible stories alive for me and many another boy with his hypnotic narrative gift. His literary hero was Kipling, and a selected group of young boys would gather on the lawn of his house, or on a bank of bluebells in the woods, or on the bare mountainside, and listen to him as he retold the *Jungle Books*. Mowgli was our Superman.

The church was St. Margaret, which was Episcopalian and a branch of the Church of England. It was felt by the majority of the working class to be the church of the bosses, and an alien importation; my English father and English mother were naturally at home in it. While I was yet a boy, the Church was disestablished as a result of Welsh nonconformist agitation in the Westminster House of Commons, and the ties with the Crown and Canterbury were severed. It became the Church in Wales; notice the "in," not "of." Suddenly it was self-supporting; in searching for its life, it found its soul. It found its roots were deeper than Canterbury, and now some of its most prominent members are very Welsh Welshmen.

But for me, St. Margaret's was a battleground for a controversy which, as I see it, breathes life into the Episcopalian Church wherever it is found—the conflict between High and Low churchmen: between those who say the Reformation changed little and those who say it changed much; between those who like to worship God with splendid ceremonial and those who like to do so in bare simplicity; between those to whom incense suggests God and those to whom it suggests the Devil. As each new vicar or assistant clergyman arrived at St. Margaret's, he was watched with inquisitorial intensity to see which way he leaned. For a long time the Low Church party won every battle; they tended to be vulgarly vocal and uninhibited in their denunciations of popery and idolatry. Shy spinsters took to crossing themselves surreptitiously, but none was brave enough to genuflect. I personified the dilemma. My parents were definitely Low Church and had much in common with their Welsh nonconformist neighbors. I was brought up to fear the Roman Catholic Church, and I hurried past its doors. I did not dare even to enter a Roman Catholic Church until I was in my twenties. This hatred and suspicion was not so much an expression of any religious conviction on the part of the Welsh miners as of hatred and suspicion of the Irish, who came to the coalfield in large numbers, which soon became larger as their families multiplied with Catholic abundance. But while my mind scorned the slightest evidence of idolatry, my theatrical heart yearned for it; incense thrilled me more than it did the devout whose prayers it helped, because for me it had the titillating attraction of the forbidden. It still has the same ambivalence for me.

I was a church choirboy for several years, and whilst I rebeled against the compulsory and excessive attendance at largely boring services—two on Sunday and one on Wednesday—I soon learned to be forever grateful for what I unconsciously absorbed: an ability to read music; the wonderful language, rhythm, and cadences of the Edward VI Book of Common Prayer; a wide, if not deep, acquaintance with the Bible. There are some parts of the Bible that every choirboy of long standing probably knows even better than the clergyman, unless he too had been a choirboy in his time; those, of course, are the "dirty" passages. They were pointed out to me, with infinite stealth, during tedious sermons. At first I didn't understand them at all, and occasionally I had the courage to say so when the service was over; whereupon, after much ridicule, I was enlightened, usually by some boy whose voice was breaking, a phenomenon which was welcomed because it betokened escape from the choir as much as because it was a sign of imminent manhood. Knowing how much the very language of the Prayer Book has meant to me in my discovery of the Elizabethan world, I abominate all attempts to modernize it. Why rob us of that lively link with Shakespeare? It's the only language that I know both our tongues uttered, albeit with different accents.

Apart from the senior colliery officials, who lived in large houses, there was one great family in Mountain Ash, and they lived in a grand house—Lord and Lady Aberdare and their son, who was for me the quintessence of an aristocratic gentleman, the Honorable John Bruce, known familiarly as the "Hon. John." Their mansion now houses the grammar school. It was long before I knew that the Aberdare family was only nineteenth century in its origins, and that it owed its title and gentility to coal. When they were in residence they came to the eleven o'clock service every Sunday morning and were obsequiously ushered into their pew, the one in front and the one behind being kept discreetly empty. And on the first Sunday in the month they ran the gamut of the choir as they came up to the altar rail to partake of Holy Communion. Every eye watched their every move, without seeming to do so. But the greatest excitement took place when a brother of Lord Aberdare was also present, General Bruce, the famous mountaineer who led two early Everest expeditions. He was the kind of man around whom stories grow at sight. He had an extraordinary physique, and we boys entertained one another by attributing to him fabricated feats of strength, swearing they were true and vouching for their authenticity with such authorities as "My Auntie Mary works in Lord Aberdare's kitchen, and the butler told her. . . ." What was certain was that his servants were Ghurkas, and he sometimes brought these foreign-looking men to church with him, complete with their murderous-looking kris. Their skill with the kris is part of the legend of Empire, but it could not begin to equal our accounts of it. Here were Kipling's jungle tales alive in the pews of our own church!

For a time I sang soprano solos in the festival anthems at the church, and when the Aberdares were there to hear me, Keats' nightingale could not rival my full-throated ease. And then, one Christmas, I was invited to sing at the great house for the Aberdare family and guests. It was the nearest I ever got to a Royal Command Performance at Windsor Castle. My jealous choirmates pointed out that Lady Aberdare was deaf, and that this alone accounted for the invitation. Nothing remains for me now of what must have been an exciting experience except my father's reaction when I returned home, clutching a Christmas bag of fruit and candy given to me by Her Most Gracious Ladyship. "Was that all she gave you?" he said. Was that all, indeed! But then my father was fast becoming a mild socialist, of the quiet-reading rather than the noisy-shouting kind.

It was at this time I first heard a name that was in years to come to mean much to me: Bernard Shaw. He was already a famous figure to the miners of Mountain Ash, but as a politician. He had shared the stage of the Workmen's Hall for a Sunday afternoon meeting with the first Socialist Member-of-Parliament, Keir Hardie, and another gentleman whose name I never knew but who was always referred to as "The Vicar of Radstock," a parish in Somersetshire near my mother's birthplace, Midsomer Norton. A socialist vicar at that time was a unique phenomenon, and I can imagine that my father was very proud of him.

One story about Bernard Shaw I particularly cherish. A pacifist meeting was held on a Sunday afternoon. When it was his turn to speak, Shaw strode forward in his unconventional breeches and Norfolk jacket, his red beard abristle, and said, "I believe in war." He then went on to explain that for anybody with money to invest, war was a good proposition, and that the way to control war was to control the armaments industry. The men who were there that afternoon chuckled for years over his shock tactics. He often used the same trick in his plays with the same result.

And my boyhood reading? The usual: adventure stories and school stories. I still remember gratefully the school stories of Talbot Baines Reed, particularly *The Fifth Form at St. Dominic's.* But even then I had little patience with the inevitable birthday book, *Eric* or *Little by Little,* a Victorian homily that families deemed it their bounden duty to give in morocco-bound volumes to their children. *Tom Brown's Schooldays* was little better. The greatest reading excitement for me, as for most young boys, was discovering the ability to enjoy books not intended for my eyes, even innocent books. There was one such book that I virtually learned by heart: Jerome K. Jerome's *Three Men in a Boat.* What a perceptive phrase that is, "learned by heart"; the words most readily committed to memory are those one loves. For years I would thrust passages of *Three Men in a Boat* upon the unwilling ears of young and old. I particularly liked the incident in which an embarrassed man found great difficulty in disposing of a strong cheese. And, too, I remember what a salutary effect the opening of the book had on me. I had just scared myself by reading, in secret, one of those *Every Man His Own Doctor* books, and I was saved from despair about the frailty of the human body by reading in Jerome's book that a similar experience had conclusively proved to the hero that he suffered from every known ailment except housemaid's knee, the lack of which seemed perversely to disappoint him. Then there was the wonderful excitement of coming upon a book about which one knew nothing in advance and which thrilled one into a vague awareness of artistic strength and stature and significance. The book was *The Gadfly* by A. L. Voynich. I could not have been more than twelve when I first met this book, and the afterglow of that meeting is still warm within me. I have several times been tempted to reread the book to test my untrained taste, but have resisted from fear of disappointment.

I am lastingly grateful that I was never taught Dickens, but was introduced to him by Fred Duxbury. The introduction led to a rich and abiding friendship. Dickens, too, shared my joy in public reading. He was as compulsive a performer as Dylan Thomas, who also reveled in portraying the grotesqueries of human behavior. Emlyn Williams has brilliantly re-created the excitement of the readings by Dickens, and I'm sure that in many parts of the world many a young boy has reacted to the Dickens-Williams magic as I did to that of Fred Duxbury, and I'm certain that from the experience the young boy knew, as I did, that the theatre, in some form, was to be the most important thing in his life.

she believed that the fumes were good for the lungs. I held my breath and closed my eyes, but the tunnel was too long for the one and curiosity too strong for the other. Then there was the arrival at Lichfield and being met by a horse-and-trap and by a distinguished and bearded old gentleman. He looked and talked like Lord Aberdare, but was in fact my own grandfather. But neither he nor his home fed my hunger for theatre in any way.

My father was my mother's second husband. By her first she had borne a son. He was older than I by eighteen years, and was as like his spare Scottish father as I was like my brawny English one. He loved the theatre, but never had any desire to practice it in any department. But he had a theatrical instinct, for whenever he tells the simplest anecdote—and he seems, even at eighty, to live every day fully in order to talk about his adventures every night—he does so by recounting every conversation in direct dialogue. " 'Don't be so bloody daft,' I told him. 'Who the hell are you calling daft?' he said. 'You, you silly bugger,' I said."

This half-brother of mine, Will Wilson, worked in the colliery from the time he was a young boy. Young boys, the smaller the better, were used to crawl in and bring out the coal after the collier's pick had pried it loose. Sometimes they worked in a hand-hewn tunnel less than two feet thick. One of the men for whom the wraith-thin young Will worked was a remarkable man, characteristic of the time and place. To begin with, he was such a good workman that, as a result of getting paid for the amount of coal he cut rather than for the hours he worked, he became comparatively well-to-do. But more important for the boy who worked for him, he was well read and had a good mind and a fluent tongue. In his service to his fellow miners, he scorned God, King, and Capitalism. In his search for freedom and justice, he had even crossed the Atlantic to the coalfields of Pennsylvania, but after a few years had come back disillusioned to resume the fight at home. Inevitably, he became a union official, but did much for the cultural life of Mountain Ash too. He saw to it, for instance, that there was a good public library in the Workmen's Hall, in the days when such modern necessities were hard-fought-for luxuries. It was this man who left a permanent impression on the mind of young Will, and I believe it was he who first told the boy about great plays, and great players, and told him they could be seen in Cardiff when they toured. Some years later, the young man that Will became saw much great theatre in Cardiff, and did so at incredible cost. Instead of coming up from the depths of the mine after the day shift, he would stay down and work on through the night to make enough for the trip to Cardiff. He would have almost no time for sleep because he had to catch a train to see the Saturday matinee. He would hurry to the theatre and stand in line for "early-doors," sixpence extra, in the pit, the back rows of the orchestra. In the case of a popular attraction, it was absolutely essential to get in early-doors, because by the time "ordinary-doors" were open, a half hour before the performance, no seats or standing room would be left. One received a square of metal from the box office which was surrendered to the ticket taker inside. As soon as he got inside, Will would ask the person who happened to be sitting next to him to wake him up when the play started, and then he would snatch a nap. Sometimes a great star would come down from London with his company in the midweek for a "Flying Matinee"; Will rarely missed one. And at last came the day when he took me with him to a Saturday matinee. Only now do I realize how generous this was, because I must have been a considerable embarrassment to a young miner who, without me, would have been free to taste the delights of the big city on a Saturday night.

There were three theatres in Cardiff—the New Theatre, the Empire, and one whose name changed as successive owners tried to make it viable; I remember it most gratefully as The Playhouse. It was the New Theatre at which I saw my first major production and had most of my early experiences of first-class, and occasionally great, theatre. My first Cardiff show was a real Arabian Night's entertainment: Kismet. Strangely enough I can remember little of the play, probably because the plot was too complicated for my theatrical immaturity; all is lost in the wonder of the opening scene, a crowded, colorful and noisy street, with Haji, the beggar, crying, "Alms, for the love of Allah!" Such a scene at the opening of a musical invariably draws applause now, although the crowds on stage even in the most lavish production are much smaller than they were in the old days when it was the practice to draw upon nonprofessional "supers." Why do we find mere numbers on stage so impressive? When the Rockettes in Radio City Music Hall finally get into one long line stretching the whole length of the huge stage, the audience invariably breaks into applause even before the girls have displayed the precision of their high kicking. Is it that we are gratified at getting our money's worth? Conversely, I have heard of people avoiding a play because there were only two characters in it. Even Shakespeare would have liked more actors for his crowd scenes so that he would not have had to present a great battle with "Four or five most vile and ragged foils, Right ill-disposed in brawl ridiculous." I suppose it is the child in all of us that finds spectacular staging exciting. But what lighting effects can rival "But look, the morn, in russet-mantle clad, Walks o'er the dew of yon high eastern hill"? And yet there is magic in the stage imitation of reality that can excite wonder in people whom reality itself leaves cold. Many people come out of a Broadway matinee having been moved by a stage sunset, completely ignoring the beauty of the sunset over the New Jersey Palisades. Human need as seen on stage can turn people into Good Samaritans, but when they come outside they again revert to their normal pattern of passing by on the other side. But not always. I like the story that when the old Yiddish Theatre in New York played their version of *King Lear*, the banks used to stay open late to enable conscience-stricken playgoers to send money to their old parents left behind in Europe; the impulse might have died by the next day. It was this power of theatre that prompted Bernard Shaw to write:

> I am convinced that fine art is the subtlest, the most seductive, the most effective instrument of moral propaganda in the

world, excepting only the example of personal conduct; and
I waive even this exception in favor of the art of the stage,
because it works by exhibiting examples of personal conduct
made intelligible and moving to crowds of unobservant un-
reflecting people to whom real life means nothing.

The first major actor I remember seeing at the New Theatre
was Sir John Martin-Harvey, "The Last Romantic," as his biog-
rapher was later to call him. I think he came twice a year for a
week at a time, and people went over and over again to see him in
the same plays. To my lasting joy, I saw him in several of his
famous parts, at the rate of one a year. A typical repertoire, a
different play every night, would open with a tried melodrama
such as *The Corsican Brothers,* adapted from the Dumas novel,
and giving the leading actor a field day as twins. In *A Cigarette
Maker's Romance,* adapted from a novel by Marion Crawford,
Martin-Harvey charmed us all as a mildly lunatic Russian count.
Then there was *The Breed of the Treshams,* a Cavalier-Round-
head melodrama, in which the famous scene showed the devil-may-
care Cavalier being tortured; this play was written, surprisingly, by
two ladies from Boston, Massachusetts. Of considerably more importance than these and their ilk was Maeterlinck's *The Burgo-
master of Stilemonde.* It came out of World War I while the war
was still on, but its life lasted long after the war was over. In this
play, Martin-Harvey dispensed with his usual romantic bravura
and played with a quiet dignity, but he was as memorable as ever.
There was usually one Shakespeare play in the week's offerings,
Hamlet or *Richard III,* but unfortunately I saw neither, and often
there was a revival of a play that Irving had made famous, such as
The Bells or *The Lyons Mail.* Martin-Harvey had learned his craft
from years of apprenticeship with Irving, whom he the more
revered the longer he knew him, despite being chained to small
parts for years. But whatever else was in the week's repertoire, the
engagement would end on the Saturday with two performances of
Martin-Harvey's most famous production—*The Only Way,* an

adaptation of Charles Dickens' *A Tale of Two Cities*. I saw it a few times over several years and, in spite of a growing sophistication, never ceased to be deeply moved.

I am glad to have seen true greatness on the stage. Rarely have I seen even a shadow of it since I became a mature theatregoer. I have seen many excellent performances by first-rate actors and actresses but seldom true greatness. It is a matter of the stature of the artist as a stage personality. Voice, physique, and looks seem to have little to do with it. It is the result of a demonic possession so that the possibilities of the human spirit, for good or evil, are expanded beyond the identifiable. It is possible that in this skeptical and debunking age we are incapable of the necessary suspension of disbelief; our eyes are too firmly fixed on the feet of clay ever to see the godlike hero. And the actors themselves cannot but share this mentality. Not knowing greatness, we applaud excellence. From the days of Ibsen, the playwright not the player has become supreme. Most of me approves the change of values, but there is still a part that bewails the passing of the Irvings and Martin-Harveys. It is true that they stood in the way of important new playwrights, who were not interested in providing them with vehicles. I suppose that only once did great player serve great playwright: Shakespeare's first Hamlet, Lear, Othello, Macbeth, Antony—Richard Burbage.

The question is often asked: How great would the great players of the past appear to us today? Would we dismiss them as embarrassing "hams"? That word "ham" in itself reveals our attitude to unusual displays of emotion in "a part to tear a cat in." Would we laugh at Bernhardt, Mrs. Siddons, Garrick, Burbage? I don't think so. A "ham" is only hammy when his playing is not true, whatever the convention, whether it be Kabuki, ballet, or nineteenth-century melodrama. And for performing of any kind to be true, it does not have to be naturalistic. There is no such thing as completely naturalistic theatre anyway; all theatre is a tissue of conventions; it is only a matter of the nature and degree of the conventions. The test of truth in a performance is like that of a tamer in a cage of lions; if the lions are doped and lethargic, no matter how great a parade of danger and bravery the tamer puts on, we are not convinced, but if the danger is patently real, the tamer is aware of that only, not of creating an effect.

Martin-Harvey's most famous stage speech was Sidney Carton's last utterance as he climbed the stairs to the guillotine: "It is a far, far better thing that I do than I have ever done; it is a far, far better rest that I go to than I have ever known." Even today scoffers mimic it as the ultimate expression of empty theatricality, but it is remembered because Martin-Harvey filled it with a radiant certainty that transcended theatre.

Only once did I have a chance to apply mature judgment to a performance by Martin-Harvey; it was at a revival of *Oedipus Rex* at Covent Garden when the actor was seventy-three years of age, and I was relieved to find that I had not been wrong. The remembered magic was still there. I was embarrassed by his final exit, as he groped his eyeless way on buskins down the long aisle, his closed eyes heavily bloodied, but then I have never been comfortable when actors rush by my seat in the audience. For me, all attempts to break the physical barrier between actors and audience destroy the necessary illusion rather than intensify it.

Another fine artist I remember affectionately from my first New Theatre days was Fred Terry, who with his wife, Julia Neilson, delighted more than one generation of theatregoers with a beguiling adaptation of *The Scarlet Pimpernel*. He returned with it repeatedly and we went repeatedly to see him in it. After our first visit we hoped to have a newcomer seated next to us so that we could point out Sir Percy Blakeney in the first scene, in which the hero was disguised as an old harridan bluffing her way through a revolutionary barricade with a cartload of escaping aristocrats.

Fred Terry's disguises during the play drew forth much applause and showed the appeal of acting at an elementary level. Martin-Harvey never disguised his handsome face; the marked differences in his character came from within. But the obvious virtuosity of protean performers such as Lon Chaney is admirable only when the transformation achieved by the makeup artist is the mirror of a transformation from within, as it is, for instance, in the case of Peter Sellers.

But Fred Terry did not rely on makeup. His great asset was stage charm. Only one artist in my later experience equaled him in this quality—Marie Tempest, a high comedienne of exquisite presence who first made me realize the delicious delicacy of comedy timing.

There is a story about Fred Terry that I treasure. I don't know where I first heard or read it, but it illustrates the power of the stage over those whose natural life it is. In his later years, Fred Terry was crippled by arthritis, but he played *The Scarlet Pimpernel* long after it seemed possible. He made his way to the theatre with difficulty, dressed and made up with pain, walked in agony to the wings, and at the call of his cue entered with no visible sign of his disability, even dancing the minuet with his old elegance. I deeply regret that I never saw Fred's famous sister, Ellen Terry. It would seem that stage charm was a family inheritance, for the grandnephew of those illustrious Terrys, Sir John Gielgud, has it in abundance.

The Cardiff Empire was one of the famous chain of Moss Empires. Usually they played twice-nightly variety bills, but occasionally a play was booked. It had to be a very special and popular attraction, for the capacity of the Empire far exceeded that of the New Theatre. The actor I remember best from the Empire was one I had seen in earlier years at the New Theatre—Matheson Lang. Here was an actor with extraordinarily compelling power on the stage who deliberately forswore his first successes as Othello and Shylock to appear in theatrical rubbish, which his talent and presence made memorable. His greatest success was *Mr. Wu*, a melodrama in which a Chinese gentleman's scheme of revenge goes awry and he finds he has taken the poison he intended for another; the virtuosity of his lonely death scene was spellbinding. I don't know how long it lasted, but the death was a slow one and completely riveting in its effect. The absolute silence

28

of a captivated audience is a thrilling experience; the spectators are welded into one person, with one pair of eyes, one beating heart. Matheson Lang did this feat of magic time and again, but most memorably when he died as Mr. Wu. He achieved a similar long-lasting success with *The Wandering Jew*, but this was an elaborate production and therefore was booked at the Empire, where I saw it and again marveled at his power.

Obviously for a man like Matheson Lang the theatre was a game that he made pay. Like Hollywood producers, he even tried to follow one success by repeating the formula. Thus, *Mr. Wu* was followed by *The Chinese Bungalow* and *The Wandering Jew* by *Jew Süss*, although this last, an adaptation from the novel of Lion Feuchtwanger, had some literary merit.

I heard a story about Matheson Lang while he was playing *The Wandering Jew* at Cardiff Empire which disturbed me at the time and which I have thought about much during the years. A student from the university who was a super in the play was standing in the wings waiting to make an entrance, probably to arrest, torment, or torture the poor Jew. Matheson Lang completed a highly emotional scene which had shattered his audience. He turned upstage and, as he did so, he deliberately winked at the supers in the wings, as if to say, "See how I've got 'em! Isn't it funny?" and completed his turn to resume the unbroken rhythm of the scene. Years later I heard a similar story about Sarah Bernhardt from a lady who had been a super with her during a London season. This lady's parents were friends of the Divine Sarah's, which accounted for the lady's being on the stage that season. The play was again comparative rubbish, *La Dame aux Camélias*, and in the middle of the famous death scene, with the audience drowning the theatre with tears, Bernhardt turned upstage as she stifled her fatal cough with a lace handkerchief and whispered to my informant that she had a present in the dressing room that she wished her to take home to her mother. Then, without a break, she continued the exquisite pathos of her dying.

Those stories, and some others like them, have given me furiously to think about acting. I still think the conduct of both artists unforgivable. It could only have occurred after too long familiarity with parts that never really stretched them. But the audience was deeply moved on both occasions, and the ultimate criterion of all acting is the effect on the audience. The exact opposite of these stories is even worse—when an actor is so self-indulgent in a display of emotion that the audience is unaffected and even embarrassed. Many an actor who is so readily moved by his imagination that tears flow easily has known the experience of losing control and breaking down completely; it is worse than breaking up in laughter. Control is essential to all art, and yet the Lang-Bernhardt stories reveal an excess of control.

There is a contrary story about Edith Evans and John Gielgud in the days before they had received their present well-merited titles. Whether it is apocryphal I don't know, but it deserves to be true because it is so illuminating. Miss Evans was playing the Nurse, and Gielgud, Romeo. One evening, in the desperate cell scene in which the distracted Romeo throws himself upon the ground, Gielgud thought he had done particularly well and expected to go home that night with high commendation from the great lady. She said nothing. He could bear it no longer and finally hinted that he thought things had gone exceptionally well for him that night. She smiled her ineffable smile and said, "My dear John, when you learn to cry less, perhaps the audience will cry more."

The third Cardiff theatre, the Playhouse as it was named when I first knew it, gave me one of the greatest theatrical experiences of my life: Sybil Thorndike's *Medea*. There is a halo about this woman, a sense of dedication, which is combined with a wholesome heartiness. She is a personification of the Life Force. Only a great part can contain her; she stretches lesser ones to bursting. I have seen many performances of hers since, and always with joy, but that early *Medea* was truly great; the stature of the actress matched the stature of the part and the result was a transcendent experience. Always, even now in her old age, one is aware of a mighty dynamo at work; her energy shames many young actors. Without energy no performance can compel, but it must be a relaxed energy. The relaxation comes from a sense of inner security on the stage. All good actors are nervous before their first entrance—on an opening night that first entrance is a torment that Dante should have included in the *Inferno*—but once on stage the true actor is in his natural element and all is well; his private fears dissolve in the public gaze. The energy of which I speak comes from a tremendous concentration of the imagination, the mind, and the emotions. It is the opposite of a nervous, frenetic "pushing," which betrays insecurity and a desire to impress an audience. The true energy is the expression of a vibrant life, apparent in a good actor even when he is standing still and listening.

It was in Cardiff I learned that not all theatre is for me. There is a distinctively English kind of entertainment that flourishes at Christmas and usually continues into the spring. Every city boasts its own version. It is the pantomime, an elaborate musical production loosely based upon a fairy tale. Some of the more frequent subjects are *Cinderella, Aladdin, Mother Goose,* and *Puss-in-Boots.* Among the strange traditions of a Christmas pantomime are transvestite delights; the leading comedian, usually the main attraction, plays the "Dame"—Widow Twankey in Aladdin, for instance—and the chief romantic male part—Aladdin, for instance—is played by a beautiful woman, preferably with legs not only shapely but long, seen to best advantage in a succession of silk tights. Then there is an obligatory "Transformation Scene," in which a tawdry kitchen becomes a gorgeous palace or a magic woodland complete with cascading waterfall. Of course, there is a Good Fairy and a Wicked Fairy who exchange banter throughout the show in rhyming couplets of stupefying banality. Every year the popular songs of the moment find their way into the script, eked out by specially written numbers. There are also "speciality acts" that enliven the show from time to time, without rhyme or reason—jugglers, acrobats, contortionists, ventriloquists. There is

31

a pretense that the show is intended for children; perhaps they should add "of all ages," but even that wouldn't inhibit some of the comedians.

Will Wilson, who first introduced me to theatre in Cardiff, loved pantomime, and for years made an annual pilgrimage to Birmingham, which he said housed the best pantomimes. He still talks dotingly about the great "Dames"—Wilkie Bard, Dan Leno. I never saw them, but doubt that they would have converted me.

I seemed to be so singular in my dislike of the form that it worried me. Years later, when I was living in London, I went more than once to see a much-praised pantomime, but never managed to sit one out. In the light of this reaction, it may seem strange that I thoroughly enjoyed (alas! for the past tense) music hall and vaudeville, and today can enjoy a good burlesque show. I think it must be the muddle-headedness of the pantomime that offends me. It has no unity of purpose, either artistic or commercial. Something for everybody inevitably means everything for nobody.

I saw most of my Cardiff shows during the four years I was in college there, at the University College of South Wales and Monmouthshire, one of the four constituent colleges of the University of Wales, the others being at Aberystwyth, Swansea, and Bangor. I traveled every day by train from Mountain Ash, thus missing what is probably the most important part of a college experience, the full life of the student community. I was there for the sole purpose of getting an honors degree in Pure Mathematics as quickly as possible, in my case three years instead of the usual four. The natural concomitants of Pure Mathematics are Applied Mathematics and Physics, but I had neither. Instead, the ill-assorted companions of my mathematical studies were History and Latin. I think I must have been the last person in Wales to have an arts degree with honors in Pure Mathematics, rather than a science degree. Everybody expected me to get a first-class honors degree, but I didn't; I got a third, and thereby hangs a tale of some significance. I discovered literature and thereafter spent as little time on mathematics as I had to—indeed, much less than that. And during my first year at the college, a new head of the mathematics department was appointed, who had little patience with a purely pure mathematician such as I. The dire result of my exciting affair with my new love, literature, and my growing boredom with my old friend, mathematics, was that when I came to the honors examination, six three-hour papers, I found difficulty in reading some of the problems, much less finding solutions to them. Even so, I scored a first-class in two of the papers. They dealt with a subject taught by a lecturer who was both a great teacher and a great man, a Dr. Taylor, who influenced me deeply while I was in college and for years afterwards.

Dr. Taylor's interests were too wide for him ever to have been a totally successful specialist, and so he was never given a professorial chair. His exact antithesis was the principal of the college at the time, a renowned botanist who was described to me by a cynical student as "an ignorant man who knows a lot about yeast." To the best of my recollection, I never spoke to that bearded eminence. But the day was a disappointment when I did not speak to Dr. Taylor. He was a short Scotsman, with a twisted leg, misshapen body and a scabrous skin, but in his presence you were blind to his appearance, for he had an overwhelming geniality, an exciting intelligence, and a delightful sense of fun. When he laughed at one of his own witty presentations of a provocative idea, his whole body would curl in upon itself and he would become a twinkling wrinkle. The ladies adored him, and he them. His greatest ardor was reserved for his religion; he was an intellectual convert to Christianity. It was only natural that, without bruiting it from the housetops, I had reacted against my conventional church upbringing; I had continued to go to church, but it meant less and less. But Dr. Taylor helped me to find a genuine faith to such an extent that I ultimately became the student president of the college branch of the Student Christian Movement, a liberal body acknowledging that a religion can and should face all questions and try to find answers. Through this movement I met some notable men, with two of whom I was deeply privileged to have a continuing friendship over a number of years: Professor T. H. Robinson, a well-known Old Testament scholar, and Professor C. H. Dodd of Cambridge, a famous New Testament scholar. Then there was a man that I met only for a week when he was Bishop of Manchester, but who became Archbishop of Canterbury, William Temple. In all these men it was the brilliance of their minds and the breadth of their knowledge that fascinated me, but what impressed me most, and still does, was that they never patronized me but seemed to enjoy conversation with the impudent, intellectual upstart that I was; I suppose it impresses me because I find it sadly lacking in myself; I often find it hard to take the wrong-headedness of the young. So great was the influence of these men that for a time I actually thought of becoming an Anglican priest. In that role I always saw myself preaching dramatic sermons, not visiting the sick. Bishop Temple, during a student conference in Manchester, raised the question of my becoming a priest. I said that I couldn't subscribe to the Thirty-Nine Articles. He smiled with his gentle wisdom and said: "What you don't believe doesn't matter. Find out what you do believe and stick to that and be grateful for it." I said I had no sense of vocation. He said: "That's an evasion. Use your intelligence to find your vocation. Look at the world and see its need, then look at yourself and see how best you can help to meet that need." But I didn't become a priest, and I'm sure both the church and I are the happier for that.

Although I took no literary studies at college, I was nevertheless helped there to find and follow my bent. For all freshmen at the college, a new obligatory course, General Reading, had recently been introduced. So far as I can recollect, no lectures or examinations were involved, and I cannot remember how they tested whether a student had completed the course. Perhaps they just hoped for the best. If the authorities are still interested, I can assure them I pursued the course with much more thoroughness than any I was taught. Each student was provided with a printed pamphlet containing twenty or more lists of books, each comprising a dozen titles. The idea, I suppose, was to broaden a student's interests and knowledge. We could choose whatever group of books we wished. I, naturally, chose the group that contained most plays; and so I met, for the first time, Ibsen and Shaw, Ibsen in a volume of William Archer's translation of five of his plays, and Shaw in his *Plays for Puritans*. I was so excited by them that I went on immediately to read all their plays. I particularly found Shaw's prefaces a heady wine; everything Shaw was against, I was against, including St. Paul and all doctors. There were other books in my chosen group that had a powerful influence on me, notably John Stuart Mill's *Liberty* and his *Representative Government*, Prince Kropotkin's *Mutual Aid*, and William Archer's *The Old Drama and the New*. I also met Joseph Conrad for the first time in his *Lord Jim*, and there was a charmingly informative book by a T. G. Jackson called *Reason in Architecture*, which taught me to see cathedrals with fresh eyes.

Subsequently, I have thought that my turning away from Mathematics might have been partly a subconscious revolt against the cramping of my spirit by poverty. Mathematics had been the way to the university and was to be the way to a livelihood, but the spirit within me might have been afeared that in seeking a living I might have lost life. The third class in the honors examination brought me up with a jolt. Were it not for Dr. Taylor's two papers I am sure I should have been failed. Now what was I to do? Common sense said stay a fourth year and get a teacher's certificate, but I didn't want to be a teacher. I had no academic qualifications whatsoever in Literature, but had passed the finals examination in History. Above all, my self-esteem dictated that I should wipe out the disgrace of the third in Mathematics. I went to Professor Bruce, the head of the History Department, and pleaded with him to let me take the honors History examination the following year. As I remember it, the examination again consisted of six three-hour papers, two in Medieval History, for which the texts were largely in Latin, two in Modern European History, and two in a special study of the French Revolution. In this last lay the difficulty, for most of the texts were in French, and I had never studied the language. I was sufficiently persuasive to get Professor Bruce to promise that, if by the end of the summer I could readily translate a speech chosen at random from two large volumes entitled *Orators of the French Revolution,* he would consider my request. I set to work, unaided, without even a Berlitz or a recording to help me. My knowledge of the French Revolution had been largely derived from Baroness Orczy and Thomas Carlyle, and I was enthralled to find that the truth was certainly stranger than fiction. I can still remember my shock of surprise when I came across a long and boring speech of Robespierre's, arguing for the abolition of the death penalty. Professor Bruce did let me join his honors class, and I did soothe my injured pride, at least to the extent of getting a "good" honors rating, a II A. I just missed a first, again because I could not totally forswear extraneous reading.

After four years in college, I had a peculiar double-honors degree in Pure Mathematics and History, a much wider knowledge of literature, particularly the literature of the theatre, than of either of my professed subjects, some memorable experiences of theatregoing, some good friends, no profession, and a frightening debt at the bank.

In retrospect it seems strange even to me that I took no part in the activities of the college Dramatic Society. It was largely an offshoot of the English Department, to which I did not belong, and it was the preserve of a clique to which I did not belong. I regarded this group with a mixture of contempt, because they behaved with loudmouthed and arrogant exhibitionism, and envy, because that same behavior evidenced a confidence and sophistication I lacked. But I did not approve of their attitude toward theatre; it was too much just fun and games. Even before I became one myself, my attitude toward amateurs was becoming well defined. I saw all the college productions, I'm sure, but remember only one, which took place in the Playhouse. It was an ambitious production of Clemence Dane's *Will Shakespeare*, which I had a mean-spirited pleasure in judging harshly, although one performance stood out as "professional"—that of the girl who played Mary Fitton.

If it is a surprise even to me that I did not belong to the Dramatic Society clique, it is an even greater surprise that I did belong to the hearties of the rugby football club and did play for the college team. Certain men seem to have an inherent capacity for physical games—for throwing, catching, hitting, or kicking a ball, for anticipating the move of an opponent and reacting with lightning rapidity. I always admired but never possessed this skill—I was always there when the blow came—and yet I found myself in good football teams, only because I was physically strong and did not have enough football sense to be anything but indefatigable and industrious. I was often cheered for holding on to the ball, when the truth was that I lacked the skill to get rid of it. I was at my best on bad days, when rain resulted in our playing on a field of mud; then hard work was at a premium and brilliance at a discount. I enjoyed the fellowship of football rather than the game. Several of the other players were as much as ten years older than I; they had served in World War I and had come to the university from the armed forces. To me they were the epitome of worldly experience and wisdom. They, in turn, thought I was bright, but they had much more to teach me than I them. Sometimes we went on brief tours, and then the secretary relied on me to help him get the drunken ex-soldiers to bed in preparation for the next day's game. One such game was with a theological college, and after ten minutes' play, both teams were sent off the field for bad language.

During my four college summers and for many afterwards I took a leading part in camps for grammar school boys. Indeed, I soon became a commandant of the camps and thoroughly enjoyed them. They had been started by a group of idealistic university men, many of them pacifists as a legacy of their war experiences. The object was to enable boys from different schools to meet and exchange ideas under leadership of stimulating minds. Such men as Professor Dodd came to the camps, which were held on beautiful sites along the seashores or amid the mountains of Wales. Living conditions were invigoratingly primitive: bell tents and ground sheets, not even sleeping bags. Every night there was a sing-song and chapel, but the sing-song was much more than that; it was an entertainment often requiring a deal of preparation, and here I found full vent for my propensities as performer and storyteller.

It was while I was at one of these camps that I received a telegram from Port Talbot asking me to go for an interview at the secondary school there. I had forgotten that I had even applied, and could not remember what subject I was professing to teach. I was beginning to get desperate about a job because the debt at the bank was mounting, so I went for the interview, certain I was going to be unsuccessful because I had no teaching certificate, and secretly hoping to be so. But I was appointed, and so it seemed that my life course was settled. That interview took place in August, 1925. In November of the same year, a few miles away, a baby was born. He was named Richard Walter Jenkins. Sixteen years later he was to become Richard Burton.

Chapter Three

Port Talbot

In Port Talbot one of the largest and most modern steel works in Europe stands cheek-by-jowl with relics of the centuries: a Roman road, a Norman castle largely buried in sand, a twelfth-century abbey. There is a narrow littoral separating the mountains from the sea. From the mountains came the coal, the sea brought the ore, and the little Welsh town of Aberavon became a large steel town. In the narrow valleys between the mountains the life and language are still largely Welsh, but the town has inevitably become cosmopolitan. About thirty miles to the east is Cardiff; nearer, to the west, is Swansea.

The Port Talbot I first knew did not have today's prosperity and was considerably smaller. In those years of poverty and unemployment its future seemed bleak, but I found the place stimulating. Apart from the new adventure of teaching, which I found exciting in itself—some of my pupils were almost as old as I and eager for the fun of tearing me to pieces—I immediately set about starting some dramatic activity. The school was coeducational, which was a great help, and some members of the staff were wholeheartedly with me, particularly the physics master, an excellent pianist with some talent for composition. The head-master needed persuading. Wouldn't it take up too much time? Would people come to see the shows? After a few seasons he became our most staunch supporter, because the main annual play brought reputation and money to the school. For the first two years we restricted ourselves to one-act plays and musical enter-tainments, but then I did A *Midsummer Night's Dream* with suffi-cient success to establish a tradition that was maintained after I left.

We did several Shakespeare productions. I was particularly proud of a *Richard II* we did, and the boy, Owen Jones, who played Petruchio in our *Taming of the Shrew*, won the Lever-hulme Scholarship in open competition at the Royal Academy of Dramatic Arts in London. He went on to play Laertes in Olivier's full-length *Hamlet* at the Old Vic. I'm sure he would now be known to most readers of this book if he had not died while he was an officer in the Royal Air Force.

We also did several Bernard Shaw plays. My foster son, Rich-ard, made his debut in one of them; he played Mr. Vanhattan in *The Apple Cart* and the audience loved him. On that first night began what years later he described as his "love affair with the audience." A few seasons later he was very effective, considering his youth, as Professor Higgins in *Pygmalion*.

Very occasionally we did plays by writers other than Shake-speare or Shaw, but always costume pieces. One year, proud of my self-acquired French, I had the effrontery to do my own trans-lation of Molière's *Le Bourgeois Gentilhomme*. I shudder now at my temerity, but I still rather like my title: *The Amateur Aristo-crat*. Then there was a play about Florence Nightingale, called, of course, *The Lady with a Lamp*, and another about John Brown, the American abolitionist, called *Gallows Glorious*, in which Richard played one of the sons.

As I look back on those years of plays, I am amazed by the amount of genuine talent that was unearthed. I don't know why it should be so, but I am convinced that the proportion of acting talent in that school was higher than in any comparable group I have met since. After thirty years I can still recall quite extraordinary performances by youngsters who could have had brilliant careers in the theatre, but I have never encouraged anyone to become a professional actor. My dictum, now rusty with repetition, was and is: "If you wish to become a professional actor it must be not because of encouragement but in spite of discouragement." I was even surprised when Richard told me he wanted to be an actor, but, when he persisted in spite of the frightening picture I painted, I secretly rejoiced and set to work to fulfill our joint ambition. By this time he was my legal responsibility and was living with me. There followed such hard work, day in day out for two years, that a lesser person would have changed his mind. I am patient in teaching those that mean little to me, but not with those I love; this is a cruel quirk that I deplore and do my best to mitigate. To begin with, Richard had to get rid of an ugly Welsh accent. There are some beautiful Welsh accents, but they don't belong to the industrial towns. And it is not enough for an actor to acquire acceptable English speech only for the stage; until it becomes so organic that effort is required to speak with any other speech, he will not be able to give himself wholly to his part. If he has to be conscious of the sounds he is making, his acting will be fake; the same applies to singers in musicals.

But there was one thing I did not have to teach Richard; he had an instinctive love of words, particularly poetry. Often he would find a poem and bring it home with great excitement to try it on me, and his judgment was infallible. One Sunday morning he rushed in from the Welsh chapel, which he still attended, flourishing a newspaper; I believe it was the old *Sunday Referee*. "Listen to this," he said, and he read an extraordinary poem by a young man then unknown to me. It was "The force that through the green fuse drives the flower" by Dylan Thomas. I asked him what it meant and he said, "I don't know, but isn't it beautiful?"

My gradual adoption of Richard was the single event in my life most fraught with happy consequences for me. It was never a complete legal adoption because, although we both wanted this, when it was discovered that I was twenty days short of being twenty-one years older than the boy—he was born on November 10, I on November 30—full adoption was found to be impossible. Instead, a complicated legal document was executed making him officially my ward, at which time his name was legally changed from Jenkins to Burton.

Richard's mother had died when he was one year old and he had been brought up, with adoring love, by a sister twenty years older than he. She was married to a coalminer, and had two children of her own, both girls. The language of the home was Welsh, and the enthusiasm of the home was for music; mother and daughters all sang beautifully. And thereby hangs a tale.

Richard longed to sing too, and to compete in Eisteddfodau, the famous music and poetry festivals of the Welsh people. One day, a few years before he became a Burton, he asked me to teach him to sing a song, Sullivan's "Orpheus with His Lute." It was a soprano song and his voice was "in standing water, between boy and man." We stayed behind after school to have the assembly hall for ourselves. I sat at the piano and he faced an imaginary audience; we could not see each other's face. The song began and soon I was red with suppressed laughter; a string or two of Orpheus' lute was certainly broken. Finally the dam on my laughter burst; I was helpless. Richard, furious at himself and me, and as uncontrolled in his anger as I in my laughter, stormed off the stage, flinging back at me the exit line, "I'll show you. Someday I'll show you." I soon forgot the whole incident, and had to be reminded of it some fifteen years later when Richard said, "Well, I showed you, didn't I?" He made the remark in his dressing room after the opening performance of *Camelot*.

Richard had won a scholarship to the secondary school where I was a teacher, but times were hard and unemployment was rife; Richard had to leave the school to add in some way to the family coffers. At that time I was not aware of him, and would have continued in that state had he not been brought back to school. He had become a member of a boys' club, the leader of which recognized a great potential for something in the boy and thought it imperative that he should be returned to school. To this end he interceded with the family and the school authorities, and Richard resumed his education.

The man who achieved this quite difficult feat is now dead, but both Richard and I owe him a great debt of gratitude, for it was he who brought us together. His name was Meredith Jones. He came to see me when Richard's return to school was certain, because there was one thing that troubled him about it. During the boy's interlude in the workaday world—he had been an assistant in a clothing store—he had taken several jumps toward manhood, and Meredith was afraid that he might find the return to school discipline irksome to the point of rebellion. Apparently I was the teacher Richard most respected, and Meredith asked me to keep an eye on him. Thus began the relationship that altered both our lives. Once, when an interviewer for a magazine asked me in Richard's presence when I adopted him, he broke in with "He didn't. I adopted him." This did not mean that he conducted a clever campaign to ensnare me. It was just that he had a hungry need which I could best satisfy; in so doing, of course, I also fulfilled myself.

Mr. Lewis, the headmaster of the Port Talbot School, was a character of Dickensian richness, and I shall always be grateful to him for defying regulations on my behalf and taking me from the Mathematics Department and putting me in charge of the English Department, for which post I had no paper qualifications whatsoever. Life took on a new excitement; now I could share my enjoyment of great writing with eager young minds and could talk about Shakespeare in the classroom as well as in the theatre after school hours.

I tried one experiment in the teaching of Shakespeare that I like to think had some significance. There was one form, politely known as "The Remove," which was a dumping-ground for non-examination material; it was considered hopeless to try to get these students to acquire a school certificate of the Central Welsh Board. Consequently there was no pressure on the pupils or on the teachers who taught them, and I was given a completely free hand to see what I could do with them. They were a pleasant and amiable class, not at all depressed by their status. For them school was fun; for their friends in other forms it was hard work, much too hard work, in my opinion; most secondary school children in Welsh schools, at least at that time and probably still, put in more hours of concentrated work each day than their fathers.

I decided to teach *As You Like It* to the Remove by putting on a production of the play, which they would produce, design, and act. My choice of play is interesting. It was the very one that bad teaching had taught me to loathe, a crime I wanted to expiate, I suppose. I managed to excite the class about the project and was content to let the play itself win them gradually. I would not force the pace or even promise them an audience. I would not even explain the text in advance, but would only answer questions as they arose. It worked marvelously. It was decided for practical and economic reasons to do the play in modern dress, and this was a great stimulus to their imagination. Thus, Touchstone, a sort of "my man Jeeves," would never take off his prim bowler hat in the Forest of Arden. They even found some dull and difficult arithmetic was necessary for mounting and budgeting the play. The final result was quite astonishing and several public performances had to be given. Years later I met one of the actors; he was the director of a large factory employing many of his school fellows who had done well in those very examinations which had been beyond him.

My main dramatic activity in Port Talbot was not in the school but in the Y.M.C.A., where the secretary was an old music hall artist, a bewilderingly clever conjurer and escapologist, who welcomed my enthusiasm for theatre. We had originally met at a conference in Oxford, when it seemed I might be joining the London staff of the Y.M.C.A. We immediately formed a dramatic society, which still flourishes and sent me greetings a few years ago on the occasion of its fortieth anniversary.

The director was a delightful and stage-wise schoolteacher named Ivor Nicholas. I suppose it was I who chiefly determined the policy and program for the society in late-night sessions with Ivor, and I confess, with a blush, that I ended up playing most of the leading parts. I was determined to take the society into the rarefied atmosphere of great plays, but we started quietly with period pieces; no royalties had to be paid for them. Our first production was T. W. Robertson's *Caste*. (It was the revolution that Robertson inaugurated in the London theatre which formed the basis for Pinero's delightful *Trelawney of the Wells*.) Then we went on to Dickens' *The Cricket on the Hearth*. Occasionally we returned to Victorian plays, notably with a play based upon an episode, probably fictitious, in the life of David Garrick, but soon I was leading the company to more rewarding pastures where I longed to browse myself. We began with Shaw, *Arms and the Man* and *You Never Can Tell*, and in a few years we were tackling Shakespeare, *The Taming of the Shrew*, *Othello*, *King Lear*. We even went way out one season with Andreyev's *He Who Gets Slapped*. We interlarded the great plays with more immediately popular ones, such as *Alibi*, *Love From a Stranger*, *Thunder in the Air*.

During these years in Wales there was a great outburst of dramatic activity such as that of the society that claimed my allegiance, and this widespread activity was focused in drama festivals. For an annual week many towns would hold such a festival. A different group would present a different play each night. People would buy season tickets, and conversation in the town before, during, and after the festival would largely be taken up with arguments about the merits of the various productions. Before the festival? Yes, because the work of previous years was remem-

45

bered, and in surprising detail. "Remember his John Gabriel Borkman? Very good, but too slow. The Archer translation is stiff enough without taking it at that pace."

Competition even to secure an invitation to a festival was fierce and did much to improve the choice of plays and the standard of productions. The basic expenses of the invited companies were paid—some more prosperous festivals with larger theatres paid more than others, and therefore were more desirable to competitors—and often substantial money awards were made to the winners. Some festivals, too, gave a silver cup for the best individual performance of the week. Only once did I win such an award—it was for my Othello—and I treasured it for a long time.

The adjudicator at a drama festival was usually a theatre critic from London. His own performance at the end of the festival was the climax of the week, and thus his ability to hold an audience by a clever and preferably witty dissection of the six productions was more important than genuine critical acumen. The successful practitioner of this art would mete out praise and blame so adroitly that after he had finished speaking about the six plays the audience would still not know which presentation was to be adjudged the winner until it was revealed at the end of the last suspenseful sentence.

After I had left the world of amateur theatre I did a good deal of adjudicating at drama festivals and quite enjoyed talking about the productions, but was always tormented by having to choose a winner. The basic conflict of values involved was that faced by every Broadway critic: How do you balance the reaction to a trifling work perfectly presented with that to a flawed masterpiece imperfectly presented?

I never made a statistical investigation, but I'm sure that the leading members of most of the dramatic societies in Wales were teachers. When I first came to America, it was a shock to me to discover the comparatively low social status of schoolteaching, for in Wales it was an honored profession. In New York, a working-class Jewish family has for its ambition that the son should be a

A partial view of Mountain Ash.

One of the coalmines in Mountain Ash.

St. Margaret's Church, Mountain Ash.

The College Rugby XV.

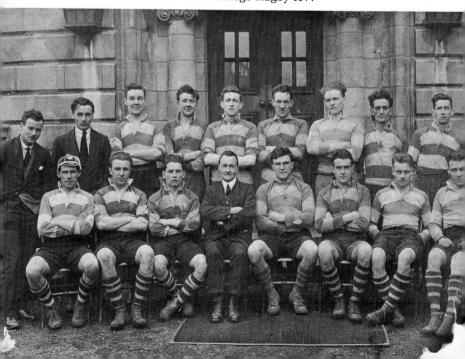

The author as Othello in 1932.
(Newark Lewis)

The final scene of the Margam Abbey Pageant.

An early studio portrait of Richard and the author. *(Newark Lewis)*

The "Main House" of Camp McArthur in Waitsfield, Vermont.

The author directing a broadcast from the B.B.C. studios in Cardiff.

The author, with Christian Alderson, in *The Caretaker*.   *(Gerald Kean)*

author, with Margaret Fairchild, in *The Man Who Came to Dinner*. (*Gerald Kean*)

The three Burtons in a rehearsal for the Poetry Reading.   *(Friedman-Abeles)*

doctor or a lawyer. In Wales, the ambition of a comparable non-Jewish family would be that the son should be a teacher. But in Wales, as in America, the chances of such advancement were very much determined by where you lived. Just as in America the standard of public education depends upon the tax wealth or poverty of the state, so in Wales differences are dependent upon the counties; a populous industrial county can afford more than can a sparsely populated rural one. I consider myself highly fortunate in having been born and reared in Glamorgan, the richest industrial county in Wales, and I should not be surprised to find that it was the county with the highest public educational standards in the whole of Great Britain. Since education was so important to the people of Glamorgan, teaching was an honored and desirable profession. Glamorgan being so pre-eminently industrial, it was, of course, the worst hit during the Depression, but, even then, the educational standards were not allowed to lag, and teaching became a still more desirable profession, now as an escape from abject poverty. Public funds provided a midday meal at the schools, and parents made great sacrifices that their son or daughter who had been fortunate enough to secure a place in the grammar school should not appear there in clothes too obviously threadbare. Thus some of the best talents in Wales became teachers, and it was their cultural enthusiasm and intellectual vigor that gave life and impetus to many community activities—political parties, religious societies, dramatic groups, choral and orchestral societies.

Certainly there were several teachers, from both elementary and secondary schools, in our dramatic society in Port Talbot. With them were some businessmen, executives and clerks from industry, and assorted wives. When we took part in a festival, the stage crew would leave with the set and costumes early in the day and the company would follow by bus in the late afternoon, often arriving just in time for a quick change and a hasty entrance.

My enthusiasm for theatre found vent in another activity in Port Talbot, and one that has become a permanent part of my life—lecturing. Just as would-be actors became preachers in nineteenth-century puritanical Wales, my thespian frustrations led me to the lecture platform.

While I was still at college, I had already done some lecturing. I had even had the impudence, when I was not yet twenty years of age, to deliver a lecture to a conference of Y.M.C.A. secretaries at Keble College, Oxford, on "The Philosophical Implications of Einstein's Theory of Relativity." Fools rush in, indeed! But it was as a result of that adventure that Zwingli Willis wanted me to join his staff; it must have been my temerity that impressed him. Some may be surprised to find the "Y" associated with philosophy, relativity, and even education, for there is a mistaken idea, particularly in America, that a big-city "Y" exists solely to provide cheap lodgings, gymnasiums, and swimming pools.

There was an admirable society in Great Britain known as the Workers' Educational Association, which, often in conjunction with the universities, organized lecture courses throughout the land. Nowhere were the services of the W.E.A. more in demand than in Wales. Wherever a group of culturally thirsty people got together, an appropriate lecturer would be found for them. There was even a group of slate quarry workers in North Wales who spent several years in studying New Testament Greek.

The Y.M.C.A. secretary in Port Talbot was anxious to use me as a lecturer; he had known little enough about both philosophy and Einstein to have been impressed by my performance at Oxford. I had no academic qualifications to talk about drama, so a group was collected, again largely composed of teachers, and they applied to the W.E.A. for my services as a lecturer on Modern European History. The class was a success, but I wanted to talk about drama, and after two seasons and much pleading and persuasion at W.E.A. Headquarters, I was allowed to switch to Modern Drama.

It was a condition of the W.E.A. classes that the students should do some written work, and I still remember the opening sentence of a long essay on John Galsworthy by a clerk at the steelworks who was irritated by what he considered to be Galsworthy's ill-informed and sentimental attachment to the underdog: "John Galsworthy will live neither as a novelist nor a playwright, but as the patron saint of the Royal Society for the Prevention of Cruelty to Animals."

In addition to directing, acting, and lecturing, there was yet one more theatre activity that Port Talbot was to initiate for me—writing. I began to write plays. I have a dim recollection that while I was still a boy in school in Mountain Ash I wrote a long one-act play that was never performed. All I remember now is that it took place in the waiting room of a railway station and that two of the characters were an old man and woman who were on their way to the workhouse where they would be separated for the rest of their lives, a sentimental situation at once revealing my besetting sin as a dramatist. But in Port Talbot I wrote plays that were performed, even in drama festivals. For several years I made a fair amount of money from royalties from two of them, the second of which, *White Collar*, was written as a requested sequel to the first, *Granton Street*. When they were originally produced by my own society in Port Talbot, I am relieved to remember that I did not play a leading part in either of them; it is good to know that the dramatist in me wrote something he wanted to say, not something he wanted to play.

The scene of both plays is a miner's home in Abernansant, a fictitious town in South Wales. It was my own home. *Granton Street* takes place entirely in the "front room," which was carefully reserved for special occasions, like family gatherings and funerals. Our own front room is forever fixed in my mind as a place of death, for there I saw the laid-out corpse of my father when I was a boy and of my mother when I was a man. The sickly smell of flowers, lighted candles, and dead flesh in the darkened room still lingers in the memory of my senses. *White Collar* takes place in the kitchen of the house. The central incident of the first play is a parliamentary election, and of the second, a threatened strike. Both plays, as I read them now, are old fashioned in subject matter because they deal with social problems that have largely been solved, and they are old fashioned in form because they derive from the Ibsenite well-made play. Both plays tell me a lot about myself, in particular my protest against a class-conscious society and the problem of my innate liberalism, which is the paralyzing effect of seeing both sides of a coin. I castigated my own failure to be an out-and-out socialist with this aphorism: "A liberal is a man who wants to be a conservative because it's respectable but is prevented by what remains of his conscience." I invented a character, Uncle Jim, a well-educated bum who lives by his wits, of which he has a plentiful supply, and who holds up to ridicule all those solid-citizen virtues to which I was afraid my poverty and need might condemn me. Here are some typical observations of Uncle Jim: "The sacrifices most people have to make to get on rob them of all power to enjoy their success. . . . Life is a goodly wine but it requires a delicate palate really to appreciate it. So many people drink the wine of life as if it were beer—or, worse still, water. . . . Most people nowadays are so worried by Life that they forget to live, and then, when they get older, they are so frightened of Death that they are afraid to live."

Granton Street is a Romeo and Juliet story. The Romeo is a young medical student put through college by the sacrifices of his mining family. The Juliet is the daughter of the managing director of the mine. Uncle Jim, in trying to persuade Romeo's implacably socialist brother to withdraw his violent hostility to the match, sums up the theme of the play, albeit in a speech so pontifical that only my raw and immature fervor can excuse it: "Since the realms of higher education have been opened to the children of every class, there has arisen a new division in society—that between the cultured and the uncultured. Lack of culture is not any longer the characteristic of any one particular class alone. The members of this new cultured class are drawn from the ranks of all the old classes, and they are more in sympathy with one another than with the uncultured of the class from which they come."

In *White Collar*, there is a comment about teachers which came straight from my early classroom experience. "There are only two kinds of teachers: those who are so happy that they are unwilling to die and go to Heaven, and those who are so unhappy that they are willing to die and go to Hell." The daily agony of a teacher who is a weak disciplinarian is a torment of the damned, and I saw such agony in a young teacher who probably had to face forty years of it. Fortunately, I soon found my own solution to the problem, and it had much to teach me in later years when I had to command an audience from a stage or a lecture platform. I began in the worst possible way by shouting down a noisy class. I progressed to domination by the threat of punishment. Then came the cruel phase of withering sarcasm, for which even now, after all these years, I feel the need to apologize. As I became more secure, I graduated to gentle sarcasm, which even the victims enjoyed then and quoted long after they had left school. But there is no problem of getting and holding attention, in either the classroom or the theatre, if one is excited by a subject and eager to get others to share that excitement.

I wrote several plays subsequently and in only one of them did I break away from my own early Welsh setting. That one, *Storm in Summer*, is set in an English manor house, but again it deals with a young man whose ideas are at odds with his upbringing. It is a gentle play, because I was under the influence of Tchekov when I wrote it, and yet it deals with the outbreak of war in 1939.

It was the writing of a pageant, not a play, that altered my life and finally took me out of Port Talbot, first to Cardiff, then to London, then to New York. The year 1937 marked the eight-hundredth anniversary of the founding of Margam Abbey, the ruins of which lie on the eastern outskirts of Port Talbot. Part of the old abbey is incorporated in the structure of the present church, but the most impressive part of the remains is the roofless but still exquisitely beautiful and unique octagonal chapter house. The abbey was virtually at sea level, but a few miles inland. Some very old farms lay between it and the sea and it is still possible to find in the walls of the farm extensions, like the pigsties, stones from the dismembered abbey, stolen when, with most of the other monasteries throughout the land, it was dissolved by Henry VIII in the 1530's.

On a slight hill above the abbey is Margam Castle, an elaborate nineteenth-century construction; there are several such buildings throughout industrial South Wales. They were built to house and flatter the new aristocracy, who needed castles to match their new peerages. In 1937, Margam Castle was the seat of the Talbot family, who had given their name to the town. The lord of the manor then was Captain Talbot Fletcher.

It was decided to hold a pageant in the abbey grounds to commemorate the notable anniversary of the founding of the abbey, and I was asked to write and direct it, with the research assistance of the history master at the school where I taught. He was a delightful man who spent his summers excavating the Norman castle of Kenfig from the sand that had buried it centuries before, and bid fair to do so again as soon as his back was turned. This castle was roughly as old as the abbey and lay between it and the sea.

The cast of the pageant was all amateur, and class distinction was to determine the apportionment of parts; peasants and monks were to be played by peasants, and gentry by gentry, but oh! the suffering of the in-betweens who jealously guarded every symbol of social position, such as costumes, billing, and place in processions. I found my imagination much stimulated by the fact that the peasants of the twelfth century were being impersonated by people many of whom were almost certainly their direct descendants. I worked with them for months, for they had to carry the bulk of the action, and there was plenty of that: medieval festivities, including the performance of an old nativity play; medieval disasters, such as the Black Death and overwhelming sand storms; social upheavals, such as the Peasant Revolt. I remember a fiery sermon by a Lollard, who was played by the man who had been equally fiery as a socialist in my *Granton Street* and *White Collar*;

he himself was an employer of labor and an ardent member of the Conservative Party. The pageant ended with a vision of the Virgin Mary high in a ruined window of the chapter house; the cast of hundreds, led by the unseen organ in the abbey church, joined in a hymn to her. She was played by Captain Fletcher's wife, an exquisite lady with the most beautiful complexion I had ever seen.

The pageant was played for a series of afternoons. Of course, both players and audience were open to the elements and, of course, rain canceled some performances, but to the last of them came a man who was to alter my life. He was T. Rowland Hughes, the Features Producer in Wales of the British Broadcasting Corporation. Those were the days when television was still a whispered back-room experiment. A "feature" in the B.B.C. sense of the word is a documentary, and it was allowed a wide latitude in form so that at one end it was hard to distinguish it from a play and at the other from a product of the news or the talks department.

Since the B.B.C. will figure largely in these pages, I should perhaps give some brief account of it, for its constitution and operation are fundamentally different from those of broadcasting companies in America. Although commercial television now exists side-by-side with that of the B.B.C. in Great Britain, radio broadcasting is still the sole prerogative of the B.B.C. There is a misconception abroad that the B.B.C. is government-controlled and therefore suspect. It is, in fact, a particularly happy example of the British genius for compromise, because although it is completely financed from licenses for radio and television sets collected by the Post Office, and although its Board of Governors is appointed by the government, it is independent of the government in its operation. Several times Parliament has tried to exercise control and every time the independence of the B.B.C. has been upheld. Appointments to vacancies on the Board of Governors are laudably above consideration of political party affiliation. Due regard is also paid to the regional needs of the listeners and viewers, for six almost autonomous regional bodies exist in addition to

53

the main body in London, and they are given the power and the means to produce programs to encourage local talent and cater for local needs. Such a regional unit of the B.B.C. is Wales, with studios in Cardiff, Swansea, and Bangor.

Rowland Hughes was a remarkable man. He was the son of a North Wales quarryman and as such an alien in the South. Why is it that in so many countries there is such disparity, and often hostility, between the North and the South? Nowhere is this more apparent than in the tiny principality of Wales. They speak English with markedly different accents and when they speak Welsh they are almost unintelligible to one another. Temperamentally they seem to belong to different species, the typical Northman being reserved and suspicious, and the typical man from the mining valleys of the South being outgoing and friendly. It suddenly strikes me that there is something of the same difference between a Vermonter and a Virginian, between a Breton and a Provençal, between a Prussian and a Bavarian. Rowland Hughes was a typical Northman, slight in build, and deep in spirit. He had learned English almost as a foreign language and yet had made it his principal study, doing brilliantly in it at Oxford. His knowledge of English poetry was wide and deep, and I learned much from him over the years. But his special affection was reserved for the London magazine writers of the early nineteenth century, and in particular for the gentle Charles Lamb.

I was backstage after the final performance of the Pageant of Margam Abbey, flitting from one group to another with thanks, congratulations, and quips, when I was told that a man from the B.B.C. wanted to see me. It was Rowland Hughes. He told me later that I kept him waiting quite a time. If I did, it speaks well of him that he stayed, because an official of the B.B.C. was a distinguished visitor, indeed. I had no idea what he wanted to see me about, but I'm amazed that I didn't go running to him. After all, he was a visitor from the professional world, and a word of praise from him would be doubly sweet. He probably did praise me—I have never known anybody to come backstage after a show with other than praise, although they often speak poison when they get outside the stage door—but his purpose was different; he wanted me to write a radio version of the pageant. I was dumbfounded; literally. He thought I hadn't understood him, so he said it again. I sputtered and stuttered that it couldn't be done; the whole thing had been conceived in visual terms. He pointed out that there was a good deal of dialogue and music. The pageant had even started with a sonnet; yes, I had actually written a sonnet, the only poem of mine ever to reach the public ear, and every line of which is mercifully erased from my own private memory. I reluctantly, although with deep inner excitement, promised that I would try to write a feature program about Margam Abbey. I was to write over one hundred full-length radio scripts subsequently—thirty, forty-five, sixty, or ninety minutes long—but none was more difficult than that first one. In learning to solve its problems, which I did with the patient and knowledgeable help of Rowland Hughes, I learned much about the exciting art of radio writing.

And so I was launched on a new career, which for several years was to be a profitable sideline. After Margam Abbey I did a dramatic triptych on Shakespeare and the Welsh, making much of the fact that the boy Shakespeare had had a Welsh schoolmaster, Thomas Jenkins. The first script dealt with a fictitious incident in Shakespeare's boyhood, when the James Burbage players came to Stratford-on-Avon. Three young boys were needed for the cast to play Will Shakespeare, Richard Field, another Stratford boy who was to be the publisher of *Venus and Adonis,* and Richard Burbage, for whom Shakespeare was to write many of his greatest parts. I was allowed to cast them from my school, provided I would guarantee that they would sound like English boys, not Welsh. Obviously the boys had to come from the junior school and my knowledge was restricted to the upper school; therefore, a notice was posted inviting any young boy whose voice had not broken to come to an open audition. Many came and all but three had to be disappointed. One of them still holds it against me that I turned him down; his name was Richard Jenkins.

My first day in the Atlantic was Easter Sunday but for me it was Good Friday, for I was so seasick that I would have settled for death to end it. And it continued for three days, on the last of which I was able to read, but not to move. I never used my deck chair, which experienced voyagers had told me to hurry to hire, to be sure of getting it well placed. Bertrand Russell has said that one of the few compensations he had found in getting old was that seasickness became progressively less of a terror with age, and in later years I was to find that this was true in my case too. But oh! that 1939 voyage. The book I first felt strong enough to want to read was Noël Coward's *Present Indicative,* and somehow it was a reassuring omen to find that he, too, had first crossed the Atlantic on the *Aquitania* and that his first stay in America was five months long. I remember the sense I had of trying my luck and testing my stomach in tackling my second book of the voyage, one by Richard Hughes, for whom I had had a great admiration from the time he had awarded a prize to my play *Granton Street* in a drama festival. The book was *In Hazard,* a terrifying account of a storm at sea. A few years later I was to write and direct a radio version of the book in which Hughes was to play the Narrator, and I still remember the last-minute crisis he caused. We had completed the final run-through and there was a half-hour before we went on the air at quarter past nine in the evening. The program had been given the important period following the nine o'clock news. In those days, British radio had the luxury of multi-studio technique, each studio having its own acoustic quality and none of them being visible from the control room. A minute before transmission, a worried actor popped his head into the control room to say that Richard Hughes was missing, and he was to open the program. I dashed out and found him waiting, with apparent nonchalance, at the reception desk where an adamant official refused to allow him to go further without his permit, which he had mislaid. Those were the days of war and such were the stupidities it engendered in the inflexibly zealous.

My first sight of America was under perfect conditions—a

balmy spring evening with the lights lending their fairyland magic to the sight that never ceases to amaze me. First there is the Long Island shoreline, which seems by night to be an endless pleasure beach, but it is Manhattan for which no photographs or films can ever fully prepare you. My first impression was of a gigantic fireworks representation of a battleship, with the downtown skyscrapers as the massive hull and those in midtown the bridge. There was great excitement in the river when we arrived, and it transpired that a fellow passenger had been Lindbergh, whose privacy aboard ship had been jealously guarded.

I had decided to spend my first American night on board, but when all my voyage friends left the ship, I did too, and found my way by midnight to a Y.M.C.A., Sloane House. I spent two months there and learned much about America. Those who lived there were either starry-eyed or disillusioned—those young and confident enough to believe that the future was theirs and those old enough to have been robbed of their future by the Depression; several of these cynically disappointed ones felt that their only hope was in Canada. I was gradually surprised to find that most of the young men working in Sloane House were doing so to help themselves pay for education and training in their chosen fields. I continue to find this an admirable expression of American independence and self-reliance, and at that time it was totally unknown to me in Britain. I heard the world talk in that Y.M.C.A., for I listened to men as varied as an Eskimo pianist and a man who had fought in the Boer War on the side of the Boers; he had been captured by the British and at the end of the war had been offered either repatriation or imprisonment on St. Helena; he bitterly regretted not having chosen St. Helena, because ultimately it would have led to British citizenship, whereas he had cast his lot with a people "who do not and never will belong to the twentieth century."

I was up early that first morning and walked to Central Park, but my devotion to the open air has always been more dutiful than enthusiastic, and it is quite characteristic of me that on that first beautiful day I went indoors to see three shows. They could scarcely have been more varied: the Planetarium, a play—*The Flashing Stream*—and the circus at Madison Square Garden.

I had never been to a planetarium before and I was profoundly impressed. From childhood, the immensities and mysteries of space have terrified me. Of all the verses I learned to chant in church, the one that found the readiest echo in me was, "When I consider thy heavens, the work of thy fingers, the moon and the stars which thou hast ordained, what is man, that thou art mindful of him?" Whereas most of my childhood is a blank, I still remember some of the climactic adventures of my imagination, and none more vividly than the lonely, star-bright night when I looked through the sky and found I could not comprehend either an end to space, with nothingness beyond, or endlessness. I was frightened by the inadequacy of my mind, and that feeling has never left me. It has made me sympathetic to the mystical and super-rational; if my mind cannot grasp the physical universe, it dare not set arbitrary limits to experience.

Not only did the Planetarium itself impress me, but also the audience with which I shared the show. It was largely composed of teen-age school children, who took part in a broadcast quiz show on astronomy. Their knowledge astonished and shamed me, but then the knowledge of children interested in mechanics, engineering, and science always has this effect on me, for I am still not quite certain how an automobile works. I console myself by remembering that even I know more about physical phenomena than Shakespeare did; knowledge changes but wisdom remains.

The Flashing Stream, a play by Charles Morgan, was an importation from London where it had had a great success. Indeed, I had twice failed to get in to see it. When I sailed from Southampton, the production had not opened on Broadway; I arrived in time to see the last matinee. The play was very well done and had the same leading players as in London, Godfrey Tearle and Margaret Rawlings. In London the critics had found the intellectual content of the play stimulating, but in New York the same quality had been dismissed as pretentious and boring—and I found my-self agreeing with the New York critics. Had I seen the very same show in London, my reaction might have been different. I believe I am the kind of person whose reaction is much conditioned by my expectation, and also by the atmosphere of the general reac-tion around me. At the same time, being well aware of this weak-ness in myself, I sometimes strive too hard to be objective; I think it is healthier, and certainly more enjoyable, to give oneself over wholly to the experience, whatever conditions it. Professional theatrical criticism seems to me to be an essentially crippling ex-perience because one cannot fully experience anything if at the very same moment one is analyzing that experience.

The different receptions of the same productions in London and New York are a matter of endless fascination, and I am the first to acknowledge that acquaintance with the theatre in the two cities has given me no powers of prophecy. I predicted disaster on Broadway for both *The Boy Friend* and *Witness for the Prosecu-tion*. But I have a feeling that the differences have dwindled since 1939 to a fair measure of predictability. Nowadays, a popular Broadway musical is likely to get popular acclaim when trans-ferred to the West End, whatever the London critics might say about it, and an English play that has won critical acclaim in London is likely to be well received by the New York critics, whatever the paying playgoer might say about it.

Occasionally I think it is possible to understand why a success in one country is not repeated in the other. A classical instance is *Death of a Salesman*. When I saw the original production in New York, it was one of my most memorable nights in the theatre, but an excellent production in London, with that admirable actor Paul Muni as Willy Loman, certainly failed to make the same impres-sion. I think this was due to the different values brought to the experience by the two audiences. The high standard of living ac-complished by the American economy is largely based on planned obsolescence. And so the salesman is a pivotal and respected figure in the life of the country; if he cannot constantly persuade us to buy the latest, the economy will suffer. Thus an American audience finds in Willy Loman some of their basic values put on trial, and his failure and death achieve tragic stature. But in England the salesman is traditionally a comic figure. I think of the little man who "travels in sardines" in John Drinkwater's *Bird in Hand*. To an audience with this deeply embedded attitude toward salesmanship, *Death of a Salesman* seemed a disproportionate fuss about an unimportant person. Failure and death in themselves do not constitute tragedy; they are much too common for that. They only achieve universal significance when they happen to a person of stature. Galsworthy had tried to make a tragedy in *Justice* from the downfall of a little clerk, but he had moved us to pity, not to awe. When the gods crush a man, he must be a lion, not a beetle, to be remembered.

It should be remarked that the national differences between audiences can be paralleled by differences within the one country. More than once in New York I have heard actors dazed by failure say, "I don't understand it; we wowed them in Boston"; similarly in London, "They loved us in Brighton."

My third entertainment on that first day in New York was the circus. For me, the old Madison Square Garden in itself was more exciting than almost anything it could display, always provided that it was full; I find it embarrassing when a show plays to acres of empty seats. I imagine I should have felt the same about the Colosseum in ancient Rome. Did the circus I saw have five rings, or was it only three? Whichever it was, anything above one would have exasperated me, and the more rings, the greater my exasperation. I find myself looking frantically from ring to ring for fear of missing something and often succeeding in doing just that, applause drawing my eyes to a ring in time to see the performers bowing after some stupendous feat that I have just missed. (The new Madison Square Garden, with its admirable organization to deal with its thousands of patrons, lacks for me the warmth and humanity of the old one. When I enter the new one, I feel I am being processed in a factory.)

Radio City Music Hall, like the Empire State Building, must be seen by every visitor to New York, and I was a visitor. The Empire State Building was a pathetic victim of the Depression. Only 28 of the 102 stories were occupied, and bitterness had renamed it the Empty State Building. Incidentally, I have never heard a convincing explanation of why New York is called the Empire State. I went to the Music Hall for the first show on my second American morning, and I confess that I was astonished and thrilled. I say "confess" because it is de rigueur to be appalled by the vulgarity of the Music Hall shows. Of course they are designed to impress and please the unsophisticated multitude, but at their best they do so brilliantly, and there is something aesthetically satisfying to me in the precise deployment of a large number of trained and disciplined bodies, even though it serves no high artistic purpose. Years later I went backstage at the Music Hall and was dazzled by the intricate and accurate organization of the multifarious activities that go to make up the show. But, of course, the impact of mere size and precision diminishes with repeated visits until ultimately one goes to see the movie, and inasmuch as the film is also chosen to please the same audience at which the stage show is aimed, one doesn't go frequently.

During my first sojourn in New York, I saw more than sixty shows of very various kinds. All that was missing was any production of a classic. The nearest I got to that was a very lively forty-minute version of *The Taming of the Shrew* in the reproduction of Shakespeare's Globe Theatre at the World's Fair. Yes, it was the year of the World's Fair, of which my most vivid recollection is the opening of the Polish Pavilion, at which I was present. I remember it because it was almost the occasion of an international incident; the workmen on the nearby and still unfinished Italian Pavilion did their best by noisy and excessive industry to drown out the Polish ceremony.

The year 1939 was also the occasion of the visit to New York of King George VI and his queen. In connection with the visit, the British Broadcasting Corporation did a series of broadcasts from New York on the city, and I was asked to talk about Broadway. Twenty years later I listened to the recordings of my talks and it was interesting to find out what had impressed me. The performance I could not find enough superlatives for was that of Ethel Waters in *Mamba's Daughters*. It was in a theatre that is now no more—one of the few theatres that was actually on Broadway—the Empire, and outside it was a large display of words of praise heaped upon Miss Waters by leading actors and actresses. The fact that the New York audience needed such an inducement to buy tickets should have taught me a lesson I was slow to learn and which has become ever more true with the years. Compared with London and Paris, for instance, there is little interest in New York in the art of acting as such. The merit of the play is paramount. I am sure this is a worthy thing, but had I applied it throughout my life to determine what plays I went to see, I should have missed some very exciting nights in the theatre.

Two American playwrights, the first of them hitherto unknown to me even by name, called forth high praise from me: William Saroyan and Clifford Odets. I was completely enchanted by Saroyan's *My Heart's in the Highlands*, and in my broadcast talk I prophesied a bright future for a fourteen-year-old actor in the cast. I was right in my prophecy, but the boy became a director; his name was Sidney Lumet. Odets' play was *Awake and Sing*. I suppose it must have been a revival of the play, because I had read it some years before in England, as I had other of his plays. Odets' vigor and power were unmatched by anybody writing in English at that time.

In some seasons nowadays, English artists seem almost to monopolize Broadway, but even in 1939 I was able to tell the British listeners that some of their own favorites were equally admired in New York. Beatrice Lillie was delighting the town in Noël Coward's *Set to Music*, Laurence Olivier was being brilliant in *No Time for Comedy*, and Robert Morley was giving probably his most memorable performance in *Oscar Wilde*. I gathered one of my first examples of the kind of colorful conversational invective that spices theatrical talk in New York when I was discussing the production of *Oscar Wilde*. I asked an actor what he thought of a certain performance in the play. He said, "It stank on ice." I felt his grammar was faulty, but I agreed with his sentiments.

Perhaps the thing that impressed me most about the Broadway theatre in 1939 was the Federal Projects Theatre. In a time of economic recession, the theatre is the first to suffer. Even in the prosperity of the sixties, it is a sad thought that the great majority of New York's residents have never seen a Broadway play and that each season soaring prices carry the theatre out of the range of medium-sized pockets. But in the penny-pinched thirties, many of the theatre's usual patrons had to suspend their patronage, and it was wholly admirable that Washington provided employment for out-of-work artists and technicians in the Federal Projects Theatre as the W.P.A. did for other unemployed workers. There was little money available for the productions, but the imaginative skills of theatre artists have often been quickened by small budgets. I marveled at how much was accomplished with so little. Yet there is a sad end to my recollections of the Federal Projects Theatre. I had just finished a recording for the B.B.C. in which I had praised George Sklar's *Life and Death of an American*, not only for its own considerable theatrical merits, but also because the very fact of its production with a government subsidy seemed a triumph of democracy at a time when democracy was being strangled in many places, for this play was a bitter and trenchant attack on government and society. Alas, as I came out into the street, still aglow with the enthusiasm that my own words had rekindled, I bought a newspaper and saw on the front page that, because of the leftist tendencies of some of its productions, the Federal Projects Theatre was being terminated.

For many people, I'm sure, the highest point of my experience of the American theatre in 1939 would have been *Tristan and Isolde* with Melchior and Flagstad at the now deceased and lamented theatre that then housed the Metropolitan Opera, but I remain partially deaf and blind to the glories of opera. For

Wagner and his followers it is total theatre; for me it remains bastard theatre. I suppose it is true that words mean more to me than music, but also the singing is such a preeminent value in opera that in my experience the acting rarely escapes being embarrassing. There was a singer in my native Mountain Ash with the most extraordinary bass voice I have ever heard. He was known in the world of Welsh singers as "Jack Basso." He was as simple as a child and sang as a child plays on a beach, for the sheer exhilaration of it. He would sing his heart out for the joy of giving pleasure. He did not even need the drop of a hat. Had he accepted one of the numerous offers made to him by noted impresarios, the world would have heard and remembered his voice, but the offers involved training and discipline, and these were impossible for him. I once persuaded him to go to Cardiff to hear Chaliapin; he dismissed that great artist as a "bloody actor." But for me, a Chaliapin is necessary to make opera really palatable.

The ostensible purpose of my visit to the United States was to observe the place of drama in the schools and colleges. I suddenly awoke to the fact that I had better do something about it, and quickly, because for the greater part of my stay the schools and colleges would be closed, except for certain limited summer activities. I made arrangements to visit some varied schools in the New York district, and "varied" is the key word. Indeed, it is this aspect of American education as a whole that is least understood by Britons. At that time a higher percentage of the population went to colleges in the United States than went to secondary schools in Great Britain, so my inherited conception of colleges and universities being places for the intellectual elite had to be basically revised. The accepted diversity and disparity of talents and endowments among pupils in British secondary schools also obtains among students in American colleges. Unfortunately, the more frivolous and nonacademic activities of students in colleges catering for the less gifted have received most publicity abroad, particularly in films, and I have found it very difficult to persuade members of the general public in Great Britain that, at the other

66

end of the scale, the best university education in America is second to none in the world. Their eyes have been blinded by spectacular football games decorated with curvaceous, baton-swinging drum majorettes, their ears have been deafened by brass bands, and their prejudices have been strengthened by jokes about college courses in flower arrangement.

Of the New York schools I visited, four had special significance for me: the first for its special problem, the second for its size, the third for its uniqueness, and the fourth for its high achievement in the kind of education to which I was accustomed.

The first school was in a poor district of immigrants. Most of the children came from homes where they heard little or no English, only Italian or Polish. (I visited no "blackboard jungle" schools, because I was unaware of their existence, and I was unlikely to have been guided to them by Americans whose understandable desire was to show their country at its best, or at least to avoid showing it at its worst.) At this first school I was struck by the fact that the teachers of English, in common with those of other subjects, had not merely to teach their subject but also tangentially to inculcate a sense of nationhood. The confusion of loyalties in the parents, whose roots lay centuries deep in Europe, resulted in a rootlessness in the children. If this is neglected, it can lead to antisocial bitterness in the child, as is so evident today; on the other hand, proper education can induce a fruitful spirit of ardent nationhood, for there is no zeal like that of the newly converted. This positive approach is also, of course, fraught with great dangers, for everything depends upon the qualities of being American that are inculcated. The responsibilities of teaching the young are too little realized, even by some teachers, and American society as a whole pays insufficient regard to it.

I was pleased to discover that dramatic methods were being used in the school to bring a knowledge of the United States to the children whose parents had come from Europe. In one class I visited, two children were supposed to be taking a trip throughout the country. The other children had been assigned different regions of the country, and it had been their task to find out all they could about the locality in which they were presumed to live, so that they would have the knowledge to answer the questions of the "visitors." The teacher had industriously gathered material, chiefly pictures, to supplement—and sometimes correct!—the information provided by the "inhabitants." The idea was much more exciting than the results were rewarding, because very few of the children rose above a listless participation, and the idealistic teacher had my sympathy.

The large school I visited dumbfounded me by its size, nearly six thousand pupils. There were almost as many teachers as there had been pupils in my own school in Wales. The principal, a delightful man, gave up his whole day to me; I was not only flattered by this, but also impressed that, with such a vast empire to rule, he could spare the time. An amusing and revealing episode took place during our tour of the premises. We met a man in a corridor and the principal stopped to ask him his business, only to discover that the stranger was one of his staff.

I understand that in recent decades there has been a movement in Britain toward large "comprehensive" secondary schools on the American pattern. While understanding the idealistic concepts upon which this movement is based, such as flexibility of curriculum and the avoidance of attendance at an academic school becoming an intellectual status symbol, I am not at all convinced of the desirability of large catch-all schools. It may be that I am merely prejudiced in favor of the size of school I attended, which had a strong sense of unity and community, but I do have a deep fear that large schools inevitably tend to become dehumanized educational factories. I also fear that raising educational opportunities for the many must result in leveling down those for the few; society's obligation to the gifted few is at least as great as that to the army of the average.

The third school I visited was the exact antithesis of the second. It was only one quarter of the size, but, even so, was much larger than I expected. It was the Music and Art School, where those specially gifted in music and art were gathered from throughout the city school system and given a thoroughly rounded education in addition to having some hours of instruction and practice each day in the field of their special gift. (As I should have expected, there was a conflict of claims upon the pupils' time between the academic and creative teachers; I had a willing ear for both sides.) Naturally, I spent nearly all my time at the school observing the artistic work. One art class was working on a huge mural, and I was memorably impressed by both the imagination and the skill shown. Then I went to the symphony orchestra room, and was amazed by the excellence of what I was told was a first sight reading of Beethoven's *Coriolanus* overture. I must add that when the conductor-teacher tried to show off with a well-rehearsed Brahms symphony, the brass let him down with more than one sour crash.

It was the fourth school, the Horace Mann School for Boys, where I found myself most at home. Here was academic education of the kind I recognized, pupils of the caliber of those I had taught. I felt immediately at home in both the classroom and the staff room. But there was a fundamental difference between this school and the ones I had known as a pupil and teacher in Wales. The Horace Mann School was private, and only the comparatively well-to-do could afford to send their sons there; even so, I was told the competition for entrance was keen. I found that most of the boys came from cultured homes where books were a necessary part of living, and so they had an initial advantage denied to boys from other well-to-do homes. One of my saddest observations about American life is the number of prosperous homes I have been in throughout the country where books were not in evidence.

The headmaster at Horace Mann took me into an English class where the subject being taught was the Romantic poets. I was induced to take part in a discussion and I marveled at the range and depth of the pupils' knowledge. Too often I have found that the products of American education in literature know everything about an author but his work. I am of the school that believes it is better, in the restricted time available, to work in depth on representative work of an author rather than to skate superficially over his whole output. After all, the object of all education, even at an advanced stage, is to teach us to read. But the Horace Mann teacher had solved the problem in an admirable way: Each of the pupils had been given a special assignment, which had involved work in depth, but the sharing and discussion of all the assignments in class also covered a wide range of the subject.

It was May 26, 1939, that I first visited the Horace Mann School and took part in that English class. I could not possibly have foreseen then how important an event it was to be in my life. The teacher whose class I visited was the head of the department, Alfred Baruth, and he and his family were to become very good friends of mine through the years. First I admired him as a teacher. His pupils caught from him his zest for knowledge, which remains undiminished with time, his love of literature, his angry contempt for the superficial and the shoddy, his Herculean energy and enthusiasm. His love of English literature had induced in him a love of England. For him the whole island is a Poets' Corner. He knew intimately every cathedral, every church, every castle, every cottage, every tavern, every tomb associated with an author. In his presence I am always ashamed by my vast ignorance of such hallowed places. (He has the same first-hand knowledge of art in Italy.) For him, I was another bit of England, and he seized on me. It took me a long time to convince him that Wales is not England, and I think he still chooses to ignore that unwelcome fact, as do most Englishmen, although he must know that when Napoleon had closed Europe to the Grand Tour, some of his own beloved Romantics ventured cautiously into Wales as into a foreign land.

I left Horace Mann that first day laden with school publications: copies of the newspaper, the magazine, the yearbook. This field of school activity was quite new to me, and I still keep on my shelves a book I garnered that day, an impressive hard-covered volume, edited by Alfred Baruth and called *Prospectors*. It is an anthology of prose and poetry culled from the quarterly magazine for the years 1917–1929. Several of the writers have matured into importance in the academic and literary worlds, but the young author of two of the poems bore a name that was to become tragic: Eugene O'Neill, Jr.

Alfred Baruth took me home that first day to meet his wife and two young daughters. I was immediately welcomed as a member of the family, which I have remained to this day. His wife, Charlotte, was a beautiful and charming Southerner. She was herself of British ancestry from Mississippi; her forebears had been among the founders of the state of Tennessee. His parents had come from Germany. The Baruths had met in their late teens in the theatre in New York, a fact that immediately commended them to me as my kind of people. He had been a young actor with the Theatre Guild in its exciting, early days, and she had embarked upon what could have become a notable career, in silent films. When they met, she had already appeared in a film with Richard Barthelmess. But when the starry-eyed young lovers had finally found a justice of the peace who consented to marry them—they eloped to New Jersey to find him in order to avoid parental interference—they both gave up their thespian ambitions, Alfred because his strong streak of puritanism was outraged by the conduct of some people he met in the theatre, and Charlotte simply to please Alfred. He went to Columbia University to get a degree, and from it a job commensurate with his new responsibilities as a married man, and she worked in stores to help put her new husband through college. This was the couple I met seventeen years later, and through them I came to know and fall in love with the United States. Without them I doubt very much if I should have found my way back here.

To swell the family bank balance, the Baruths had instituted an annual tour of Europe on which they took some twenty or so boys from high schools. But these were not just moneymaking ventures; the Baruths love traveling and sharing their enthusiasm for places and objects of beauty and historical interest with cultural neo-phytes. One has not seen even Manhattan until Alfred Baruth has shown it to him.

The crisis in Munich in 1938 had scared American travelers away from Europe, and the Baruths came up with another idea: an automobile exploration of the United States. They repeated this trip in 1939 and, when I met them, there was one place left in one of the cars, which they invited me to take, strictly at cost. It was the perfect opportunity for me to see the country—we were also to go to Mexico City—and I seized it with gratitude and excitement. The three of us with nine boys set off in two cars on June 27, to return on August 30 after a journey of some fourteen thousand miles.

To one brought up in a narrow Welsh valley, the size of the United States is an overwhelming experience, comparable with that of a street ant setting out to climb the Empire State Building. Of course, if he happens to get on an elevator his experience will be very different, in much the same way as that of a man crossing the United States in an airplane. Jet planes annihilate not only distance but the sense of it. A country can only be truly discovered from the road. Even so, to travel across America by car can only approximate in exhilaration, adventure, and awesome terror the slow conquest of the distance by the wagon train of the pioneers.

It was not only the size of the United States that I found hard to assimilate, but also its extraordinary variety. My standard of height had been Snowden's 3560 feet. Now I was to see large cities perched on plateaus much higher than that, towered over by permanently snow-covered mountains. Within one landscape I was to see frozen peaks and arid deserts, and to learn that on the same day the country could have subtropical and subarctic weather. The same country was to show me man's most ambitious conquests of nature together with nature's oldest living things; in Boulder City, American engineering skill had made the desert rejoice and blossom as the rose, and in the Sequoia National Forest, I stood in fascinated contemplation of living trees which were almost twice as old as the Christian era. Too many people have bewailed the monotony of life in America; for me, the contrasts have an unparalleled excitement—dangerous poverty at the very doors of the wealthy; luxuriously designed houses on the very edge of the habitat of wild beasts and venomous reptiles; communities that have preserved age-old and outworn beliefs and customs being forced to rub shoulders with groups pursuing the latest fads; Cadillacs swerving to avoid vultures swooping down to claw up run-over snakes. There is the joy of living and the violence of killing in the scenery, the weather, and the people.

In most Americans the word "socialism" provokes anathematical denunciations, but the system of the United States National Parks is an admirable example of socialism, for by it land is owned and controlled by the government for the benefit of the community as a whole. I am filled with admiration for these parks, not only for their endless beauty and inexhaustible interest, but also for the facilities available to tourists of varying means and the knowledge and courtesy of the specially trained ranger-guides.

In that summer of 1939, I visited many national parks and still retain lively memories of many: the processes of geological time as illustrated by Glacier National Park, the Painted Desert, and the Petrified Forest; the awesome terror of the Grand Canyon; the ominous silence and stillness of Crater Lake as night descended quickly and caught me on the shore at the bottom of the bowl; the varied and delicate delights of Yosemite Park; the vivid hues of the rainbow trout in the Emerald Lake of Lassen Park; the deeply felt emotion of people as they gathered for the regular eruption of "Old Faithful" (I saw it three times, the last time by floodlight); the eeriness of the Carlsbad Caverns climaxed nightly by the emergence of myriads of bats. It would take a lifetime of vacations for an American to get to know the natural beauties of his own land, and too few, even of those who can afford it, devote even one vacation to it; a diet of seeing the works of man abroad should be varied with one of seeing those of God at home.

While it is true that the U.S.A. is a comparatively young

country—although it is too often forgotten that as a political unit it is older than either Germany or Italy—I found its historical sites peculiarly stimulating to the imagination. Ancient Rome and Stratford-on-Avon affect me profoundly in different ways, the one by the sense of actual contact with antiquity and the other by its associations with Shakespeare's world. But the fact that the great events of American history happened only yesterday gives the sites of those events a thrilling authenticity and immediacy. The Battle of Bosworth Field we must conjecture; the Battle of Gettysburg we know. I sometimes get the feeling that the whole country is a colossal setting for vast Hollywood Technicolored epics of improbable adventures—which actually happened.

Many places stirred my imagination. Notable among them were the Alamo, where Travis conducted his hopelessly gallant defense against the Mexican army when outnumbered about twenty to one; the shack of "Judge Roy Bean," who administered "Law West of the Pecos" in a highly individual way by recourse to one law book and a six-shooter between whiles of serving as a barman; the occasional little cemetery of pioneers, most of them with Anglo-Saxon and many of them with Scottish names (their tombstones said they were killed by Indians or disease, but I felt that many must have succumbed to hopelessness in the desert); Sutter's Fort in Sacramento, with its memories of the '49 Gold Rush and the incredible hardships of the immigrants, epitomized in the story of the Donner party, which resorted to cannibalism in the struggle to survive; ghost towns, such as Virginia City, with its silent and decaying opera house where the world's greatest artists had performed, to be paid in nuggets of gold; Salt Lake City, the Mecca of a new religion, complete with saints and miracles, specially adapted to call forth the sacrificial devotion of hardy pioneers in a new world.

I went, too, into Mexico. I must go back there because, even though I am sure that great progress has been made since 1939, I am equally sure that my jumbled impressions of the country at that time are jaundiced and unfair. I suffered from altitude sickness in Mexico City—it hit me as I was climbing the Great Pyramid at Teotihuacan—and this may account for the fact that my pleasant memories of such places as the Floating Gardens of Xochimilco are outweighed by remembering the characteristic corruption of the police officer who stopped us for speeding on our return and bargained with our driver to avoid booking us. The legacy of the fight between Church and State was very much in evidence; when I saw the anticlerical murals of Diego Rivera at the Presidential Palace, they were fouled with eggs and tomatoes. At Puebla we saw the "Hidden Convent," and marveled at the courage and ingenuity of the nuns who had maintained their religious life in secret during the period of proscription of the Church by the State. My sympathies between the two sides in the struggle wavered; on the one side there was the glorious Chapel of the Virgin of the Rosary in the "Golden Cathedral" at Puebla, and on the other the inerasable memory of another Church where I was clawed at in the semidarkness by grotesquely malformed beggars as I looked at glass cases containing wax effigies of Christ clad in feminine nylon underwear, bought by desperately impoverished peasants to bring them good luck.

My outstanding Mexican memory is of a man, a Hungarian, who had become a Mexican citizen. He was our guide for much of the time we were in Mexico City and had led the kind of life I find incredible even in fiction, but somehow I believe his every word, and not even distance lends skepticism. He attracted adventures like a magnet, and in his company even I had some. At sixteen he had been a novitiate for the priesthood, but three years later he had fought with the Red Army. He and a friend had later joined the Foreign Legion, from which they had soon tried to escape; he had succeeded but his friend had been shot. Then there was Cuba; at first he had worked on a sugar plantation, but, tiring of that, he had found employment on the estate of a wealthy lady as a keeper of apes, which his employer used for unmentionable purposes. And so to Mexico, where he seemed to have settled permanently. His main occupation when I knew him was hunting, but which he did as an employee of the Government. While we were there he disappeared for two days to hunt a jaguar that had been causing trouble to a village. I visited such a village with him, walking off the dirt road a couple of miles along a jungle path. I noticed that several of the Indian villagers had pairs of pocklike holes in their faces. My hunter-friend—I forbear giving his name, because I think he would wish me not to do so—told me that these were the bites of whipsnakes that hung unseen from the trees. He assured me that the Indians had an unfailing antidote for the poison of the bite, which he had found completely efficacious even against the poison of more deadly snakes and tarantulas. Far from reassured, I practically crawled back along that jungle path on my hands and knees. Then there was the time he took me to see a secret pulque distillery. He left me in the car while he disappeared into a thick wood to get permission from the law-breakers for my visit. Across the road was an estate of some kind completely surrounded by high walls; it showed no sign of life. Tired of waiting, I went over to investigate; I supposse I must have found the spirit of adventure catching. There were forbidding double doors and a bellpull. I pulled it; I still can't believe that I had the temerity to do so; I'm just not that kind of man. But I did ring that bell. Almost immediately the large doors began to open, but apparently without human agency. I caught sight of a pleasant courtyard with a fountain playing, and beyond it some low buildings, but no sign of life. I was about to make a cautious entry when I heard my friend shout to me. I turned and ran back to the car. He told me I was about to walk into a leper colony. I looked back. The doors were closed.

The adventure of his that was most vivid to me happened in Yucatán. He was stranded on a train by floods. The train was on an embankment. As the torrential rains caused the floods to rise, all the wildlife of the surrounding jungle sought refuge on the embankment, and many of the reptiles, some of them deadly, found their way into the train where they stayed until the rains stopped and the floods began to subside. I think he said it took two days and two nights, and during the nights there was no light on the train. But nobody was harmed; the common danger had turned natural enemies into frightened friends.

The encounter my Hungarian adventurer was most proud of was a meeting with Bernard Shaw. I can't remember now how that happened, but having had that adventure myself, I discounted it in him.

In late August of 1939 we were beginning our long trek back from the Pacific to the Atlantic, but my mind was on Europe and not America, for the radio hourly told of the gathering war momentum. The unending corn-seas of Nebraska did little to distract me, nor did a visit to a clinically impressive slaughterhouse. When we crossed the Mississippi, I wondered if I should ever see it again. Such sentimental yearnings are absurdly foolish; every day we have experiences that will never be repeated. My one desire was to get back to Europe before war broke out; I was due to sail on the *Queen Mary* September 6. Even the midwestern towns we hurried through kept my mind on Europe: Paris, London, Vienna, Cambridge, Londonderry, Cadiz. Then to the industrial East, where steel mills spoke to me of war. Even the final act of sightseeing was a battlefield, Gettysburg, where that saga of courage, victory, and defeat is brilliantly evoked in minute detail, and where Lincoln's immortal commemorative words were spoken, ten sentences invited as an afterthought, but which hallow the place where they were uttered even more than the dead who prompted them.

Names became Welsh now—Bryn Mawr, Berwyn, Cambria— as we hurried back to New York under a bombardment of bad news: armies mobilizing, London bracing itself for a surprise air attack, children being evacuated to the countryside.

On September 1 came the news that Germany had invaded Poland. I spent most of the day in getting a sailing permit. As I waited in queues, wild rumors flew around. Most of the officials were openly anti-German. The *Bremen* was in dock and was detained for search. Each evening a Bund demonstration and vociferously hostile counterdemonstration took place at the dockside, while the very spick-and-span crew lined up at the rails and sang the "Horst Wessel." The pro-Nazi Bund was strong in New York, but the prevailing sentiment was that of a doctor who said to me: "I hear you are going to hell next Wednesday. Don't worry; we'll be there with you."

Sunday, September 3. War is declared. Perversely I felt a sense of relief; the inevitable had happened at last. Before leaving New York two months before, I had agreed to address the Sunday morning meeting at Sloane House Y.M.C.A. on September 3 on the subject of "Breaking Down Barriers." The occasion, the subject, and the news combined to make the meeting an extraordinary one. Among the many who stayed behind to speak to me afterward were a Pole and a German. Both were young men eager to fight for their countries. The Pole wanted to know if I could help him to get back home—I couldn't; at that moment I wasn't certain how I was to get home myself—and the German wanted to assure me that although the circumstances of war might mean that he would have to kill me, there would be nothing personal in the act.

On the next day, Monday, it was clear that the *Queen Mary* was not going to sail. Some new-made American friends tried to persuade me to stay, but I was determined to get back home, and I managed to get a passage on the American ship *President Roosevelt*, which was to sail on Wednesday at noon.

The Baruths picked me up to take me to the ship, the center of much attention because she was the first American passenger liner to venture across the submarine-infested Atlantic since the U.S.A. had declared her neutrality in the new war. Huge floodlit flags were painted on her holds and sides so that we could not be destroyed in ignorance by bomb or torpedo. As I walked onto the *Roosevelt*, the crew were walking off; they refused to sail until an agreement for extra war-risk pay was signed. We waited and waited and farewells lingered and lingered. Several people came to see me off, hung around for a couple of hours, and left with uncertain good-byes, because it looked as if we might not sail at all. Finally, only the faithful Baruths were left. They had been bidding me a farewell for ten hours. At last it seemed certain that we would sail and I persuaded Al and Charlotte to leave. A meal was announced; we had had nothing all day. After the late dinner, I came back up on deck to discover that we had quietly slipped away and were moving down the Hudson and out to sea.

And so my first adventure of the war was under way. The voyage was very different from the outward one—and infinitely more delightful. The shared danger developed a heartwarming camaraderie among the passengers. I was to experience the same spirit during the air raids. And although the ship went through some heavy gales, I was never near seasickness; I suppose the greater fear had driven out the lesser. I found myself at the purser's table for dinner. He was a jolly and friendly person with a schoolboy's unalloyed excitement at the possibility of being torpedoed. He was convinced that those of us aboard who were "war personnel" would never get to England; his favorite theory was that we would be stopped by an armed raider, taken aboard, and dumped for the duration of the war in South America, probably in Argentina. During the voyage the purser gave a very lively party, at which an omniscient loudmouth ascribed the war and all other evils to the Treaty of Versailles. His particular bête noire was Georges Clémenceau, "The Tiger." All attempts to silence him failed, until a distinguished-looking middle-aged blonde, who had been sitting silently apart, rose and left. Then we learned that she was Clémenceau's daughter. She was now married to an American, but she had lost her first husband in the 1914–1918 war and was hurrying back in the hope of seeing her son before he went off to war.

After we had been at sea for a day, we were told officially that there could be no guarantee that we would not be landed in a belligerent country; the prevalent speculation was that we would be put ashore in Portugal, and left there to our own devices. In fact, neither the gleeful predictions of the purser nor the direful speculations of the passengers were fulfilled. We landed, as we had hoped, in Southampton. It's true that a German submarine surfaced near us and traveled with us for some miles, obviously in a quandary about what to do; it disappeared without doing anything. And on our last day aboard we had to change course to go to the succor of a torpedoed ship, *The City of Vancouver;* when we got to the spot there was no sign of her, no life or wreckage. We learned later from a Dublin broadcast that a Dutch oil tanker had saved all but three of the crew. We found it ominous that there was no mention by the B.B.C. of the sinking.

As we steamed up the Solent to Southampton, only naval- and troopships were seen. At last we were docked in Britain at war, but our landing was delayed for quite a time. It transpired that there were some Germans among the crew, which led to several exciting theories. All that is certain is that we saw some men being taken off the ship under guard before the passengers were allowed to land.

I had scarcely set my foot on England before I was stopped by a beefy constable who wanted to know why I wasn't carrying my gas mask, the first of many idiotic harassments during the war years; Shakespeare's Dogberry proliferates in time of war.

Cardiff. That gentleman was appalled to discover that I had driven a car to see him. He tried to insist on my returning in an ambulance, but we compromised on engaging a driver to take me home in my own car, and I was forbidden to move from my bed even while the German bombs were dropping around me. My heart, I am told, recovered fully, but the week after he saw me, the heart specialist died suddenly.

Threading through all my wartime activities was a major new element in my life, Richard Jenkins, who more and more became my responsibility in fact, and ultimately, as Richard Burton, in law. If it is true that you never really know a subject until you try to teach it, I owe a lot to Richard, for he was a relentless questioner, and what he learned, he kept; his memory for poetry, for instance, is vast, but discriminating. Apart from seizing every opportunity of our private life to assuage his thirst for knowledge, he took an active part in all phases of my public life. He was my pupil at school, a cadet in my squadron of the Air Training Corps —by virtue of which he attended Oxford University, Exeter College, in wartime—an actor in the Community Theatre as well as in school plays, and ultimately a radio actor in Cardiff, where I continued to write progressively demanding parts for him.

The Air Training Corps was formed to give some preliminary training to potential pilots and navigators while they were in their last years of high school so that, when they joined the Royal Air Force, their training could be speeded up, for the war in the air created an insatiable demand for fliers. Richard was in Canada, training as a navigator, when war ended; his eyesight was not quite good enough to meet the requirements for a pilot. While in Canada, his nose was broken in a fight, a fact he kept from me for a long time; he knew it would have provoked more anger in me than sympathy, because such escapades might jeopardize his chances as an actor. He also hitchhiked with a Welsh Air Force friend to New York in search of my friends, the Baruths, only to find that they were in Vermont; so he found his way there too.

When he went to Oxford he found that the university dramatic society, the O.U.D.S., was going to do an open-air production of *Measure for Measure* in the cloisters of one of the colleges; I forget which. As an unknown, he was cast for a minor part, but in no time at all he had displaced the leading actor and was playing Angelo. After all, as I am sure he told them, he was already a professional, for he had made his debut in the West End in *The Druid's Rest*, a comedy by Emlyn Williams with a Welsh autobiographical setting. It was Emlyn Williams, too, who was to give Richard his first chance in films, in *The Last Days of Dolwyn*, in which his mother was to be played by that greatest lady of the theatre, Edith Evans. But that lay ahead unknown, and in the meantime there was Angelo, that tormented and lustful Puritan, no small task for a lad of nineteen, even though by this time he already had some years of experience behind him. I did what I could to help by letters, and somehow managed to get up for the weekend of the final dress rehearsal and the opening. After the dress rehearsal, we stayed up most of the night working on the part, and astonishingly he retained all our work in his performance the following night. I floated on air back to my room at Exeter College, waiting to share my excitement with Richard, but he didn't come. He had gone with some of the cast to a party, had been plied with strange drinks, and passed out. He came surreptitiously to my room soon after dawn. He looked ghastly, and his clothes and flesh were torn because he had become impaled on some railings as he made his regulation-defying re-entry into the college. My night of waiting had dampened my first night ardor, so I imagine it was a grisly dawn for both of us.

Richard's tutor and mentor at Oxford was Neville Coghill, "a verray parfit gentil knyght," a scholarly theatre enthusiast and the life and soul of the O.U.D.S. Some twenty years later Richard was to pay something of his debt to this delightful gentleman by returning to perform *Dr. Faustus* with the O.U.D.S., thereby raising money to realize Professor Coghill's long-standing dream of a permanent theatre for his beloved dramatic society which shared his heart with Chaucer and Shakespeare.

The Oxford performance was not Richard's first acquaintance with *Dr. Faustus*. When he was a boy in school, we had spent a summer week in Stratford-on-Avon to see the plays, among which that year was *Dr. Faustus*. Mephostophilis, which is Marlowe's spelling of that diabolical name, was brilliantly played by another Welshman, Hugh Griffith. Richard was captivated by the play and was determined that someday he would play Faustus. It is extraordinary how many of the dreams we shared have been fulfilled. He wanted to get to work on the part right away; he was sixteen at the time. So we spent our afternoons in working on the glorious final soliloquy. We were staying at a guesthouse, which was being newly run by a young man and wife. Our studio was the shaded lawn at the back of the house where we felt sufficiently alone to let ourselves go, because all the guests had disappeared after lunch on sightseeing expeditions. But we had reckoned without mine host and hostess. Apparently they watched and listened in secret behind window curtains as we subsequently discovered when they wrote a book about their adventures in Stratford-on-Avon. Should this book in turn ever be read by them, they will at last discover who the two declaimers of Marlowe's mighty lines were.

I gradually became a radio director as a result of the progressive illness of Rowland Hughes. He was stricken with disseminated sclerosis, and I watched this proud and brilliant man decline from one walking stick to two, to a wheelchair, to fireside immobility. There can scarcely be a more cruel disease than disseminated sclerosis, for the mind remains fully alert to the end, watching the slow death of the body, limb by limb. But Rowland refused to accept defeat. When he could no longer do his radio work, he started to write novels in Welsh. One of them, I am proud to say, was dedicated to me: "I'm cyfaill, P. H. Burton, gydag edmygedd" ("To my friend, P. H. Burton, with admiration"). That novel was called *Yr Ogof* (*The Cave*) and dealt with fictional characters involved in the life of Christ. His other four novels all dealt with the slate quarrymen of his native North Wales. By the time he got to his last novel, his hands were so paralyzed that all he could manage was a few painfully scrawled words on a page each day, but he finished it. Ironically the novel was called Y *Cychwyn* (*The Beginning*); it was intended to be the first part of a trilogy.

When orthodox medicine afforded him no hope, Rowland Hughes put ever renewed faith in promised cure after promised cure. This most skeptical of men traveled long distances with the help of his remarkably buoyant and devoted wife to quacks and faith healers. On one occasion he was persuaded to undergo a starvation treatment in an expensive East Anglian establishment. I visited him there. He was living on a diet of water and prunes, nothing more, and the prunes were doled out with mathematical paucity two or three times a day. I shall never forget the way he devoured those prunes, and sucked and sucked at the stones to find every last vestige of juice. He implored me, gripping my arm, to bring him a piece of cake from the hotel I was staying in. I can't remember if I did so, but I hope I did. The other abiding memory of that experience is the astonishing, almost frightening, clarity of the starved man's mind. It had always been razor sharp, but now it was honed to an uncanny brilliance.

Rowland Hughes was a proud and reserved man and both these qualities became heightened by his sickness. As his helplessness increased, he did not want to be seen. He became utterly dependent upon his wife, whose incredible cheerfulness never seemed to flag. I became his contact with the world of which he was being robbed. One of his final acts of courage was to insist on being taken to the Maida Vale studios of the B.B.C. in wartime London to direct a big radio production of a feature program on "Coal," written by me. It was for the vast overseas service of the B.B.C. and involved a large cast and a symphony orchestra. Being careful that as few people as possible saw us, I carried him from the taxi on my back to the control room, and at the end of the rehearsal, when the way was clear of curious and pitying eyes, carried him back again. He was an easy burden; he had always been a slight man, but his sickness had shriveled him to skeleton thinness.

Rowland became very possessive of me, both as a writer and a person, but this I understood and never resented. In radio I owed everything to him. He had discovered me, encouraged me, and taught me. We complemented each other; his writing instincts were poetic, mine dramatic. Like many directors, some of them very successful, he had little understanding of the actor; he knew what he wanted in a performance, but found difficulty in helping the actor give it. As I shared the control room with him during the production of my own scripts, I was able to make suggestions, and more and more he came to rely on me as an interpreter of his intentions to the actors. So, at last, when the time came that he would be too ill to come to the studio, he insisted that I take over the direction. Thus it was that I became the only director of the B.B.C. that was not a member of the staff. Prior to this, Rowland had also used me extensively as an actor, and so gradually I acquired, by practical experience, an extensive knowledge of radio.

With the end of the war, in 1945, I was free to leave school and join the B.B.C. By this time Rowland was finally incapable of continuing his radio work in any degree, and I succeeded him as Features Producer in Wales, but not without protests on the part of the Welsh-language press, for I was the first monoglot appointment by the B.B.C. in Wales in a directorial capacity; radio engineers almost entirely were monoglot Englishmen. It is little known outside Wales how vigorous and rich is the use of the Welsh language and what cultural wealth it commands, but it has to fight for its continued existence. Fortunately much of the best talent in Wales is proudly Welsh-speaking. My revolutionary appointment resulted in a distinct advantage for the Welsh-speaking public, for a parallel appointment was made of a Features Producer for programs in the Welsh language, and an exciting choice was made for the new position, Aneirin Talfan Davies, a brilliant amateur of letters who troubled the settled waters of Welsh literature with winds from the outside world. The son of a Welsh preacher, he had shocked the entrenched forces of Welsh nonconformity by deserting to the Episcopalian Church in Wales and championing his new faith with the zeal of the convert. As a bilingual Talks Producer in Swansea, he had done some memorable work. Notably it was he who had sponsored most of the broadcast "Talks" of Dylan Thomas.

Aneirin Talfan Davies has contributed much to our knowledge of Dylan Thomas, particularly in his study of Dylan's poetry in *The Druid of the Broken Body*, where he emphasizes the religious nature of the poet's preoccupations. These, I think, will contribute to his timelessness; the problems of man in relation to society change, but the problems of man in relation to the mystery of existence remain. The mention of *The Druid of the Broken Body* made me pause to go and take it down from my shelves. In opening it I was thrilled again to find something I had unforgivably forgotten; the book is dedicated to me.

The other B.B.C. sponsor of Dylan Thomas, that genius of the spoken word, was another amateur of letters, John Arlott, who worked in the Talks Department of the Overseas Service but was best known to English listeners for his commentaries on cricket matches, that most English of games, which seems to arouse the enthusiasm of many English writers. Neville Cardus, for instance, who wrote with such mastery of music and musicians, also wrote about cricket with such delightful persuasiveness as to make even me enjoy it in print, whereas the leisurely game, played for days at a time by neatly clad men in white deployed over a green field of which the central pitch was cared for with billiard-table meticulousness, left me bored. My dramatic intsinct, when I am a spectator, calls for sudden-death sports like boxing and baseball, though I am not a devoted follower of any sport.

Having reared the tousled head of Dylan Thomas, it is appropriate that I should deal with the radio program of his that I produced and directed while I was still in Cariff. My first never-to-be-forgotten meeting with him was in London. When I officially joined the B.B.C. staff in 1945, I was posted briefly to London and stationed in Rothwell House, a converted building behind

Broadcasting House, which housed the B.B.C. Features Department and, I believe, the Drama Department. The idea was that I should absorb the methods of work and administration of the department and be stimulated by contact with my creative colleagues, who proved to be occasionally creative but always stimulating. They had been recruited by the head of the department, Laurence Gilliam, who captained his brilliant crew with a proper respect for their talents and a firm hand on their artistic waywardness. The member of the team who most captured my admiration was Louis MacNeice. The war had proved to be the finest hour for radio and the department was riding high. It could not then foresee its gradual near extinction by television.

I was sitting in an imposing office in Rothwell House, temporarily assigned to me as a transient, when I was told that Dylan Thomas had called to see me. I was nervously excited because I had already fallen under the magic spell of his poetry. He for his part had come to make contact with a possible future employer; he didn't know that I had already been warned that he would eagerly sign a contract to get an advance, but without any intention of writing a word. In a self-description he was to write for me eighteen months later, I see him again: "Thick blubber lips; snub nose; curly mouse-brown hair . . . speaks rather fancy; truculent; plausible; a bit of a shower-off." Separated by a forbidding office table, we found it hard to start a conversation, but after several formal inanities, Dylan crashed through the ice with characteristic shock tactics. I asked him how he pronounced his name. He said: "In Wales they call me Dullan; in London they call me Dillan; but my intimate friends call me Shit Face." That was the beginning of a delightful relationship between us.

The program Dylan Thomas wrote for me in 1947 was *Return Journey*. It was one of a series in which writers explored their backgrounds and origins. In February Dylan and I went to Swansea in search of his youth. The center of the town had been razed by German bombs, but when we arrived there the ruins were blanketed with thick snow, and the torn ugliness was gentled into shapes of grotesque beauty. A blizzard made us spend most of our time indoors with Dylan's boyhood friends, over endless pints of beer in snug bars, countless cups of coffee in the Kardomah. Particularly do I remember sessions with Vernon Watkins, a gently profound bank-clerk poet, Fred Janes, an artist who taught art so that he might paint pictures, and the formidable Daniel Jones, who was studying Chinese between whiles of writing symphonies.

Then came the writing of *Return Journey*. Dylan was to narrate the story himself but he did not want to do so in the first person; he needed an objective approach to the boy that was. I suggested he should go in search of "Young Thomas," and so it was. But first the contract. The B.B.C.'s scale of fees was determined by the status of the writer and the length of the program. In Dylan's case the first was clear but the second highly dubious. Dylan wanted the contract to read forty-five minutes, so that he could have a proportionately larger advance, but I was adamant in making it read thirty minutes, and thus it was scheduled, for broadcast from Cardiff on June 15. When the script arrived, neatly written in a small round hand on pages torn from a cheap exercise book, I was elated. I read it aloud several times to myself to enjoy the wonder of it. It was beautiful and moving—but short. I prided myself on my accurate timing of scripts and knew that this was about six minutes short.

Dylan came to stay with me for about a week before the broadcast. I had laid in a goodly store of Guinness, which was his drink of the moment, but he took none of it, nor anything but innocent drinks in the house. Even his visits to pubs were short and respectable. Soon after he arrived I raised the subject of the length of the program. It took some time to convince him that I needed another six minutes—I couldn't wait for the first studio run-through to prove it—but he said he couldn't possibly work like that. I persisted, and pointed out that two important elements of his boyhood were missing: girls and books. Thinking to shut me up, he said, "All right. You write one and I'll write the other." He did not know that I have something of a gift for pastiche. I said,

"Good. Choose." Somewhat nonplussed, he said, "Girls." He quickly added that, if he didn't like what I wrote, we wouldn't use it. I agreed, because my acceptance of his challenge would at least have got another few minutes out of him. But he did like what I wrote. In Swansea he had taken me to a secondhand bookstore, where the owner had early recognized the talent of the book-hungry boy and had become his enduring friend. It was in that store that I set my little scene on a Saturday morning when Young Thomas encounters a preacher rummaging for sermon material on the religious shelves. There was a delightful sequel to this piece of Dylanesque writing of mine, which Dylan used to recount with great gusto. The program was enthusiastically received by all the critics, but one of them, writing in one of the most revered journals, devoted almost the whole of his laudatory review to the scene in the bookstore. When the program was finally edited by Aneirin Talfan Davies for publication in the volume called *Quite Early One Morning*, he wrote to me about the bookstore scene and we decided that it had to be omitted. By the strangest coincidence, some fifteen years after the original broadcast, I casually turned on my radio set in New York, and found myself in the middle of a rebroadcast of my original production of *Return Journey*, and my own preacher was speaking. Dylan would have liked that.

Most of the feature programs I wrote myself were done during the war. When I joined the staff after the war, I considered it the more important part of my function to find and encourage new writers, and in this field I had some very satisfying success. One writer in particular I cherished, and it is a major disappointment to me that he has not had the brilliant career I foresaw for him. So far as I know he has stopped writing. It is true that he is tragically introverted and that his marriage has collapsed, but I should have thought that his personal sorrows would have lent power and urgency to his pen; apparently what makes some men write makes others stop.

The scripts I wrote myself covered a wide range of form and

content: dramatic reconstructions of events past and present, dramatic character studies from Giraldus Cambrensis to Lloyd George, scripted interviews for magazine programs, adaptations of novels.

There was no doubt about which was my most successful script. It was *San Demetrio*, directed by Rowland Hughes and broadcast in all regions of the B.B.C. It started out as an interview for a wartime magazine program, the kind of work I least liked doing. I had been asked to interview the wife of a merchant navy man in Port Talbot. It turned out that her husband was home on leave and he told me, rather laconically, about his most recent adventure. I immediately saw in it one of the great stories of the sea. His name was Charles Pollard and he had been Chief Engineer of the *San Demetrio*, a motor-driven oil tanker of just over eight thousand tons. She had been one of a convoy of thirty-nine ships crossing the North Atlantic to England in the fall of 1940. Guarding the convoy was the *Jervis Bay*, a name now immortal in British naval annals. In mid-Atlantic, the convoy had been attacked by a powerful German battleship, the V*on Scheer*. The *Jervis Bay* was hopelessly outclassed in range and gun power. She steamed toward the enemy to bring her within range, herself a sitting duck the whole time. The first shell got her amidships. Her bridge was shot away, and soon she was ablaze from stem to stern, but she sailed on. At last the V*on Scheer* was within range. The guns of the sinking *Jervis Bay* sprang to life and kept on firing until the water silenced them. This courageous self-sacrifice enabled all but fou⁻ of the convoy to escape.

But my story was of the *San Demetrio*. The V*on Scheer* got her, and she was soon dangerously on fire and almost certain to blow up before she sank. The captain gave the order to abandon ship. I concentrated on the story of the sixteen men in the lifeboat containing Chief Engineer Pollard. They endured a night of storm and high seas; all were seasick, and by the morning some of them were already suffering seriously from exposure. They sighted a ship but failed to contact her. In the evening they sighted another ship; it was the *San Demetrio*, still on fire and adrift in a Sargasso Sea of oil. They were so desperate that they contemplated reboarding her but it was decided that that would be suicidal, and they passed another dreadful night. In the morning they sighted the tanker again, and by this time their desperation was so great that it overcame their fear, and they decided to reboard her; a quick death by explosion was preferable to a slow one by exposure. In getting aboard the *San Demetrio*, they lost their lifeboat, and were trapped. Now began the miraculous story of survival. They managed to put out the fire, get the damaged engines going, and with patched-up steering gear and no compass they began to move toward Europe. They ultimately made landfall in Ireland. There was a further happy sequel to the story, when the owners of the *San Demetrio* themselves instituted a successful salvage claim on behalf of the fifteen survivors; one had died aboard.

The B.B.C. has a strict rule that no real person may be represented in a dramatic program without his consent, if he is alive, or the consent of his nearest relative, if he is dead. This policy meant a lot of work in the case of the *San Demetrio* program, and we completely failed to contact one of the leading characters of the story, a Canadian seaman known to the crew as "Yank," a fascinatingly enigmatic character, a born wanderer, and a secret man. Prior to the disaster he had kept himself aloof and had done as little work as possible, but the fight for survival changed him. He was the first to volunteer for the dangerous tasks; he worked indefatigably and his constant good spirits and cheering wit did much to sustain the efforts of the crew. At the salvage award, the men unanimously requested that he be given the "Red Duster," the emblem of the merchant navy, which had somehow survived the havoc of shell, fire, and storm to remain flying. In our subsequent search for Yank we finally tracked him to Bristol, but all we found was the Red Duster in a locker at the Y.M.C.A. It seemed probable that Yank himself had been blown to bits in an air raid on the city.

Even for me the *San Demetrio* had a happy sequel. As we came off the air—it was a live broadcast from the Cardiff studios—we heard the announcer in London say that, as a result of the special interest of the program, it would be rebroadcast at the same hour on Friday instead of the scheduled program, and listeners were urged to tell their friends about it. Later I heard a rumor, which I did not dare to believe, that Winston Churchill had heard the program and had given the order for its early repeat.

The necessity for getting permission to portray real people had some wryly amusing results in the case of my program about Lloyd George. I had decided to concentrate on the first part of his cabinet career, when as Chancellor of the Exchequer he laid the foundations of the Welfare State, before, in World War I, he was to become one of Britain's greatest war prime ministers. But it was the pioneer social legislation that I felt to have the more enduring importance, and I called my program *Man of the People*. In the New Year's Honors List of 1945, the many admirers of the radical Lloyd George were shocked to read that, just before his eighty-second birthday, he had accepted an earldom, and would henceforth be known as Earl Lloyd George of Dwyfor. He was to enjoy his new title—if enjoy it he did, which I deeply doubt—for less than three months; he died in March. My program ended with a brief reference to the earldom. To whom should the B.B.C. apply for approval of the project? Obviously, it would have seemed, the widow, the new countess, who had begun her career as Lloyd George's secretary and graduated into becoming his second wife. But it was not quite as simple as that, for it was felt that the rightful guardians of their father's political reputation were the two children who were themselves distinguished members of the House of Commons, Megan and Gwilym. Then there was the eldest son, Richard, the new earl, to whom the father had bequeathed, willy-nilly, a title, but nothing to support it, for he had completely cut him out of his will. It was decided to send a copy of the script to each of the four people who might consider themselves aggrieved if they were not consulted. First came a gracious approval from the countess; then from the new earl, on House of

Lords stationery, some carping and minor criticisms; but from Megan and Gwilym nothing. We went into rehearsal, and shortly before transmission, telegrams arrived from Megan and Gwilym approving the script but asking that all references to the earldom be deleted. We got around this by cutting out all comments on the earldom, but the program ended with the reading of the engraving of his tombstone at Llanystumdwy, which recorded his title.

When no relative was known to exist, we would risk portrayal of dead persons. One of the writers I discovered resurrected a fascinating court case from nineteenth-century rural Wales. He called it *The Case of the Starving Girl*. A young girl had done without food for some days, which had drawn attention and perverted admiration to herself. The parents, with a sick pride, told the neighbors and the rector of the parish, and the wonder grew and grew until all were caught by their own belief. The story spread throughout the country and skeptical rationalists challenged the believers. A strict watch was placed upon the girl so that she could not be fed secretly, and, of course, she died. The parents were then arraigned for neglect leading to manslaughter, and the program centered on the court case, the author using it to stress the dangers of credulity. The program had received the usual publicity in the *Radio Times*, and on the day of the broadcast, while we were in the middle of the final rehearsal, a telephone call came from some man who insisted on speaking to the head of the B.B.C. in Wales, and did. Cryptically he threatened the B.B.C. with dire consequences if *The Case of the Starving Girl* was broadcast, and then he rang off. Somehow or other he was contacted again and this time he was persuaded to give his reason. It appeared that a younger sister of the girl was still alive, and, to avoid the inherited shame of the case, she had taken another name and another home. The program was canceled at the last minute and was never broadcast.

Sometimes research for programs led to adventures in the field. Perhaps the most exciting for me took place in connection with PLUTO, which I had been assigned to write. The Walt Disney title was misleading. It stood for "Pipe Line Under the Ocean," and dealt with the remarkable feat of engineering that laid oil lines under the English Channel from England to France to supply the invading troops. In days of peace, it would have been a considerable feat; under the hazards of war it was indeed astonishing. It was decided that I should go on a pipe-laying expedition, which took place entirely at night. I set out from a secret base on the South Coast in a speedboat to make rendezvous with the pipe-laying vessel. The sea was choppy, and the Channel has laid low much better seamen than I. It seemed to me miraculous that we found the ship at all, but we did, and then I was faced with a task that even to this day I don't know how I accomplished. I had to use a rope ladder to climb up on deck; the ladder was moving one way and the ship another, and it was dark. I must have negotiated it somehow, but I'm sure I arrived on deck in no state to take the necessary careful notes of what was going on. I have a dim recollection that I was landed on a newly liberated part of the French coast and that the noise of the French workmen robbed the clandestine operation of its appropriate atmosphere. All the time, I feel sure, my mind was preoccupied with the return journey. But when I did gratefully tread the English soil again, or rather English concrete, I found the adventure was not over for me. I was put under guard and held incommunicado. PLUTO was a joint operation of the Navy and the Army; the Navy laid the oil lines and the Army operated them. One service had cleared me for the project, but not the other, and thus I became His Majesty's guest until the matter was cleared up; a willing guest, I must add, because I was royally entertained. While I deplored the administrative muddle, I approved the caution, because I knew the location of every line.

Occasionally one sent a recording team into the field for some special purpose. Such a team once provided me with a comic dilemma, which they made the most of. I had been given the task of writing a program to commemorate the two hundred fiftieth anniversary of a famous British regiment. The regiment itself

95

marked the occasion by a splendid dinner at headquarters, at which the toast to the regiment was to be made by its colonel-in-chief, who was no less a person than the King himself, George VI. Obviously my program had to end with the King's speech, and arrangements had been made for a team of engineers to record it. But the King was taken ill and the senior colonel of the regiment made the toast in his place. The team returned to the studio with the disc of the recording; this was before the days of tape. I wanted to hear the recording, but they were reluctant to play it before the final run-through on the grounds that every playing diminished the quality. They were so insistent that I should make do with the script of the colonel's speech that I became a little suspicious and finally threatened them into playing it. A high-pitched voice piped the words, "I have here a message from His Majesty, the King," but the words were barely intelligible; the colonel had a cleft palate. I am still rather proud of my presence of mind. I took the recording in my hands and accidentally dropped it, but with sufficient force to splinter it beyond repair. An actor read the speech on the air, and an abject letter of explanation went to the colonel from me the next day.

I became proud of the group of radio actors in Cardiff. Most of them, and the best ones too, were only part-time professionals, although while I was there a full-time repertory company was formed, and sometimes actors were brought down from London. There is a tendency to despise radio acting, but I learned to respect it as a satisfying and difficult skill. The microphone, like the camera, is a microscope on honesty. The ear will immediately detect falsity of emotion in the voice of the actor, and, in watching an accomplished radio actor perform, you will observe such concentration and absorption in the imagined moment as is difficult to achieve amid the distractions of live theatre. Every politician takes to the air at his peril; simple honesty and naked intimacy are not his usual stock-in-trade.

I also acquired a perhaps exaggerated regard for radio as a dramatic writer's medium. His word is all. Theatre is a much more cooperative art than radio, and the playwright is much more at the mercy of other artists and craftsmen in the theatre. Poets like Louis MacNeice and Dylan Thomas began to find a wonderful freedom in radio. I personally find *Under Milk Wood* diminished by visual performance, while a consummate theatre craftsman like Tchekov is equally diminished by radio. How, for instance, can the impact of the silent Masha in the opening of *The Three Sisters* be accomplished on radio? On the other hand, Shakespeare's verbal magic and the flexibility of the action on his nonrepresentational stage make him take kindly to radio. Every dramatic medium calls for the writer to exploit its particular essence, which is largely determined by its relationship to the audience. Radio writers have to aim at a solitary listener whose attention must be wooed and imagination excited. President Roosevelt brilliantly captured the essence of radio when he called his addresses to the nation "Fireside Chats."

The artistic development of radio was blighted by the advent of television, which I believe has not really begun to explore its artistic possibilities. It is, obviously, the supreme medium of news, for the communication of events as they happen, but this is its journalistic strength. What are its artistic advantages? It seems to me that it has kept its eyes too firmly fixed on what it shares with movies and not paid sufficient attention to what it shares with radio, which is its relation to the audience. For instance, I used to think that radio comedy was missing the boat when the comedians played to a live audience in the studio. This reduced the experience of the listener to that of a news event; he was a mere eavesdropper on the experience of others. The true radio comedian worked directly upon the imagination and intelligence of one imagined listener—on one, and not upon the potential aggregate of millions. Television, too, reduces the reviewer to a second-class participant, watching the enjoyment of others. It compounds the felony in comedy series by adding canned laughter, the ultimate betrayal of the medium. Only commercials use the medium properly, and I feel that much of the ironic praise given to commercials

97

as a snide comment on the programs that surround them are a subconscious acknowledgment of the fact that the commercials at least are directly aimed at the viewer.

My decision in 1945 to join the staff of the B.B.C. was the watershed of my life. I am not an adventurous person and do not naturally welcome change, but my life has been full of change. I am not even an avid traveler, but I have traveled countless thousands of miles. I had been teaching for twenty years and was still enjoying it; any temptation to boredom was offset by the variety and richness of my outside activities. But I began to be scared that the pattern of my life was fixed: another twenty years of teaching, then retirement, then waiting for death. Even now, more than twenty years later, I cannot accept the fact of the inevitability of death. My mind is full of plans for the future, and I suppose they are largely a subterfuge to avoid facing the grim fact that lies in that future: death. I have sometimes said that a man is old when he looks back more than forward; if that is so, at sixty-three I am still very young. Early poverty had taught me to value financial security, and so it was not easy to give up twenty years of pensionable service. It's true that I was going to start all over again at a higher salary in another pensionable service, but this new security did not weigh with me because I felt obscurely that once I had made the initial break I should later acquire courage for greater recklessness. Of course, the overwhelming motive for the change was that at last I was being given the opportunity to become fully a professional, not, it is true, with my first love, the theatre, but with a near relative. Richard, too, had something to do with the decision. He knew then that Wales would never again be big enough to contain him, and he felt it part of his duty to me to pry me out of my rut. Thus, at the age of forty, the instinctive stay-at-home started on his wandering way, and his wanderings are not yet over.

After four successful and happy years in Cardiff, I was offered the post of Chief Instructor in the Staff Training School of the B.B.C. in London. At that time the B.B.C. had a complete monopoly of the British airwaves; hence it had to train its own staff. Had the training center been anywhere else I should have hesitated to become a teacher again, but London was my Mecca and I left Wales, never to return. The Welsh-language press that had fulminated against the B.B.C. when I was first appointed in Cardiff because of my lack of Welsh now bewailed my transfer to London. I was less disposed to account it an accolade than yet another excuse for lambasting the foreign beast in London.

What is my true nationality? In some ways I share the dilemma of twelfth-century Gerald the Welshman, who spent his life in fighting for the independence of the Church in Wales, but was felt by the Welsh to be Norman, and by the Normans to be Welsh. I was born and brought up in Wales, but my parents were both English. I am in many ways the product of my Welsh environment, my emotional responses are very much those that seem characteristic of the mining valleys of South Wales, and yet I was always aware of not quite belonging. Nor was I completely at home in London; there I was always aware that I was Welsh in my difference. When I finally became an American citizen in 1964 it was not as traumatic an experience as if I had had a definite sense of previous nationhood. I used to call myself British, but that is an evasion. Happy is the man who has no doubt that he is English like Shakespeare, or Welsh like Dylan Thomas, or Scots like Robert Burns, or Irish like Sean O'Casey.

I fully understand what might have been the heart of the mystery of that extraordinary man in a century of extraordinary men, Sir Richard Burton, when he said, "My misfortunes in life began with not being a Frenchman"; he had spent most of his early childhood years in France and in later years his enemies were to label him a "foreigner." Despite our shared surname, I have no blood relationship with the great explorer and adventurer, but I do share to some extent his lack of a sure feeling of national identity. Perhaps Burton's passion for disguise was not unrelated to his lack of a clear-cut sense of being English. I find that I have varied my name slightly with the years. In Wales I was known as "P. H.

that even Welsh youth now knows more pop tunes than hymn tunes.

It is strange to think that I was twenty-one before I saw a play in London. One of the most difficult readjustments I had to make when I came to America was to the different scale of distances. It was less than two hundred miles from Mountain Ash to London but it was more remote to me as a young man than any part of the English-speaking world is to me now. It was exciting because it was the heart of the theatre and the literature that I loved—the two places I wanted most to see were Drury Lane and Poets' Corner—and it was terrifying because of its size and strangeness.

I started to earn my living in September 1925, and by the most industrious scraping, although still with a deep sense of guilt, I saved enough to spend a week in London during my first holiday, at Christmas. I was accompanied and helped financially by the mentor who had done so much for me since the death of my father. He knew London well and I could not have had a better guide. Fortunately he liked the theatre too, at least well enough to go, I think, every evening. On later visits, when I was alone, I went to two shows every day, and there was one notable day when I managed five: a film in the morning, then a matinee, a quickly squeezed-in two hours of a nonstop variety show, another play in the evening, and finally a late-night cabaret. I found that my appetite for theatre of all kinds was less exceptional than one would expect, but then, as one gets older, it is comforting to learn that all one's most private extravagances are widely shared.

What remains of that first visit to London's theatres? A big film, a little play, Drury Lane, and a variety show. The film was the silent version of *Ben Hur* with Ramon Navarro. What impressed me most was the full orchestra accompanying the action with an exciting precision, and also the fact that we paid seven shillings and sixpence to get in. I had never paid so much money to get in anywhere; in Mountain Ash I could have gone to the cinema fifteen times for that, but there, instead of a full orchestra, I should have had to be content with a quintet in the Workmen's

Hall—a delightful show-off violinist, a charmingly demure cellist, a very adroit pianist, who managed to manipulate his cigarette with whichever hand the music would free for the moment, a most lugubrious bass player, and a virtuoso on the drums and sundry other instruments which provided the appropriate noises for the silent screen. In the Palace there was only a pianist, whose repertoire was very limited but who delighted us by ringing the changes with unmodulated abruptness between the mood pieces for chase, villainy, love, and death, for which purpose he permanently craned his neck and kept his eyes unfalteringly on the flickering screen above him.

The little play I remember from that first London visit was *The Farmer's Wife*, which introduced to the London stage Cedric Hardwicke, later to be knighted. He was a young man at the time but brilliantly played an old Devonshire codger, Churdles Ash, who delighted London audiences for, I believe, years. Barry Jackson, also later to be knighted, had brought the production to the West End from his flourishing and significant Birmingham Repertory Theatre. *The Farmer's Wife* seemed a fair gamble; it was original, simple, delightful, by an author of some reputation, Eden Philpotts, and with what should be a town-taking performance by a new actor. All the parts were beautifully played. I still remember the crusty farmer of Melville Cooper. (Many years later I was to direct him in a musical in Palm Beach, Florida.) But despite some good notices, the play languished in the opening weeks. In those days, Londoners went to see favorite or fashionable players, not recommended plays. Barry Jackson persisted in keeping the play on and gradually his faith was justified and *The Farmer's Wife* drew the town for a record run.

The success of *The Farmer's Wife* prompts two observations about present-day Broadway, because it simply could not happen there. To begin with, the expenses of Broadway production are such that it could never have been nursed to success. The most distressing feature of Broadway is that, with rare exceptions, its rule is long life or sudden death. By 1 A.M. after the opening performance it is possible, with some certainty, to forecast the life of the play, for by that time the press agent has got hold of a release of the notices, and, although they protest their own horror at the idea, the men who have written them, and particularly the one who has written the one in the *Times*, have decided the life or death of the play. When Caesar has turned his thumb down, the opening night party at which the death sentence is read is painfully ghoulish. While it is true that often the wonder is how the play ever got to opening night, there are many occasions when the play could have found its own audience if the producer could have afforded to nurse it as Barry Jackson did *The Farmer's Wife*.

The second observation occurring to me from that play is that neither the young Cedric Hardwicke nor Melville Cooper would have been cast for the parts on Broadway today. Young actors are never considered for old men, except when, as in *Peer Gynt*, the action of the play calls upon the actor to play both ages. There have been instances in my theatregoing life when young actors in their twenties have played *King Lear* successfully at the Old Vic. And a young man, Edward Atienza, made a memorably comic cartoon of the old Archbishop in *Romanoff and Juliet*, and this on Broadway, too, but then he had been imported with the production from London. It is a well-worn quip in the profession that when an actress has acquired the experience and skill to play Juliet, she is too old to look it. Unless the trend is reversed on Broadway, it will be true that when an actor is old enough to be cast for King Lear, he will be too decrepit to carry Cordelia in his arms at the end of the play. Fortunately, with the growing challenge of the burgeoning new repertory theatres throughout the United States, it is inevitable that actors will be called upon to extend their range, a frightening process to many of them because their training has not prepared them for it. At last it may be that a Broadway producer will see the actor in a man rather than just the age, and that when he has to cast Polyphemus he will not send his casting director to scour the freak shows for a one-eyed giant.

Drury Lane was my theatrical Mecca on that first visit to London. Later I learned that the theatre with the real magic of continuity is the Haymarket, but Drury Lane had the magical name. Had I not seen in Cardiff Fred Terry play Charles II to the Nell Gwyn of Julia Neilson in *Sweet Nell of Old Drury*? It somehow seemed desecration that this most English of theatres should house an American musical, *Rose Marie*. This was my first experience of a truly spectacular production and I was thrilled by the brilliant precision of the totem dance. I and the whole house with me clapped and clapped to get the Indian maidens to fall down again and again. How naïve it all seems now after the brilliant development of choreography in musicals by such creative artists as Agnes de Mille and Jerome Robbins!

The variety show took me to the tawdrily domed Coliseum, which I remember more than the show I saw there. Top billing was given not to a vaudeville act but to a one-act play. I have a vague recollection that it was about a haunted room, and that the setting on that huge stage, where I was later to see my first revolving stage in *White Horse Inn*, was much more impressive than anything that happened in it. This may have been the last instance of the invasion of theatre into music hall, by means of which the great ones of the Edwardian era had capitalized on their reputations. By appearing in a one-act play, or extracts from their famous repertoire, and sharing a bill with conjurers, comics, and performing dogs, they had found a new audience and large sums of money in their declining years.

That brief but crowded 1925 visit to London was the first of many before I finally went to live and work there twenty-four years later, and this seems the right moment to reflect on some of my experiences as a provincial-come-to-town theatregoer during all that time.

Throughout those years I sat in cheap seats, preferably in the pit, that haven of theatre addicts which has since gradually dwindled to extinction. (I never knew it on Broadway, although I suppose it must have existed at some time.) Occasionally, because I had no option, I sat in the even cheaper gallery, but the excitement of the gallery audience, who genuinely knew and loved theatre—the discomfort they cheerfully endured was proof of this —did not compensate for the bad seating and the precipitous view of the stage. And there was one production that made me vow never to sit up there again; the director had been so oblivious of the gallery that he had placed much of the action on platforms at the back of the set where it was completely lost to our view. Yet the gallery and what it stands for is an important element in theatre. The Gallery First-Nighters in the West End was, and maybe still is, an influential association. They could be cruel in their disapproval and touching in their loyalty. They saw everything, and remembered it. They could be vindictive and generous. They were quick to recognize new talent, but it took years of good work to win their abiding support. Not for nothing was the gallery called the "Gods."

There seems to be little gallery mentality on Broadway, and the theatre is the poorer. In the sense in which I use the word, there is no gallery in a Broadway theatre; no third shelf, nor any shelf of undivided benches. Not that there is anything at all desirable in either of those physical discomforts, but they did in London make theatre as available as movies. My American equivalent cannot see theatre as I did. That is very sad, but it is even sadder that he doesn't even choose to see it as much as he might. Somehow he doesn't feel it belongs to him. Even the off-Broadway theatre is moving out of the realm of his pocket and his way of life. Theatre-going in New York, as a necessary part of civilized living, is more and more restricted to the local wealthy and out-of-town expense-account visitors, both of which classes are more interested in touted successes than in theatre. Never was the stricture of Sheridan's Mr. Puff more deserved: "The number of those who undergo the fatigue of judging for themselves is small indeed."

Writing this book has made me face as honestly as I can my own values in the various aspects of my enjoyment of theatre, and it has resulted in my surprising myself. Which do I more enjoy, watching or participating? Undoubtedly, participating. But in what way? Therein lies the surprise. Possibly because I haven't done enough of it to blunt the excitement, I should at the moment have to place acting first; then, in order, directing, lecturing, reading, writing, and only finally, watching. But it was not always so. I lived in the thirties for those crowded hours in the London theatre. What has happened? I suppose I have become too sophisticated about plays and playing. Rarely does a production of a great play live up to, much less transcend, my image of the play, and rarely does a player gain more than my objective admiration. These are signs of maturity, I suppose, and Brecht would approve of them, but I miss my theatrical innocence. There are still rare occasions when I am transported beyond the restricting power of my critical intelligence, but nowadays they are more likely to happen in the cinema than in the theatre, probably because I am still fairly innocent about films.

Characteristically it is players rather than plays that dominate my cherished memories of those hard-earned and hard-spent visits to London. Some of them have since become acquaintances of mine, and some even friends, but not even that has dimmed their early effect on me. That might appear a cynical remark, but it is not meant as one. When I know an actor well offstage, it is very difficult for him on stage to transport me beyond admiration, and the better I know him, the more difficult does it become. Thus what excites me more than his performance when I watch Richard on stage is the effect he has on the audience, yet in his best moments in a good movie he can still stir me deeply.

It has always seemed to me that the more an actor remains an unknown mystery offstage the more readily can he work magic onstage. I deplore the tendency of some actors to want to prove themselves good citizens in the public gaze. An artist should be known by and in his work. Most talented writers are a great disappointment to meet. All artists are essentially lonely and when they are put on public display they tend to be either shy and mumbling or, in self-protection, loud and bombastic.

It would be self-indulgent of me and inevitably tedious to the

reader if I recalled all the performances that thrilled me during
those early years of my theatregoing, so I shall mention only those
that may still have some significance.

There is no doubt that my greatest debt of gratitude belongs to
Edith Evans and John Gielgud, both of them performers of such
distinctiveness that, when they are not at their best, one becomes
aware of mannerisms, particularly vocal ones. But at their best
they are truly great. I came to think there was nothing Edith
Evans could not do. She seemed naturally to be the quintessence
of all great ladies until one saw her as a simple peasant. She was
the wittiest of all women in high comedy and yet could portray
a primitive, even bestial, mind. But whatever she played, she filled
the stage; it was her rightful kingdom. And yet she occasionally
makes an expedition into that alien land of films, and comes back
triumphant. I used to hold a contrary idea but have now come to
believe that a good stage actor can be equally good in movies, once
he has made the necessary theatrical adjustments. Edith Evans is
the supreme example. Her name brings to mind the greatest playwrights—Shakespeare, Congreve, Sheridan, Shaw—but she also
adorned much lesser works because they gave her an opportunity
for a bravura performance. I can still see vividly her malevolent
gypsy in *The Old Ladies*, brooding over the scene like a vicious
harpy, and chilling our blood with her croak of "Bye-bye." There
was her aging and tempestuous prima donna in *Evensong*, suffering the agony of being supplanted by a newcomer and working
herself into such a paroxysm of fury as to suffer a heart seizure.
She was not a beautiful woman—she has become a Rembrandt
beauty in her old age—but when she acted a beautiful woman, as
Orinthia, for instance, which Shaw wrote especially for her, even
her face became suffused with a radiant and glamorous beauty. I
always believed her to be completely what she wanted me to
believe.

I first saw John Gielgud in a modern play, *Musical Chairs*, a
tense and absorbing Tchekhovian drama of frustration by a new
playwright, Ronald Mackenzie. Two years later he was to write a

companion play in genre and success, *The Maitlands,* again for John Gielgud. The playwright used his well-gotten gains for a motoring holiday in France and there he was killed on the road. I don't suppose his plays would stand up today—we should find their neurotic characters too theatrically conceived—but they made it possible for John Gielgud to give performances that vibrate in the memory. They called for his most obvious qualities, intelligence and introverted sensitiveness protecting itself with biting words, yet withal an inherent nobility. Nowadays, when Gielgud is chiefly associated with Shakespearean and other costume roles, it is well to remember that he first made his mark in modern clothes, and not immaculate ones either. Between the two Mackenzie plays there was a very successful costume play, but not by Shakespeare—*Richard of Bordeaux.* In Shakespeare's version of the same story, *Richard II,* Gielgud was, for me, supreme. He has undoubtedly a sublime lyrical gift, and part and player were perfectly matched when Gielgud played Richard, that exquisite of sorrow. A poetically deaf actor can no more speak Macbeth than a tone-deaf one can sing MacHeath. An instinctive command of the sensuous devices of poetry is a necessity for all Shakespeare's great parts, but above all is it a necessity for *Richard II,* written at a time in Shakespeare's development when the lyrical poet was only with difficulty held in by the dramatist's leash. Richard II was a perfect subject for Shakespeare at that moment, for he portrays him luxuriating extravagantly in the beauty of sorrow, until he is finally chastened by suffering into a moving simplicity of speech; in Gielgud, he found the perfect player. I hesitated to see Gielgud's *Macbeth* because I felt he was too frail for the robust Scotsman, but again Gielgud's lyrical intelligence worked wonders. Macbeth is a particularly difficult part to play, because it combines the apparently contrary qualities of tough ruthlessness and a vivid imagination, the latter expressed in some of Shakespeare's finest poetry. Gielgud made me see and feel things in the agony of the character that I had not been aware of before. Gielgud is also an extremely gifted director. If I had to choose one production that I found perfect in every way, it would be Gielgud's superb interpretation, both as director and actor, of *The Importance of Being Earnest*. Whoever saw it will always hear him and Edith Evans in the roles of Ernest and Lady Bracknell.

I am best known in New York as a teacher of Shakespeare for actors, and it was a performance of *Macbeth* in London during one of my theatre-visiting trips that crystallized my point of view with an enduring clarity, and gave me almost a missionary zeal in spreading the gospel of William Shakespeare according to Philip Burton. I propose to devote a later chapter to this subject, but briefly I hold that it is the duty of the director and the actor to use their best endeavors to discover the intentions of the author and then their best talents to reveal them. This may seem to go without saying, but it is not so, particularly in the case of dead authors, so long dead that they have no relatives or lawyers to protect their work against distortion. The *Macbeth* that clarified my attitude to Shakespeare on the stage had two brilliant and powerful performers in the leading roles, Henry Ainley and Sybil Thorndike, but suddenly I realized that their interpretation could not possibly have been Shakespeare's intention, for Sybil Thorndike dominated Henry Ainley in a way that no Elizabethan boy-actor could have dominated Richard Burbage. The Sarah Siddons tradition in the part must be all wrong. Eagerly I went back to the text with new eyes and new insight.

I have no hesitation in saying which was my single most memorable moment in the theatre. It was given me by Werner Kraus in Hauptmann's *Before Sunset*. The moment happened when Kraus, playing an elderly man in love with a young woman, played by Peggy Ashcroft, was being told with infinite gentleness that he was too old for her. He wore no makeup, and as he listened, the color drained from his face and he became visibly older. This, for me, was the greatest example of the power of an actor's imagination over his body. It is comparatively easy for an actor to get turkey-red with simulated anger or to shed tears of imagined grief, but only that once did I see an actor's imagination rob him of color. I

David Slivka, Philip Burton, Nancy Wickwire, Richard Burton, and the bust
of Dylan Thomas. The Poetry Center, New York: May 24, 1964.

The author at a *Camelot* rehearsal.

Gerald Kean, Philip Burton, Bruce Graham at an audition for the Clinton
Company. *(Alan Grossman)*

Slaves to parts

James O'Neill in *The Count of Monte Cristo.* *(Culver Pictures)*

Henry Irving in *The Bells.* *(Theater Collection, New York Public Library, Astor, Lenox, Tilden Foundation)*

Joseph Jefferson in *Rip Van Winkle*.
*(Theater Collection, New York Public Library,
Astor, Lenox, Tilden Foundation)*

Martin Harvey in *The Only Way.*

Laurence Olivier, Edith
Evans and John Gielgud in
Romeo and Juliet.
*(Theater Collection, New
York Public Library, Astor,
Lenox, Tilden Foundation)*

Edith Evans in *As You
Like It.* *(Theater Collection, New York Public Li-
brary, Astor, Lenox, Tilden
Foundation)*

Edith Evans in *Evensong.* *(Culver Pictures)*

John Gielgud in *Richard of Bordeaux*. *(Culver Pictures)*

remembered Hamlet's description of the Player King's emotion during the Hecuba speech; he says that at the working of the player's imagination "all his visage wann'd." Shakespeare's actors were obviously capable of this feat. That line alone should silence the slanderous suspicion that they were only capable of rhetorical bombast.

I have learned that the most difficult of stage arts is high comedy, especially keeping the brilliance and sparkle of wit shining bright eight times a week in a long run. There is a tendency for the most coruscating line to sound idiotic gibberish with constant repetition. Emotional scenes are much easier to play night after night. I was blessed by seeing some great practitioners of the art of high comedy. It is an art that is in danger of dying out for lack of practice. In a society without manners there can be no comedy of manners. Our times are those of black comedy. Of course, Edith Evans is supreme in period high comedy, but the actress who gave me most delight in contemporary high comedy was Marie Tempest. Rather like America's Minnie Maddern Fiske, she graduated from musical comedy, but unlike Mrs. Fiske, who established a new and brilliant reputation by introducing several of Ibsen's dramatic heroines to America, Miss Tempest remained true to comedy, but in words without music. She combined an ineffable charm, a scintillating mind, a glorious humanity, and a faultless technique. Whatever she was in, I saw. Her final curtain was in itself a feast of artistry; her slow, full curtsey was the perfect symbol of constitutional monarchy—she was our queen, but at our behest.

My unbounded admiration for Marie Tempest led me to write a play for her and her husband, W. Graham-Browne, who always acted with her and often directed her plays. I called the play *Cedar So Strong*. It was a quotation from a novella by Thomas Lodge, the son of an Elizabethan mayor of London, from which Shakespeare took the story of *As You Like It*. The full quotation is: "There is no diamond so hard but will yield to the file, no cedar so strong but the wind will shake, nor any mind so chaste but love will change." I wrote it for the trio who had enchanted me in *The First Mrs. Fraser*: Marie Tempest, Henry Ainley, and W. Graham-Browne. It dealt with the conflict in an ambitious writer between a career and a home. After success, he returns in middle age to try to find what he had thrown away. It probably was a question that was troubling me at the time. I knew nothing then about the difficulty of getting scripts read, much less accepted. I was still schoolmastering in Port Talbot, and knew nothing about the maze of middlemen in the theatrical jungle. It was even before the B.B.C. had found me. With blithe confidence I sent the script to Mr. Graham-Browne at the theatre where he was currently playing. Or did I have the temerity to send it direct to Miss Tempest? Anyway, a miracle happened, and although it later turned out to be a somewhat stillborn miracle, the glow I basked in for several weeks was worth the writing of the play. Within a week of sending the script I received a telegram from Graham-Browne congratulating me most warmly on the play; a telegram, no less; he was too excited to write a letter. It is only now that I am inured to the heartbreaking hardships and incredible chances of the theatre that I realize that that telegram was a miracle, for which the memory of W. Graham-Browne shall always be gratefully enshrined by me. But after the telegram there was silence. I went with a school trip that Easter to Paris. (I remember being outraged by having to tip the ushers who conducted us to our seats in the theatres.) We returned on a Sunday, and as we passed through London I bought the *Times* and *Observer* and, as usual, eagerly turned to the theatre pages. Somewhere there I read a note that Marie Tempest had found a new play by a new author. Immediately I saw my brilliant future in exciting detail; I have never lacked the ability to fantasize madly; every dream of mine that comes true, and some of them have, always disappoints. But the snippet in the newspaper was followed by another silence. At last I could bear it no longer, and I wrote to Mr. Graham-Browne. My letter did persuade him to write to me. He was charming but discouraging. He was still enthusiastic about the play and said that

Miss Tempest shared his enthusiasm, but the theatre was about to celebrate her fiftieth year upon the stage and she felt that never again could she play a forty-nine-year-old part. She never did. Mr. Graham-Browne suggested I should come to see him when next I was in London. My visits were so infrequent that I couldn't wait for that. Somehow I managed to get up for a weekend soon after receiving the letter. As I emerged from Paddington Station I read on the newsboy's billboard: "Famous Theatrical Figure Dead." I asked who it was and was told to buy a paper and find out. I did. It was W. Graham-Browne. *Cedar So Strong* was never done professionally. Our amateur company in Port Talbot did it, but without Marie Tempest it proved to be small beer. As for its chances now, it would prove stale and lifeless small beer.

The moral of that tale for would-be playwrights is to write plays because you have something you must say, not because you have parts you would like someone to play. Also, if the playwright is like me, the completion of the task of writing is its own satisfaction, and he lacks the drive and the temperament doggedly to market his wares; that's why agents were born.

Cedar So Strong did not teach me my lesson. I continued to write plays for particular stars whom I admired. From what I said earlier, it will be no surprise that I wrote a play for John Gielgud and Edith Evans. It's my favorite among my plays, *Storm in Summer*, which I have already mentioned. Without any intermediary or introduction I sent it to Mr. Gielgud. He not only read it but wrote to me about it. Now that I know how theatre men of his stature are pestered with scripts, I am amazed by his interest and courtesy. He said, quite rightly, that when everybody's mind was exercised by the continued delay in establishing a Second Front, it would be difficult to enlist people's sympathy and interest in a young man tormented by doubts about the war. He suggested that the time for it would be some years after the war. It has waited for its time, and still waits, in my drawer, where it has become a musty period piece.

I even wrote a play for Richard, *The Dark Wood*, about a

young Welsh religious revivalist, but when I wrote it he lacked the position and power to get a production for it, and now that he has the position and power, he is too old to play the part. But that script did not completely die of neglect. The B.B.C. did a successful production of it on television, as a result of which the play was optioned for Broadway, and even got so far as an announcement in the Sunday *Times*, but that was the last I heard about that.

I wrote other plays too, all of them aimed at the West End, and all of them missed their target. This raises the perennial and important question of whether good scripts fail to get a production because they are lost in the hazards of the commercial theatre. One thing is certain: bad scripts find productions. My own feeling is that no scripts of genuinely outstanding merit remain forever hidden, but that there are scripts which deserve a chance but never get it. Even the best of my own scripts was not of that rare quality to fight its way to life by its own merits, but my lack of sufficient determination to fight for it sealed its doom. I have now had some years of experience on the other side of the game; I continue to receive a depressing number of playscripts to criticize, to dissect, or to recommend. Many of them have merit and deserve production, but there has never been one that so excited me that I would fight for its production, and I should find it much easier to fight for someone else's work than for my own. Yes, I believe that many scripts of viable mediocrity never get their chance, and viable mediocrity is a just description of most that do. As for the bad plays that get to Broadway, or die in their initial airing on the way to it, I remain baffled. Doesn't anyone ever read them before they go into rehearsal? Sometimes a star, desperate for a play, does read it, and in seeing the possibilities of a part remains blind to the play. Sometimes the author has money or has access to it. Sometimes it is a hollow imitation of a last season's success. Whatever the reason, when a bad play is staged and meets the fate that anyone with theatrical intelligence and objectivity could have foretold for it, it is an embittering experience for the unproduced writer of better plays, especially when he reads that periodic correspondence in theatrical columns, which assumes that, because so many produced plays are bad, there are no good unproduced ones. Let the frustrated playwright take comfort from the stories of later established playwrights who waited years for their first production, and of the many scripts that became dog-eared and decrepit by being passed from office to office and reader to reader before finding an appreciative eye and a courageous sponsor.

But it is not only bad plays that fail. Wrong casting, wrong direction, wrong timing, can ruin a good play's chances. Even a good production of a good play can fail to draw the town, and drawing the town is the criterion of success. It is not the only one. Good work well done brings its own rich and deep reward, even though it may not pay bills. The best books do not sell the most copies.

My comparative success as a radio writer compensated to a large extent for my failure to get my plays produced in London, but I sensed, even when I accepted the post of Chief Instructor at the B.B.C.'s Staff Training School in London, that the writer in me would become stifled when my energies were expended in organizing training courses and teaching. But I wanted to get to London, and this was a way to achieve that. Besides, Richard was married and living in London now, and well launched on his career. I found an apartment only a five-minute walk away from his.

I thoroughly enjoyed my work as Chief Instructor of the B.B.C. I met, as students, a bewilderingly numerous and varied welter of people from many countries, and, as lecturer, most of the leading people in the B.B.C.—administrators, planners, producers, engineers, writers. The head of my department was exceptionally congenial. His name was James Pennethorne Hughes, and he was almost my exact antithesis in background, upbringing, and temperament. He was tall, fair, and good-looking, typecasting for a product of the best English public schools. It was said that several generations back royal blood had found its way illicitly into the family veins. From the beginning we got on well together because we both enjoyed his considerable wit, which he paraded shyly. He was a shy and diffident man, his inner life dominated by ambition and gradually soured by frustration. (He had written two books. The punning title of the first showed his delight in verbal contortions: *While Shepheards Watched*, an account of Cairo in wartime. The second, *Witchcraft*, revealed his delight in and wide knowledge of the esoteric.) Finally despairing of promotion to the top levels of the B.B.C. hierarchy, he left to live a writer's life in a quiet village of the West Country, which he had come to love with an admirable passion. But after a few years, and too young to do so, he died.

My work in the Staff Training School was to organize short training courses, six weeks or less, and to do a deal of teaching, as lecturer, chairman of discussions, and demonstrator of production techniques. Most of the scripts for the productions I wrote myself. The basic activity was the General Course, which served to initiate newly appointed staff members into the mysteries of radio and the mazes of the B.B.C. Then there were special courses for such categories as announcers and producers; these were especially interesting because they brought together the experience of the practitioners. Perhaps the most interesting, and always the most difficult, were the Colonial courses. To them came native men and a few women from what had once been the British Empire. In their hands lay the awesome power of the radio medium in their new countries, and I felt a great sense of responsibility in dealing with them. It was our task not only to teach them the technical use of the medium, but also to inculcate something of the B.B.C.'s code of ethics; for instance, the truthful and objective presentation of news. I always tried to encourage the students to adapt to radio the material, attitudes, and approaches of their own cultures. I remember sadly the deep differences dividing people who shared a racial inheritance. Complex West Indians seemed to have an attitude, at once contemptuous and envious, toward simple West Africans. Even within the artificially created new countries that were preparing for independence there were deep hostilities; to me

116

Nigeria was Nigeria until a Hausa and an Ibo, both of them likable men, confided to me privately their opinions of each other . and each other's people.

I learned far more than I taught as Chief Instructor. The specialists who lectured on the various subjects were the heads of departments or their designates, but occasionally a crisis would prevent any of the appropriate people from turning up, and usually I had to be the last-minute substitute. In this way I became, or at least sounded, knowledgeable on almost every aspect of broadcasting and the B.B.C., except engineering, about which I retain an impenetrable stupidity, and such specialized subjects as the translation of modern terms into classical Arabic, the lingua franca of the Middle East. I can still see the smug smile of the translator who solved the problem of "parachute" by substituting "umbrella of escape," and his dismay when confronted by "parachute troops."

One of my last tasks as Chief Instructor had been to organize the first television training course, chiefly aimed at personnel from several European countries who would be involved in the development of the new medium in their own countries. I suppose the motive was to woo them to the use of the British system of transmission rather than the American one. It is little known in America that there was a B.B.C. television service operating from London in 1937, but it had to be suspended because of the war. Beyond the schedule I could contribute nothing to the television course, except a long list of questions, and a new instructor was appointed to deal solely with television courses, which soon burgeoned.

I stayed in the Staff Training School for two years and three months, and then resigned. I received offers of promotion to persuade me to stay, but the advancement meant moving even further away from the microphone and creative work into the remote stratosphere of administration. The irony of all branches of show business—and some august members of the British Broadcasting Corporation would be horrified to learn that they are in that business—is that the ones who call the tune, not those who play it, have the power and the money, and sometimes the callers are tone deaf.

The decision to leave the B.B.C. was a difficult one, and I still don't quite know where I found the courage to make it. I was forty-seven at the time and was leaving for limbo, but the limbo of freedom, which had become obsessively desirable. Knowing how my spirit had been shackled by the fear of insecurity, I could only overcome that fear by defying it and abandoning security. It wasn't easy, yet I have never regretted the decision, and now every job that spells security irks me. After all, the place of maximum security and least worry is prison.

But in those first months of freedom, when for the first time in my working life I did not have the anodyne of regular work and regular payment, I found it difficult to enjoy whole days and weeks of leisure. I could not refrain from counting my dwindling capital and being reluctant to leave the house lest a phone call should bring an offer of work. Yet I did go out to see a lot of plays and films, but the usual result was that I felt I had wasted time that should have been spent at home writing. I did not seek work; by some absurd reasoning I felt that to do so would be a confession of failure. It has taken me years of comparative success to teach me to enjoy leisure without twinges of conscience, and I doubt if I shall ever learn the lesson completely.

Of course, those phone calls did come, chiefly from the B.B.C. in London and Cardiff. Now I had to start learning another lesson: I had to learn to say "No," and this I still find very difficult. I was invited to write feature programs on subjects that didn't interest me in the slightest—open-pit mining, for instance—and the only satisfaction I gained from the work, apart from the very welcome payment, was that of turning in a professional script. I knew very little about television, except what I had learned by attending the courses I had organized, but one of the first contracts I was given was to write the initial and establishing episodes for a weekly series for Children's Hour. It was called *The Apple-*

yards. I did twelve scripts, but with little enjoyment, apart from that of learning something about the new medium. I found the restrictions of the audience crippling, and still more those imposed by the producers; the director was a delight to work with, but I became reluctant to send in a script because of the rewriting that would be called for, and I am temperamentally a disgruntled re-writer. Of course, what I went through was as nothing compared with the writer's agony in American television, where the necessity to satisfy conflicting criticisms and avoid offending anybody re-sults in ulcers for the writer and mediocrity for his work.

An experience I did enjoy in television was telling a fifteen-minute story, and at an hour which made it clearly not for chil-dren. Algernon Blackwood had made this genre popular, by retell-ing some of his *Tales of the Uncanny and Supernatural.* It seems to me a particularly appropriate use of television. In my first tale I told of a childhood adventure of my own. A friend of mine, Rhys Davies, a writer of novels and brilliant short stories, used it as the basis of a story he called *Fear.* It was another story by Rhys Davies, *River Flow Gently,* that I used for my second television solo appearance.

I had come to know, like, and admire Rhys Davies very much. His early courage in staking all on his writing ability did much to shame me in my days of doubt and fear. When he was a very young man he had left the Rhondda Valley to become a writer in London. He was the first Welshman to make such a decision without compromise. One or two others before, and several since, have become writers but with the safeguard of a private income or another profession, such as journalism or teaching. Rhys made a total decision, and abided by it. He had done some writing for me when I was the features producer in Cardiff, and I always enjoyed working with him. He shrewdly observed the follies and hypoc-risies of men with a wry twinkle, but was himself generous and thoughtful. Occasionally he would allow a brief peep into his past, and would thrill me with some anecdote about D. H. Lawrence and Frieda, with whom he had lived on the Continent for some time. After I had left the B.B.C., when the program director in Wales asked me to do some scripts for them, I suggested, as one, that I should write and direct an adaptation of *Marianne* by Rhys Davies. It was a powerful tale of revenge based on a true story, but there was a surprise development at the end that strained the credulity of both reader and listener, and yet that surprise was a part of the true story. Fiction dare not have the haphazard, chance quality of life. Fiction must be well made; life isn't.

At last, the kind of work I most wanted came my way. I was offered a part in a play, and in an imporant production at that— the so-called All-Star Coronation Production of Oscar Wilde's *A Woman of No Importance* at the Savoy Theatre. The cast was filled with names of people well known to me and, in several cases, admired—Clive Brook, Isabel Jeans, Athene Seyler, Nora Swinburne, Jean Cadell, Aubrey Mather. I was to play the small and dull part of Mr. Kelvil, M.P., but it was exciting to rehearse and play with such a distinguished cast, and it was a constant sop to my vanity to know that Aubrey Mather's part was even smaller than mine, although not so dull. The director was Michael Benthall and the producer was Hugh Beaumont, then at the height of his extraordinary and well-exercised power in the London theatre. He was known in the profession as "Binkie," a most misleading appellation for such a charming and suave czar, but many a young actor who would have quaked in his presence used it familiarly as a guarantee of his own professional status, in much the same way that "Gadge" is bandied about in New York by actors who wish to imply a friendship with Elia Kazan. Binkie's production of the Wilde play, which was almost certain to lose money, was his lavish contribution to London's celebration of the great event of 1953, the Coronation on June 2 of Queen Elizabeth II. The text of the play had been edited by Paul Dehn in an endeavor to tone down some of the more melodramatic exchanges and to incorporate even more of Wilde' epigrams.

We opened, to mixed notices, four months before the Coronation, and for some time it seemed that this elaborate production which had been designed to grace the royal occasion might not live to see it, but Hugh Beaumont was determined that it should, and it did. During May, London became more and more crowded, and the theatres more and more empty. London in her Coronation dress was what people had come from all over the world to see. Why spend time and money on an indoor show when the streets and the squares and the parks were so much more colorful and exciting? But once the great day was over, a day on which television came magnificently into its own, the happy crowds flocked into the theatres, and gave our limping show energy for a fresh spurt that carried us along for another two months.

My favorite memory of that production of A *Woman of No Importance* concerns Sir Winston Churchill, who came to see it one evening and sat in the front row. Sitting in the row behind him was Esmond Knight, whose beautiful wife, Nora Swinburne, was playing the title role. Esmond Knight, a handsome romantic actor with an engaging vitality both on and off stage, had been a naval officer in the war and had been blinded when H.M.S. *Hood* was sunk. Incidentally, he bore his affliction like a hilarious saint, and told very funny stories about his misadventures. Later, when a faint glimmer of light returned to his eyes, he resumed his acting career fearlessly. On that night in the theatre, Sir Winston spotted the blind hero and invited him to sit next to him in the front row. Sir Winston himself was deaf by this time, and so in the front row we had one man who couldn't hear us and another who couldn't see us. Throughout the performance the war leader carried on a very lively and light-hearted conversation with the war hero, and it had nothing to do with the play, nor was it modified in any way by the fact that the play was going on. The great man's deafness made him unaware of his loudness, and his greatness made everybody else pretend to be unaware of it. At the end of the performance he applauded us generously and was led out of the theatre by his entourage. As he left, some representative of the theatre hoped he had enjoyed the play. He replied, "The play? Oh, yes, the play. . . . I must read it."

When *A Woman of No Importance* closed, there was a suggestion that I might play Claudius to Richard's Hamlet at the Old Vic. I think the suggestion came from Michael Benthall, who was in charge of the Old Vic at the time, but it is possible that I may have plucked up enough courage to make the suggestion myself. Anyway, nothing came of it; Michael decided that my presence in the cast would make both him and Richard nervous. Richard's Hamlet had long been one of my most cherished dreams, and our work on it together in my London flat gave me great joy and satisfaction. The production opened at the Edinburgh Festival, where it was played on a "thrust stage," although it had been designed for the Old Vic's "apron stage." On the opening night, I was sitting in the front row at the side of the stage and was infuriated by being presented with the back of Richard's head at critical moments. I have never been wholly converted to "theatre-in-the-round." I know the academic arguments in favor of it, but they all pale for me in the light of the fact that at every moment of the play some people are robbed of the visual focus of the action, the actor's face. Only once did a theatre-in-the-round production completely enthrall me, and that was the Circle-in-the-Square production of O'Neill's *The Iceman Cometh.* I had decided, in reading the play, that it was overlong and repetitive, but that brilliant production proved me wrong.

Richard's London Hamlet in 1953 and his New York Hamlet in 1964 were very different, although equally successful. Both scored record runs, which filled me with pride. The London Hamlet was much more conventional than the Broadway one, more lyrical and romantic, and to me more satisfying, but the later Hamlet had an excitement all its own. Richard would only have essayed the role a second time in a completely new and challenging framework, and the conception of a modern-dress rehearsal setting gave him a real freedom to experiment, of which he took full advantage. I saw the play several times, in Toronto, Boston, and New York, and every time he thrilled me with moments of fresh insight; even on the last night things happened that I had never seen before.

One evening in 1953 stands out vividly in my memory, and a sequel to it increased its significance. It was October 11. Dylan Thomas came to spend the evening with me; he was leaving for America the next day. He wanted to discuss an idea he had for a stage play. He told me that he felt he was coming to the end of his lyrical impulse and wanted to turn to dramatic forms. The play's tentative title was *Two Streets*. It was to be in one long act, for Dylan had no patience with intermissions; playgoers might at least emulate the endurance of moviegoers. The setting was to be two nearby streets in a South Wales town, and at the same time a boy is born in one and a girl in the other. The play depicts the forces that shape their lives as they grow up. At the end of the play, they meet and fall in love. As we talked that night, a dominating Dylanesque figure emerged; he was to be a cheapjack selling the Welsh valleys in the Depression, an evangelist launching a revival, a recruiting officer seeking soldiers, a politician seeking votes, a circus barker seeking patrons. Time and again as Dylan's imagination and invention soared, I had to remind him of stage practicalities. At one point, with exasperated rotundity he exclaimed: "For God's sake let me start with two prodigiously pregnant women!" We also discussed the libretto he was to write for a Stravinsky opera; the subject was to be the rediscovery of life by a few survivors after an atomic war had virtually wiped out mankind. Dylan had readily agreed to the project because some foundation had promised a handsome down payment to commission the work, but Stravinsky had decided that they would do much better subsequently if they completed the work without having any prior strings attached to it. Dylan was much chagrined by this decision because he was always more interested in ready than in future money. While he was with me he phoned Richard to "borrow" two hundred pounds from him. When I asked him why he was going to America, he said it was to make money. When I pressed him further and asked him how much he would bring back, he smiled his sad self-condemnatory smile and said, "Nothing." During the evening we discussed many things in addition to the play and the opera: Wordsworth ("What a pity for his poetry that he lived so long"), some additions to *Under Milk Wood*, *King Lear*, and pornography. After we had been talking for some hours, he asked if he might lie down, and he went into my bedroom to do so, asking me to wake him after a half-hour, which I did, but with great difficulty. I even became alarmed. But at last, after a vigorous shaking, he slowly became awake again. He seemed not surprised that sleep had claimed him so deeply. When he left the house—I had to give him a pound for his taxi—he was full of excitement again about *Two Streets* and said he wanted to get together with me about it as soon as he returned from America. But he never returned. Within a month he was dead.

Early in 1954 I was involved in two memorial programs to Dylan Thomas. On a Sunday afternoon in January at the Globe Theatre, a most distinguished audience listened to readings from Dylan's work and about him. Somebody remarked that a bomb on the theatre that afternoon would have wiped out London's cultural and artistic life. It was a particularly exciting afternoon for me because it was the only time Richard and I had performed on a stage together. Two months later I arranged at the Old Vic a reading by a very distinguished cast of *Under Milk Wood*. I had hoped to take an active part in it, but by that time I was on tour with a new play. I did get back from Blackpool on the Sunday in time to see the performance. I was particularly impressed by the work of Emlyn Williams and Rachel Roberts. It was that evening that aroused the interest of Emlyn Williams in Dylan Thomas, and from it grew his delightful recital from Dylan's works.

The play that took me out of town was John Whiting's *Marching Song*. I had been an ardent admirer of his since he had excited actors and puzzled critics with his play *Saints' Day*, which was awarded the prize in a competition organized by the Arts Theatre. I found his new play equally exciting, and longed to be in it. It was to be produced by the Hugh Beaumont management, and I made my enthusiasm for John Whiting known to the casting director, Daphne Rye. At that time she had great power in the London theatre and used it to good purpose. Many a young talent was discovered, nurtured, and shaped by her. Richard owed much to her and it was through him that I came to know her. She was a joy to know because she was shrewd and knowledgeable about theatre, amusingly acidulous about actors, and warm and generous in her hospitality. She arranged a reading for me with the author and director, and I was offered the small part of Father Anselm. There was nothing else for me in the play, except the best part, Cadmus, for which I was in any case too young, but they were anxious for me to understudy it. I was very dubious about undertaking that frustration, but Daphne assured me that I was almost certain to play it. That distinctive and delightful actor and man, Ernest Thesiger, was to do the part, but he was already old and frail and they were afraid that, at best, they should expect many absences from him because the play was to have a long pre-London tour in the rigors of an English winter. Of course, Mr. Thesiger was the only member of the cast who never even sniffled with a cold, and he took an impish delight in telling me every day how well he felt. But the joy of his company did much to compensate for his absurdly good health. He had a passion for royalty and prepared me, in hushed tones, for days to meet a member of the exiled Romanoff dynasty. I expected a frail and wispy relic of the centuries, and was dumbstruck to be greeted with a paralyzing handshake by a large and tweedily jolly woman. That encounter took place in the theatre bar in Brighton, a unique bar that was reserved for the company. In addition to Brighton, the tour took us to seven other towns and cities: Cardiff, Cambridge, Glasgow, Blackpool, Bournemouth, Liverpool, and Oxford. I thoroughly enjoyed the adventure of theatrical "digs," those private houses which for years had specialized in housing members of traveling theatrical companies. Old-timers kept jealously guarded lists of the good ones, and reserved their places far in advance. The best were very good indeed, far better than any hotel, for they catered for the odd hours demanded by the profession. In most hotels at that time it was impossible to get a meal after the performance, but the landladies of the best "digs" reserved their best culinary efforts for midnight.

Marching Song opened in the St. Martin's Theatre, which I shall always remember because eighty-eight steps separated my dressing room from the stage. Once again John Whiting puzzled the critics, and this time there was no Arts Theatre following to support the play; it closed after forty-three performances. Selfishly I wasn't sorry, because by this time I was convinced that if we had run for years, I should never have played Cadmus.

The following week I impulsively decided to spend the summer in America, and, before I could change my mind, I went to the Cunard office and booked a passage on the *Mauretania*, but I deliberately chose a crossing two months ahead, to give me time to finish some writing for the B.B.C. and to make plans for the fall. I had not the slightest idea that my intended two months in America would turn into a permanent stay, so permanent that ten years later I should happily choose to become an American citizen.

Chapter Seven

America Again

My visit to America in 1954, the one in which the visitor became
an immigrant, was not my second but my seventh. I had bid
"Good-bye" to the Baruths from the deck of the *President
Roosevelt* in September, 1939, and I doubted if I should ever see
them or America again. But throughout the war we maintained a
correspondence, chiefly as a result of the loyal determination of
Mrs. Baruth to do so; I received far more letters than I sent. She
frequently sent over much-appreciated parcels too, but German
submarines prevented many of them from arriving; and at irregu-
lar intervals would arrive a copy of the New York Sunday *Times*,
whose vast size seemed a symbol to my friends in Port Talbot of
all that was incredible about that Brobdingnagian country of
America. The copies of the *Times* accumulated in formidable piles
waiting to be read. The same still happens with the several magazines that arrive at my home; news becomes history before I get
around to it. The Baruths maintained a lively interest in all my
wartime activities, and sent a trophy, the Baruth Cup, to be com-
peted for by the Flights in my Air Training Corps Squadron.

At last the war was over, and I began to think of visiting America and the Baruths again. I finally managed to do so in the summer of 1948, at which time I was working for the B.B.C. in Cardiff. Thereafter, with the exception of 1953 when I was playing at the Savoy Theatre, I went over every summer until 1954, when I did not return.

The war had prevented the Baruths from continuing their summer student tours. Instead, they had opened a camp in Vermont named, with wartime fervor, Camp MacArthur. In the first years the main activity of the campers had been to help the local farmers in harvesting, but their leisure hours had been spent in dramatic activities. It was this work that the Baruths developed after the war and that enabled me to join them again. They bought a farm property in Waitsfield, Vermont, which was admirably suited for their purpose; there was a large main house, a beautiful old barn, which became the boys' dormitory, and the "Brook House," which became the girls' dormitory. The whole venture became a respected part of the community life, and the village hall was the center of the dramatic activities. A competent professional staff was engaged each summer, and well-rehearsed productions were toured within a radius of one hundred miles for one-night stands. Two or three major productions were produced each season. The campers were largely high school seniors, but members of staff also acted in the plays. During the years I myself played two roles: Sheridan Whiteside in *The Man Who Came to Dinner* and George Radfern in *Laburnum Grove*, which in Randolph was billed as *La Burnum Grove*.

Randolph, some thirty miles south of Waitsfield, contained, and probably still does, a magnificent old theatre, totally out of proportion to the size of the community. If every man, woman, and child in the township attended a performance, a play would not run a week there, and my experience leads me to believe that rural Vermont is not theatre-conscious. The Randolph theatre had been built to accommodate touring companies for one-night stands, but I cannot understand how the most optimistic entrepreneur could have hoped that it would be viable. In several places in this country I have seen large and hoary theatres mysteriously stranded in theatrical deserts.

I began my transatlantic trips as vacations, but increasingly I began to feel a pressing urge to interpret the United States to the United Kingdom, and because there was a dearth of dollars in Britain I worked out a plan with the B.B.C. enabling me to stay longer in America so as to bring back radio documentaries of American life at no dollar cost. I used the money I received from the Baruths for my work in Vermont to get the programs, with the cooperation of the B.B.C. office in New York.

I suppose the most important program I did was *State Capital*. I wanted to illustrate the states' rights versus federal control issue, which is a major and abiding one in American political life. Vermont was a perfect state for my purpose, because there is an independence as strong as the native granite in a typical Vermonter. His state had been born in such a fierce spirit of independence that she had not even been represented in the Continental Congress, and subsequently had even contemplated joining Canada. And at that time the state virtually belonged to one party; the current joke was that the Democratic Party met in the living room of one of the members.

The party structure in America is very difficult for an Englishman to understand. He is used to a party label's signifying certain beliefs; he knows, without asking him, where a Socialist or a Conservative stands on a specific question. But not so a Republican or a Democrat; it largely depends upon what part of the country he comes from. I found a dramatic example of this fact for my documentary on Vermont; a certain prominent politician there whom I got to know well had to be a Republican to get into office at all, but in Britain he would have been a Socialist, because his main concern was to promote cooperative activity among the farmers. I came to the conclusion that the driving force in American politics is the value of opposition for its own sake; the function of the "outs" is to criticize and curb the "ins." There is no

sectional interest that votes solidly because one party better sup-
ports its cause; not every Catholic voted for Kennedy, and I know
an intelligent Negro who voted for Goldwater.

In Montpelier, the state capital, I recorded interviews with the
governor, several state officials, the mayor, sundry voters, and a
few colorful characters, all of them proud of their state and most
of them violently suspicious of the octopus in Washington. I was
lastingly impressed by two widely held opinions about the small
farmer in Vermont. He had largely been put out of business by
refrigeration. In the days of quick decay of vegetables, the Eastern
cities had been the market for his produce, but now he could not
compete with the large-scale farming of the Midwest, whose
markets, through refrigeration, were every city in the United
States. As a result, Vermont relied less and less upon farming and
was becoming more and more a resort state. Many of the people I
interviewed were saddened by this change; to cater to visitors
meant virtually to become servants, which went much against the
grain of an old-time Vermonter. But the state government did its
best to protect the local farmers. I remember that ice cream in
Vermont was unusually delicious because the law insisted on a
very high cream content, and margarine was not allowed to look
like butter; it looked like most unappetizing lard, and the package
contained a globule of coloring matter which the purchaser could
knead into the white lump to produce an illusion of butter. The
Baruths themselves were examples of "out-of-staters" who had
bought a farm for other purposes. Subsequently, they sold it and
gave up their summer enterprises. If they had kept it, they would
have made much more money, because after they had left Waitsfield, it became a center of the new and thriving skiing industry of
Vermont. The comment of the deterioration of the soul of the
Vermont farmer when he was forced to cater to visitors was one
of the opinions that has lived in my memory; the other was that
the Great Depression had meant less to most Vermonters than to
most other Americans because it only made life a little harder for
people to whom life had always been hard. It was sad on walks

through woods to come across, as one frequently did, derelict homesteads that had been reclaimed by the forest primeval. A vivid sense of the past is always with me in New England. When I see that curious road sign "Thickly Settled," my mind jumps back two hundred years.

A Vermont documentary radio program which gave me great pleasure to make was one I did especially for the B.B.C. Children's Hour. I called it *Yankee Tommy Tucker*. Tommy Tucker, for that was indeed his name, was the son of a Waitsfield farmer. He was about eight years old when I made the recordings, and thus would be about twenty-eight as I write this, probably with a young Tommy Tucker of his own. The idea was to present a day in the summer life of a boy on a small American farm. I followed him around with the recording machine from his early rising in the morning to his bedside prayers at night. Tommy was an ideal subject, neither self-consciously inhibited nor an unpleasant show-off. He knew me well before we made the recordings and so was used to having me around; nor did he know when he was being recorded and when he wasn't. The resulting program I, at least, found delightful. The thing that most impressed me and my subsequent listeners, both young and old, was to find that eight-year-old Tommy drove a huge tractor on the farm. I suppose it was illegal, but perhaps it wasn't, provided Tommy never drove the tractor off his father's property. Anyway, drive it he did, and with consummate dexterity. This staggered me, who never succeeded in driving a simple car with relaxed ease and have always refused to attempt to drive one in America. This prompts the speculation that Americans are now born with an inherited aptitude for managing machines, because it has become such an essential part of their lives. I know of the biological doubt about inherited characteristics, but I remember the consternation that the early cars caused among sheep and cows, and now even lambs and calves are suckled contentedly in fields bordered by busy highways.

There is a large Welsh colony in Vermont, attracted from North Wales by the slate and marble quarries, which called for their native skills. I went in search of them with the recording machines and found them with their Welsh tongue and traditions intact, and, as in their home country, their culture centered around the chapels. Even their American English was spoken with a North Welsh coloring, and that is very different in sound and spirit from the Welsh accent I acquired in my childhood. But the Welsh Vermonters had a South Walian delight in choral singing, and most of the programs they sang at home and far afield consisted of items that they had brought with them in their luggage and their memories, and which they sang in Welsh: stirring calls to battle, charming folk songs, and the inevitable hymns. The younger generation, I found, no longer spoke the language, but they acquired enough of it, parrot fashion, to sing in the choirs; I wonder, but doubt, if they still do. The Welsh were not the only people for whom the quarries were a magnet; side by side with them lived and worked the Italians. I made recordings at the marble quarries where the only languages heard were Italian and Welsh, and each of the disparate peoples had a rudimentary fluency in the other's language.

With my interest in coalmining, which was a part of my birthright, I inevitably wanted to do a program about the American miner, and my machine and I went in search of him in Pennsylvania. Again I expected to find many Welshmen working "on the coal," to use a phrase which is old on my tongue, but I had come a generation too late. Almost all the immigrant Welsh colliers had by this time become officials, of high and low degree, and on both sides of the bargaining table; John L. Lewis had to be a Welshman. With great triumph I ultimately tracked down a recent Welsh immigrant who was actually working on the coal, but he was looked upon as a strange survival of a species thought to be extinct. I secreted my microphone in the men's showerhouse and was later told that the babel I recorded was largely Polish, the substance of which did not lend itself to broadcasting. I remembered the narrow seams from which men and boys had ripped the coal in South Wales, carefully gathering the nuggets of black gold, and so, as in many other aspects of American life, I was struck by the apparent wastefulness of the coal-getting system. But in this instance I applauded, because it seemed to reduce the rigors and the dangers of the miner's life; yet, even as I discussed this fact with the manager of one of the mines, the news came that a man had been killed underground.

When I took my American tapes back to Britain they caused much amusement to the B.B.C. engineers, because, quite unconsciously, my accent had changed in every case to take on the color of the person being interviewed. Of course, it had the advantage of putting the victim at greater ease, but I had no such conscious purpose. Why did I do it? The answer probably has some unflattering implication about my "identity problem."

When I sailed to America in July 1954, I had no other object than to enjoy a two-month holiday with the Baruths, who had already sold the farm in Vermont by that time and had not embarked on any other summer projects. After my maiden crossing of the Atlantic in 1939, when I had been prostrated by sickness for most of the voyage, I had thoroughly enjoyed the sea journeys to and fro. Occasionally I had had, for lack of time, to come by air, in the prejet days of those tedious flights by way of depressing Gander, Newfoundland. But the sea trips had been delightful. There was the sense of physical well-being engendered by the bracing air, there was very good food and drink, the guiltless indulgence of casual reading, a movie every day—although they are never seen at their best aboard ship, and even less in the air—sometimes good leisurely conversation, and occasionally a shipboard friendship that was congenial and deep enough to endure on land. I was particularly grateful to one voyage on which I had formed a lasting friendship with a gracious and delightful family from Cleveland.

Yet the voyage in July 1954 was the least pleasant I had made. The ship seemed to be full of the most objectionable kind of American tourist, loud in complaints about Europe and Europeans. For them the glory that was Greece and the grandeur that was Rome meant only tough steaks, hot rooms, no showers, thieving guides, and their only satisfaction was that of being able to say that they had done Europe. There was one particularly loud-voiced and proudly self-made businessman who sat at my dining table and who was distressed because I always seemed to be reading, although not, I hasten to add, in the dining room. He insisted on trying to convince me of my mistaken sense of values, and he boasted that he had read only one book in his life. When he told me that that book had been *St. Elmo*, I understood why he had never gone on to a second. I myself had once-upon-a-time been nauseated by that too, too moral story written by the Georgian novelist Mrs. Wilson, which told of the taming unto marriage of a worldly sophisticate by a pious prude, and which had been so admired in the South that its incredible popularity is still evidenced by a rash of "St. Elmo's": towns, hotels, streets, and even men. But to return to the poor company on the S.S. *Mauretania*.

I was even embarrassed by the English barber on board, who, while he was cutting my hair, delivered a diatribe against all Americans at such a pitch that the Americans waiting for his services could not but hear him. My replies in their defense they could not hear. I have always been acutely embarrassed by people who indulge in loud private conversations in public places, and yet I have envied, too, their lack of self-consciousness.

I thoroughly enjoyed that first leisurely month in New York City, which I had not really explored since 1939. Al Baruth and I went in search of the little known. I remember being astounded by the primitively rural conditions still existing in the back roads of Staten Island and found it hard to realize that they were a part of the greatest modern city in the world. Equally out of place yet in sharp contrast is the Dutch colonial town of Richmond in the center of Staten Island, its original old buildings still, in 1968, in process of being excellently restored. It is true that in New York City the present aggressively pushes out the past, but there are still delightful nooks and crannies of survival to be found even in raucous Manhattan.

After I had been in New York about a month a meeting was arranged for me with two gentlemen who had just formed a film company. I think it wiser that I should leave them nameless, even though I am still friendly with both of them. One of them was a well-known Hollywood producer and the other an equally well-known scion of a wealthy family, who had used his wealth, acumen, and knowledge to acquire an extraordinary collection of paintings. I liked both men, and still do. After several meetings, they invited me to take charge of the script department of the new company with the added inducement that I was to have a practical and financial interest in productions. Negotiations took nearly a month and were finally concluded three days before I was to return to England. The terms were, by English standards, very generous, yet the decision to break completely with my life in London was not an easy one to make. I tried to have the agreement tentative for six months, but my would-be employers would have none of that; three years with renewal options was the least they would settle for, but even that, much to my later regret, was never signed. My visa status was that of a visitor, but it was changed to that of an immigrant without my having to leave the country: apparently a flattering case was made out for the unique quality of the services I could render, and the desirability of my immediate employment. And immediate it was. Before I was fully aware of the implications of what was happening, I found myself ensconced in a beautiful room, which was insulted with the name of "office" and which contained a large Corot, a Van Gogh self-portrait, and a Mary Cassatt; the waiting room was dominated by an El Greco. I had not even had time to fly back to London to tie up my affairs there.

It was obvious to me from the beginning that my new employers had an ulterior motive in securing my services; they protested too much to the contrary. They hoped my being a part of their venture would make Richard more readily available for some of the films they hoped to make, and, if their company really got into active production, this might have been so, but it soon became apparent that the two partners were not going to be able to work together, and within six months all their energies were devoted to dissolving the partnership with the least hurt to their individual selves, and I was left holding an empty bag, sitting in a beautiful chair, manufacturing pointless work for myself on an exquisite desk, and contemplating my dire situation as I gazed at famous paintings. But all that lay ahead, and we started with high hopes. My first assignment was a very pleasant one. Richard was in Hollywood at the time, making the film about Edwin Booth, *The Prince of Players*. I was to go out there to interest him in a projected film about Von Luckner, "The Sea Devil," the outmodishly chivalrous and romantic German naval commander of World War II. The whole idea was too tentative for any commitment on Richard's part, but my visit was a particularly pleasant one; it was the first time I visited the homes of Hollywood people whose work I admired, and as people they did not disappoint me. I especially remember with delight the meetings with Humphrey Bogart, James Mason, and George Cukor. I remember the relaxed humor at the Bogarts'—the house had been taken over by television engineers for the elaborate preparations for one of Edward R. Murrow's "Person to Person" programs, and the maze of cables and the apparent confusion led, surprisingly, not to domestic exasperation but to family fun. I remember the stimulating and wide-ranging conversation at the Masons' and the dinner-table wit at the elegant home of George Cukor, with the appropriately sensational after-dinner view of Los Angeles at night from his high-perched Italian garden.

But Hollywood is not my city, and I don't think it ever could be. I have visited it a few times and have never been reluctant to leave. To start with, walking is frowned upon. Twice I have been stopped by police while taking a walk in Beverly Hills; they wanted to know where I was going and why. Unless I am free to walk, I am not free, and because I refuse to drive a car in America, Hollywood is a prison to me. Then there is the stratified social life, in which invitations to parties acquire the professional significance of "billing" in a movie, and there is the all-too-frequent predatory conversation: "Who loses and who wins; who's in, who's out." New York is big enough to put the theatre in its place, but Hollywood is all movies, and even the top salaries paid to actors on Broadway are very small compared with the fortunes paid in Hollywood, and so the New York actor leads a much more normal life than his equivalent in Beverly Hills.

Richard Burton was not the only star my film company sought. They also had high hopes of a three-picture deal with Gina Lollobrigida. At a preliminary conference with Miss Lollobrigida, to which she came attended by the usual business entourage and at which I was present to suggest some possible subjects for the three movies, the beautiful one remained silent during the cascade of words expressing a two-way enthusiasm for her talents and the artistic excellence of the films to be made. I wondered whether her Sphinx-like detachment was caused by her rudimentary knowledge of English. Finally she was directly appealed to, and she swept away all the froth with two words: "How much?"

I am not a fast reader, and I have but one speed, which perhaps partly accounts for my sense of guilt when I use precious time to read the latest best-seller, which I rarely do, but in my function as scriptman for the abortive film company I wrote a conscientious report on "properties" at an average of one a day, and my concern for every writer was such that I pursued the dreariest prospect to its boring, lifeless, or limp end. In addition, I also wrote several screen treatments of properties in which my employers became interested; this I thoroughly enjoyed and derived some sense of accomplishment from it, even though, with every passing week, my sense of frustration and futility increased.

Almost exactly six months after I started to work in my beautiful office, the film company was no more. There had been a mounting series of comically tragic crises in the relations between the two partners, and the climax occurred when the wealthy partner refused to advance any more money and literally locked out the producer. While I had worked, to no purpose, on my reports and treatments, I had become aware that an end was inevitable, but by this time I was owed several thousands of dollars, and I had to wait for a settlement between the partners to get it. I finally received half of what was due me.

All this time I had maintained my flat in Belsize Park in London, and I now decided to return to it. Accordingly I booked passage on the *Scythia*, but at almost the last moment I impulsively and quixotically changed my mind. I canceled my passage and cabled London to terminate my lease of the flat. At the same time I wrote to some relatives of mine in Wales to ask them to go to London to arrange for the packing and transportation of my goods and chattels for storage in Wales. Why did I decide to stay in America? Even now I'm not at all certain, but I have never regretted the decision. I enjoyed my life in New York and the new friends I had found there, but then I enjoyed my life and friends in London too. Certainly I should have had some sense of failure in returning, and there was an exhilaration and an excitement about being stranded far away from home at fifty, but my American future was so uncertain that for some time fear kept me sleepless. Furthermore, I was living in a hotel which was much too expensive for me in my imminent poverty.

My wealthy and erstwhile employer generously afforded me office space for as long as I should need it and I set out to make a living as a writer. A friendly agent, whom I had met through the evanescent film company, got me involved in dramatizing an interesting novel, but we failed to secure a production for it, and it brought me no money. She then got me an engagement as a director in a summer theatre for the forthcoming season, but the rules of the actors' union, Equity, forbade my employment because I had not been a "resident alien" long enough. One of the assistants in the film company had been an ambitious and knowledgeable young man who aimed at becoming a theatrical producer and he persuaded me—with nothing else to do I did not need much persuading—to work on a dramatization of Dorothy Canfield's novel *Bonfire*. It was a challenge that brought me great satisfaction, particularly because it resulted in a stimulating correspondence with Mrs. Fisher (Dorothy Canfield). I was delighted that she found my dialogue authentic enough to be surprised when she learned that I was not an American, and her complimentary approval of my final script gave me great pleasure. But the satisfaction of accomplishing a difficult task and the pleasure of approval were the total reward; no production eventuated and so no money came. The would-be producer had an idea for a musical to be called Las Vegas and persuaded me to attempt to write the book for it. He also enlisted the services of a composer and lyricist who wrote some very good numbers, so good that, when Las Vegas proved to be abortive, they incorporated the numbers into another show which became successful on Broadway, but since the numbers had grown out of my book, I received a minuscule percentage of the successful show, a most welcome source of income.

In February 1956, almost a year after the film company had disintegrated without coalescing, the spirit of adventure, never strong in me, made a brief appearance. I have already mentioned that my wealthy patron, for he had become my patron in allowing me free office space, had a notable art collection. It had been arranged that one hundred of his pictures—there was so much discussion in the choice of the one-hundredth picture that finally both candidates for the position were included to make the total one hundred and one—were to tour for exhibition in the art galleries of some of the major cities of the United States, starting in Portland, Oregon. To submit several millions' worth of irreplaceable art treasures to the hazards of travel, and repeated packing and unpacking, and all this in the middle of an American winter, was a logistics problem of extraordinary delicacy and difficulty. It was decided that the pictures should travel by road in two specially prepared and temperature-controlled vans. No insurance company would insure the paintings for more than one-third of their market value; as some slight added protection the drivers were to be armed. Fortunately, the revolvers never had to be used, which was just as well, because if we had run into any trouble, the first problem would have been to find them; they were always getting mislaid. The owner of the pictures suggested that he and I should accompany the precious cargo, riding one in each van. I agreed, whether eagerly or reluctantly I cannot recall. But, somehow or other, I ended up going alone. One of my motives in going was that the adventure would provide material for a very salable article. I even went armed with a camera, in the manipulation of which I am absurdly inexpert. I did write the article, a lengthy one, and I did take pictures, some of them recognizable. I failed to sell the article at my first attempt and, as usual with me, gave up any further attempt, and now it seems that I have lost it, for a thorough search of my manuscripts has failed to find it. I did come across my snapshots and a yellowing page of pictures from the *Oregon Journal,* in one of which I am looking lasciviously at a Maillot bronze of a female torso, and another of which shows Monet's *Nympheas* above the caption: "What on earth is it?"

To avoid the rigors of a northern winter it had been decided that we should travel to Oregon via Texas, but, as if our journey had been plotted by a power that delighted in playing tricks, the North had comparatively good weather and we had to contend with floods in Louisiana and a blizzard in Texas and New Mexico. I had been warned that I should find the trip rough and had been counseled to buy some strange articles of apparel, including a polo belt. But I had been promised that I should sleep in motel beds, yet never once did I do so. My driver wanted to make time so that he could spend a few days en route with his wife and children in California. Such sleep as I snatched was among the pictures in the van, and they were packed far more comfortably than I. Particularly did I come to resent Monet's *Nympheas,* for it measured 237.25 inches, a statistic that is embedded in my body and my memory.

I gained an unbounded admiration for the drivers of long-distance vans. I did not know that in most cases it is only the van itself that is owned by the van company; the detachable front part supplying the traction is owned by the driver; the cabin is his home, the shelf behind the driver's seat his bed, and the motor his life, and all are usually heavily mortgaged. He is paid by the size of the cargo and the distance of the journey, and so, to make the most money, he must get there sooner than strict adherence to the law will allow. Each driver must carry a relief driver, but, if my experience has any general significance, the owner-driver is very reluctant to entrust his wheel to anybody else. He could not sleep anyway; he prefers to drive himself with the aid of benzedrine. We traveled by night and day with brief stops and an occasional lay-by for a few hours' general snooze. My driver—I shall call him Joe—was a friendly and high-spirited young man, very proud of his wife and three children; the relief driver, whom I shall call Tom, was somewhat heavy and taciturn, but he repaid the effort of getting to know him. A business venture of Tom's in Arizona had failed and he had decided to try long-distance hauling. This was an apprentice trip; quite naturally he was disappointed that Joe was reluctant to let him drive. Despite our enormous detour and days and nights of endless rain, Joe got us to his California home in five days.

The first myth to be exploded by the trip was that truck stops provide good food. They don't. Dinner after dinner consisted of tough meat, soggy vegetables, and tired pies. Some were slightly better than others in that there was less left on the plate at the end of the meal; there was one in Meridian, Mississippi, that was memorably good by comparison; we even stayed there long enough to shave. I couldn't understand the extraordinary popularity of one place in the South. Joe insisted on postponing the dinner stop until we got to this paradisiacal café. It was nearly midnight before we arrived and the place was surrounded by dozens of trucks and vans. True, there was a maturely attractive Eve inside who seemed to know every driver from every state in the Union, and there was an abundance of raucous good fellowship, but even my starved stomach was not deceived by the food; it might have been the leavings of what we had had the night before. After we had left the place, I learned the secret of the stop's popularity; the drivers could lay in a supply of particularly effective under-the-counter stay-awake tablets there. I, too, was a stay-awake potion for Joe. My world was as foreign and fascinating to him as his to me, and he plied me with endless questions, historical, artistic, and literary. Why were the pictures so valuable, especially that funny stuff by Picasso? Why did we have a king in England and not a president? Did people really like Shakespeare, or were they pretending to? How many really understood his old-fashioned language?

Joe was touchingly solicitous of his tractor. (That doesn't seem to be the right name for it, but it certainly describes its function.) The very size of the van involves hazards unknown to the driver of a car. The ordinary driver has to be aware of what is happening in four directions—front, back, right, left—but the truck driver has to add a fifth: up. Joe became careless for a few minutes in Washington, D.C. He was preoccupied by something he had discovered at the last stop. The usual rates of payment would not apply to this very special cargo, and he found as the result of a phone call that his special deal was inadequate. After a whole day and night of worrying, he finally called, at midnight from Chattanooga, Tennessee, a vice-president of the company, and demanded and got a better deal from the irate and awakened man. But in the first minutes of his worry he had become careless, and the roof of his cabin was ripped by a low-hanging tree. There were other enemies, too, of which he had to be wary. After we left El Paso, Texas, he was hell-bent for home, but even he had to submit to a strong wind in Arizona, and stop by the roadside, fuming with frustration: even though we were stopped, the wind, pushing against the large area of the van, threatened to topple it.

Then there were the planning and plotting to avoid having to buy the more expensive gasoline. State taxes on gasoline varied widely and every effort was made to fill up in the cheaper states, but this was not always easy. Some states insist on long-distance motor vehicles crossing their territory on gasoline bought in the state, and to ensure this, the vehicle is stopped at the border and its gasoline is measured with a dipstick. If the tank is full, a proportionate tax has to be paid. I was amused by Joe's stratagem to avoid this payment in one state in the Southwest. Truck drivers exchange helpful information at truck stops and by complicated hand signals as they pass each other, and Joe had discovered that an amenable old guard was on duty at this particular checkpoint. We pulled up in the early hours of a very cold morning with a full tank. Almost before we had stopped, Joe was out of the cabin and in the guard's shelter. I heard him hail the old man as if he had found a beloved and long-lost father. Then he shiveringly described the bitterness of the cold outside. Thereafter the conversation became a mumble unintelligible to me, but the ruse worked because the old man made the briefest of appearances just to bid Joe a safe journey.

I had a delightful three days in Los Angeles, where some friends had been warned of my strange approach and gave me a good time, the most welcome part of which was a comfortable bed. One night I took Joe and his wife to a nightclub; their enjoyment and gratitude were endearing. Tom had dropped off in Arizona to see his wife; he was to meet us three days later in a suburb of Los Angeles to resume the journey. With Tom out of the cabin, I became, for visual purposes only, the relief driver; had I been forced to function as such, it would have been the end of me, Joe, and the art collection.

We had rarely seen our companion van during the five-day journey, but we virtually traveled in convoy from Los Angeles to Portland. We started out on a Saturday morning and arrived at midnight the next day, and this despite the fact that Oregon provided the greatest hazards of the whole trip: deep snow, slushy and slippery roads, steep gradients and sharp bends, and sudden and swirling mists that blotted out vision. Here, at last, we were made very conscious of the value of our cargo, for we were under constant police surveillance. Our reception in Portland was warm and exciting. Tom Colt, the curator of the Portland Art Museum, and his wife, Priscilla, were most gracious to me, but Joe, Tom, and the driver of the companion van had thoroughly adopted me as a member of their fraternity and were most eager for me to stay with them at a truckers' hotel; I could not but agree, because I took it as a great compliment. After two days in Portland I decided to return to New York on the *City of Portland,* my first experience of a transcontinental train. On the day of my leaving I tried hard to contact Joe to say good-bye, but failed, and I have not seen him since. I heard subsequently that a week later he had had a serious accident in British Columbia. I did hear from Tom again, and in New York. It must have been about two years later. He phoned me from a hospital in Brooklyn. He, too, had had an accident, and he feared that his tractor was wrecked beyond repair.

Back in New York from Portland, one after another promising possibility arose but all of them came to nothing, and again I began to think of returning to London. I booked a passage on the *Mauretania* in July, only to cancel it the next day. In a final confrontation with my dilemma it became clear to me that I wanted to stay in America. I had made several satisfying and stimulating friendships and, although no big opportunity had come my way since the film company had dissolved, I seemed to be surrounded by exciting possibilities. Even the uncertainty was a heady wine. To be fifty-one and starting out all over again in a new country is in itself rejuvenating. Symbolically, I stopped going to the office which had so generously been put at my disposal; I wanted no charity. I managed to make a simple living from modest advances on a few projects that came to naught. In particular, I did a great deal of research and writing for the producer-partner of the dead film company on Simón Bolívar, who is a wonderful subject for more than one film. For over a year it seemed that a large-scale film would be made with the cooperation of some South American governments. I wrote synopses, film treatments, and conference memoranda, but all for nothing.

Then I was introduced to the head of a very exciting theatre workshop. He was a leading teacher of acting in New York, an exceptionally good one, and the workshop consisted, by invitation, of his best students over the years. They were eager to embark on classical work, and I was invited to give six lectures to the workshop on Tuesdays at 11:30 P.M., so that members working in the theatre could attend them. It seemed that once again circumstances were deciding that I was to be a teacher. I found the audience very stimulating and was delighted when it was suggested that I should become a permanent part of the workshop; it was felt that the head of the group and I were complementary in our approaches to theatre. A productive and delightful association resulted and some good work was done. But there is a limit to healthy work in a theatre-studio, and there must come a time when that work results in theatre productions to be seen by the public. Such was always the aim, and at last it was decided that I should direct a production of A Winter's Tale. Everybody was excited, the play was cast, and we went into rehearsals. But the actors could not afford the luxury of leisurely and unpaid rehearsals, however much they longed to do the work, and soon we began losing them, chiefly to television in Hollywood. Finally there was a rehearsal at which only one turned up, and he has since become a successful Hollywood director. The production died, signaling the lingering death of the workshop, by which the New York theatre was made the poorer.

My lectures on Shakespeare had been such a success that I arranged to give a series of twenty at Steinway Hall. They were aimed at the same kind of audience that I had had at the workshop and were entitled "The Actor's Shakespeare." Rarely have I enjoyed work more than that involved in the preparation of those lectures, but they have resulted, in the profession, in an association of my name with Shakespeare, which, although flattering, has been somewhat limiting. This association might have been professionally disastrous, for directors are typechosen as much as actors, if my first theatre production had been a play by Shakespeare, but, almost by accident, it wasn't.

One day in November 1956, I was called by Noel Behn, the

manager of the well-known Cherry Lane Theatre in Greenwich Village. He wanted to know if I would be interested in acting a leading role in a production of Sean O'Casey's *Purple Dust*, which he and three other men were about to produce. I told him I would be much more interested in directing it, and was sufficiently persuasive to get him to meet me. I convinced him that he would be a fool to think of anybody else as a director, and he in turn convinced his partners. The chance I had been waiting for had arrived, because, although I had been sidetracked in London into radio and in New York into films, my natural world was, is, and will be in the theatre.

Purple Dust, although not a major O'Casey work, is nonetheless a theatrical delight, if played with an exuberance of spirit, alternately comic and lyrical. I longed to get to work on it, but first there were literally hundreds of people to be auditioned, a painful and difficult task. During that ordeal one fact emerged that was astonishing to me; a high percentage of the actors and actresses we saw could not carry a tune, and yet they offered themselves for parts in which they knew they had to sing. In my vocabulary they were tone-deaf; the new euphemism is that they had a "pitch problem." This phenomenon, which I have encountered often since, even in people who present themselves for training in musical theatre, is particularly puzzling to me who was brought up in South Wales where singing was as natural as speech. What accounts for it? I can only surmise that in too many American homes childish efforts at singing are discouraged by laughter.

Auditions are always a cruel ordeal for actors, but in America they are at their worst. I have known of really well-known actors who have been called for auditions when it should have been obvious to anyone with a knowledge of their work whether they were suitable for the role. For the unknown, it is hell, for there are so many of them swarming after every part, no matter how small and dull. Only recently I was told of an experienced casting director who kept fifty actors waiting six hours in a room in which there was no chair, and then cursorily dismissed them one by one.

This was an instance of a particular abomination known as an "open call." Perhaps from too much sympathy for the actor's agony, I go to the other extreme; most actors leave my auditions buoyed up by the conviction that their chances of getting the part are excellent.

The rehearsals of *Purple Dust* were enjoyable, but we did not get to the first night without a series of crises, which resulted in our opening with a cast somewhat different from the one that was engaged. A crisis mentality seems to be a part of commercial play production in America. Fortunately, our script was already published and therefore couldn't be rewritten. Most new scripts in America undergo a metamorphosis between the first rehearsal and the first night on Broadway, and I have known instances where the changes have not resulted in a better play but have merely been dictated by the panic of a financial gamble, which tends to believe that any change will improve the luck.

Purple Dust was a success and ran for over a year. (Its success was such that one inquirer at the box office assumed from its title that it must be a Western.) It is a lamentable irony that that production of one of his minor works, playing in a small theatre with fewer than two hundred seats, brought Sean O'Casey more money than any single production of any other of his plays. During the run of *Purple Dust* I went to Britain for six weeks, sailing there and back on the *Parthia*. I dashed all over the place, visiting my roots in Wales, my friends and the theatre in London, Richard on the French Riviera, and Sean O'Casey in Torquay. I had been told to expect in O'Casey an irascible old curmudgeon, but instead I found a delightful, lively, warm, generous, good companion. I gave him as vivid an account as I could of the production, from inception to fruition, told him of the brilliant inventiveness of the designer, Lester Polakov, in creating the illusion of a vast baronial hall on a small stage, confessed somewhat fearfully that I had reshaped some lines to get surer laughs and received from him not only plenary indulgence but delighted gratitude. One shadow marred our weekend together. A short time before we met, his beloved son, Niall, had died quite suddenly in London. That in itself would have been a bitter tragedy for O'Casey, but it was made much more poignant by the fact that when the young man had last been home, he and his father had had their only quarrel and had parted without a reconciliation. The disagreement had been about the Hungarian revolt. O'Casey had held to the official communist position that the revolt had been fostered by outside capitalist influences, but Niall's communism had been very sharply shaken. I had decided carefully to avoid any mention of Niall, but O'Casey wanted to talk about him, not with morbid recrimination or bootless protest but with glowing love. I remembered O'Casey's tribute to the courage of his mother when he dedicated *The Plough and the Stars* "To the gay laugh of my mother at the gate of the grave." Sean shared his mother's courage.

When I returned from Europe, I took the first opportunity to visit *Purple Dust* and was appalled by what I saw. In my six-week absence, several members of the company had left and been replaced, but, even worse than that, the stage manager, who had been at my side throughout rehearsals, had also left, and the newcomers had had no sure and knowledgeable hand to guide them. This situation is one of the deplorable conditions of off-Broadway. The basic pay is so small that no one can be signed to a run-of-the-play contract, and any member of the company can leave with two weeks' notice. An actor who scores a big success is likely to receive some tempting offers, so the bigger the success of a play the less likely is the cast to remain intact. I took the largely new cast of *Purple Dust* in hand and virtually had to direct the play all over again.

Purple Dust brought me several offers to direct plays, but I was not sufficiently interested in any of the scripts. I did direct two plays that summer. The first was for the Theatre Guild. It was a cleverly condensed version of Bernard Shaw's *Back to Methuselah*, which is really five plays requiring five evenings in the theatre. The actor Arnold Moss had contrived to cut, trim, and squeeze it into one evening's entertainment, and I was sufficiently impressed by the resulting script to undertake its direction. It certainly was not normal summer theatre touring fare, but when it found its right audience, as it occasionally did, it proved to be an exciting evening in the theatre. The play, stretching within two and one-half hours from "The Garden of Eden" to "As Far as Thought Can Reach," provided the excellent leading players, Celeste Holm and James Daly, with a range of parts in which I think they surprised even themselves, for American actors rarely get a chance to break the mold into which they are poured early in their profession.

The other play I directed that summer was a charming little musical, originally called *The Small Servant*, but I persuaded the authors to change the title to *A Pound in Your Pocket*. It was fashioned from some characters and incidents in Dickens' *The Old Curiosity Shop*, and the music and lyrics were by Charles Strouse and Lee Adams who, a few years later, were to gain fame with a very different subject, *Bye Bye Birdie*. The producer of the show, Philip Barry, Jr., had Broadway hopes for it, and asked me to do a tryout at the beautiful little John Drew Theatre in East Hampton. Small though the cast was, I had to use some socialite amateurs, one of whom at one performance, having liberally acquired Dutch courage to speak her one line, missed a chair and sat on the floor with great aplomb. I subsequently did another production of the play at Palm Beach, Florida, with an almost totally different cast, but, although both productions were quite well received, neither engendered the necessary enthusiasm to be brought to New York, where I still feel it belongs, but in an off-Broadway theatre.

In the fall, it was decided to send out a national tour of *Back to Methuselah*, starring Tyrone Power, but for various private reasons I decided not to do it. Instead, I accepted an invitation to direct *Interlock*, which the author, Meyer Levin, described as "a psychological melodrama." We gathered a very exciting cast— Celeste Holm, Maximilian Schell, Rosemary Harris—the rehearsals were rewarding and hopes were high, but critical acceptance was lukewarm out of town, and finally in town, and the play closed after four performances. I have done much thinking since about that failure and have decided that the play would have stood a much better chance in either London or Paris. The values of the play were essentially theatrical, in the pejorative sense of that word. It afforded opportunities for thrilling performances, but that is not enough for American critics; for them content comes first. This is probably a sign of maturity of critical judgment, but I feel there should still be a place in the theatre where it can be wholeheartedly and unashamedly theatrical. I am grateful that my own early theatregoing often took me to such a place.

When a director's first play on Broadway fails, he is unlikely to be offered scripts with any measure of built-in success. His hopes will be tied in with those of producers and authors desperately trying to make it. In the next years I was induced by producers to work with authors, on rewriting plays, sometimes for months. Occasionally the projects got as far as announcements in the press and auditions of actors, and then, with one exception, the projects expired for lack of financial sustenance. In no case of an abandoned project was I paid a penny for my work. This was, and to some extent still is, a common experience of directors. A certain amount of preliminary unpaid consultation is necessary so that producer, author, and director may find out if their ideas are happily mated before any contracts are signed, but often a director will let them go on to the point of exploitation when he is looking for work and is offered a script with exciting potential. Directors and choreographers need mutual protection as much as actors or any other band of workers, and in 1959 the Society of Stage Directors and Choreographers was formed to provide such protection. It took the society over three years to secure a contract for a minimum basic agreement with the League of New York Theaters, which is an association of Broadway producers. I joined the society soon after its inception and have taken an active part in it ever since. For two years I was its executive vice-president. As Broadway shrinks and the American theatre expands, the society now seeks to extend its protection to directors and choreographers working in such fields as regional theatre and off-Broadway. For an artist, the work itself is even more necessary than its reward, which renders him very vulnerable to commercial exploitation.

I said there was one exception to the abortive plans for new plays with which I became involved. One came to fruition, and I wish it hadn't. It was the dramatization of a fascinating novel set in West Africa. It dealt with the rise to power and subsequent fall of a fictitious native leader, clearly suggested by Nkrumah. My enthusiasm for the subject and the novel made me forget, as a result of the continued persuasion of the producer, that my initial reaction to the script of the play had been one of disappointment. The young dramatist, too, was charming, and he tried to be as cooperative as his possessive pride in his work would allow him to be. He had a very good grasp of dramatic construction and a facility for pedestrian dialogue, but more was needed. Yet neither his work nor mine reached the bar of critical judgment; disaster overtook us. The producer failed to raise enough money for a Broadway production—it involved a large cast and elaborate staging—and decided to do the play first in London, where it could be put on for much less money; the idea was that success in London would guarantee a Broadway showing. I readily agreed to move operations to London; apart from anything else, I was interested in finding how I would adjust to life in the old place again. Our theatre was to be the Lyric in Hammersmith, with the prospect of transferring to a West End theatre after three weeks. But the Lyric itself was to me almost a hallowed place, for there I had enjoyed some of my most memorable theatrical experiences, and it was there that Richard had played two of his first starring roles in London, in *The Boy with a Cart* and *Montserrat*.

Rehearsals were exciting and hopes were high. Tony Walton designed the production and made his first brilliant use, aided by the lighting of Richard Pilbrow, of slide projections to suggest the many settings. For the crowds we had authentic East Africans, and I found them a joy to work with. I had to scold one for frequent lateness at rehearsal. I overdid it and immediately repented. After rehearsal I took him for a drink. He was a Moslem, but coffee, too, is a drink. I asked him the meaning of his long name. It was "The one that lived." He had been the only one of many children to survive. I repented still more for my sharp tongue.

All the leading parts in the play were African, but there were several smaller white parts, all played by excellent English actors. A foretaste of disaster occurred during the last weekend of rehearsals; a London actor playing an important part was stricken by a heart attack and taken to hospital. A replacement was found and fitted in during the feverish final rehearsals. Then came the opening night. The burden of the play fell upon Earl Cameron in the Nkrumah-like part, but there was a second and crucial character, a nationalist and idealist in exile, who returned to his country at the time of its liberation. This part was played by a leading Negro actor. Five minutes before the curtain was to rise, when it had been established that Kenneth Tynan and his fellow critics were seated and ready to pronounce judgment, I was nervously pacing at the back of the dress circle. An urgent whisperer came to tell me that I was needed in the dressing room of the second player. There I found that gentleman moaning that he couldn't go on. I still don't know what was wrong. There was some story that a doctor had given him too strong or too wrong a sedative to steady his first-night nerves. I also heard subsequently that he had been known to cause such a crisis before. Whatever the cause, the actor was certainly bemused, listless, and perhaps in pain. While I tried to stir him into activity with the old show-must-go-on adrenalin, the curtain was held for fifteen minutes, which was not calculated to ingratiate us with the critics.

The play opened with an intriguing prologue, during which all our sick actor had to do was stand briefly with his handsome face in a spotlight; this he managed to do. The next scene, really the first of the play, was a farewell party to him in London. It was the scene that had worried me most in the play because it was so expository; its only hope was a lively attack and brisk pacing, but as the life and soul of the party fumbled his way through, the scene sagged like yeastless dough. The next scene was on a street in East Africa. To make this vivid and colorful I had worked hard and successfully to get the Africans to re-create their own experiences, and as I stood nervously in the wings, I hoped that the play might yet be revived from the near deathblow it had already received. But the Africans had become infected by the atmosphere of crisis backstage and they played with a muted nervousness. All was lost, but grow old along with me; the worst is yet to be. The second act of the play opened with the triumphant return of the exiled leader to his liberated country. He entered, staggered, and collapsed. The curtain was rung down, leaving him half outside. He was dragged in by the legs from the public gaze and I had to go out in front of the curtain and tell the audience that the performance had to be abandoned; I have an idea that mine was the best-received speech of the night.

Even in those comparatively lean years after my initial Broadway failure I was given a number of very satisfying engagements. In particular, I remember pleasurably a Shaw Festival in Greenwich Village and productions of *King Lear, Twelfth Night,* and *Macbeth* in the Library of Congress. However good the Shaw Festival might have been, it could not have succeeded because it took place in the summer in a theatre that was not air-conditioned. The person responsible for this folly was an actor who put his own money that he could ill afford into an idealistic enterprise. We got good notices but poor audiences. Nevertheless, week-by-week the producer poured more and more money into the doomed adventure until there was none left. I hope he derived some satisfaction from his admirably quixotic and dedicated sacrifice. We did the American premiere of Shaw's last play for live actors, *Buoyant Billions;* he did follow it with a playlet for puppets. We also did *Getting Married, Over-Ruled* and *The Shewing Up of Blanco Posnet.* We rehearsed for six weeks in a loft on the lower

153

East Side, and I remember that our comings and goings made one policeman very suspicious. Finally he confronted me, and it gradually emerged that he suspected we were making pornographic movies. When I told him we were rehearsing a play called *Getting Married*, the title did not entirely allay his suspicions, so I invited him to sit in on a rehearsal; he came but did not stay long.

I think the most difficult play I have ever directed is Sean O'Casey's own favorite play, *Cock-A-Doodle Dandy*. The management was virtually the same as that which had produced the very successful *Purple Dust*. Again I had the stimulating cooperation of Lester Polakov as designer, but we did not repeat our first success. I believe now that this was due partly to miscasting but also to the fact that, although our production occurred ten years after the play was written, it was still before its time. It was a comparatively expensive production for off-Broadway, and it needed almost capacity attendance to sustain it. It limped along for a few weeks with rather more than half-houses, but this was not enough. We opened in Toronto, Canada. (One opening-night telegram I received read: "How far off-Broadway can you get?") We had been chosen to open a new theatre, and quite a large one. This in itself was asking for trouble, because the play has such a special appeal that I doubt if it could have a run in a large theatre anywhere in the world, much less in a new and unknown theatre in a somewhat depressed and depressing district of Toronto. To complicate the situation, the Roman Catholic authorities in the city forbade the faithful to see the play, and some of the more exuberantly faithful paraded posters of the ban outside the theatre.

Nearly three years after my first brush with Broadway, I had my second, but this time it was only tangential. Richard was appearing in a musical, *Camelot*. It not only opened in the vast O'Keefe Center in Toronto, but also opened it. It is rare, indeed, for a Broadway musical to open out of town, no matter how far away, without sadistic whisperers in Manhattan reporting with a gloating shake of the head that it's in trouble, but *Camelot* was in real trouble. And at that moment the director, Moss Hart, was taken ill and soon after died. In the three weeks before the Broadway opening I was called in to help, chiefly in Boston.

The task of making radical changes in a play while it is still giving eight performances a week is forbidding, but in the case of a musical it is nightmarish. The pressure upon the authors and composers would not seem to be conducive to good work, and yet Alan Jay Lerner and Fritz Loewe in a matter of days wrote several new numbers, two of them my favorites in the show. The company has the particular difficulty of playing the old show by night while rehearsing the new material by day until such time that the changes are safe enough to be incorporated in public performance. The changes in the text of *Camelot* were so drastic that Oliver Smith had quickly to design a new set and it had to be built and painted by round-the-clock work. Several completely new costumes also had to be designed and made. Rather to my own amazement I discovered the hectic activity to be exhilarating. By day I rehearsed the company for five hours (less on matinee days); then watched the public performance (twice on matinee days), hurrying backstage as soon as the curtain was down to "give notes"; then I returned to the hotel to work with Alan Jay Lerner on the fruits of his day's writing labors. The indefatigable industry of Lerner and Loewe, the willing and amiable cooperation of the large company led by Richard and the adorable Julie Andrews, the eager readiness of the choreographer, Hanya Holm, to try new ideas, achieved a near miracle, although I still think that further work for a week or two might have made what was a very good show into an even better one.

All this time I was getting older but feeling younger. During those few weeks of never-ending work on *Camelot*, tired people remarked how tireless I was. Sometimes I even have a comic sense of guilt that the man I am does not accord with the man I look. My attitude to death is immature and unrealistic; it's something that happens to other people. But when I was fifty-seven I faced my own death for twenty-four hours, and I think I grew up a little. The possibility of sudden death has increased in this twentieth century, but it has not stopped me from riding in a car, flying in a plane, walking in a street, or sleeping through an air raid. But when the enemy strikes from within, one cannot evade the personal implication. My doctor is a comparatively young man in whom I trust completely. A painless canker appeared on my tongue. After a few days I was persuaded to go and see him about it. After being assured by me that, to the best of my knowledge, it could not have been caused by venereal disease, he arranged for me to see a well-known specialist. That gentleman took one look at it and at a swollen gland in my throat, and disappeared from the room. In a minute or so he returned with two other white-coated gentlemen, one of whom held a camera. With clinical detachment they proceeded to take pictures of my tongue, and, in low asides, to make excited comments on the perfection of the case. The doctor just had to show these pictures at an approaching medical convention; my tongue at least was about to acquire enduring fame. The doctors went out of the room, leaving me in a cold sweat of fear. After a few minutes the specialist returned with a nurse bearing instruments. He told me that he had arranged for cobalt treatment to begin next day, but he was virtually certain that part of my tongue and the lump in my throat would have to be cut out in two weeks' time; immediately he needed a part of the canker for a biopsy. I stammered, "Cancer?" He tried, but failed, to lull my fear by being vague and evasive. In reply to my question, he said that I should alert those I felt should know. Among others I told Richard, sending a night-letter telegram to Rome, where he was filming *Cleopatra*. But Richard's lawyer, Aaron Frosch, who also looks after me in ways far beyond the requirements of his profession, phoned him in Rome. Between them they decided to oppose the operation, on the grounds that without my tongue I was better dead; a dubious compliment at best. But I would have insisted on the operation; my love of life is so great that I think I should adjust to living under any handicaps. Within an hour of leaving the doctor, I had lost my voice; I have always been extraordinarily subject to psychosomatic influences. At the time I was rehearsing one production, *The Three Sisters* at Brooklyn College, preparing another, *Macbeth* for the Library of Congress, and auditioning artists for a revue I had compiled, *Picnic on Parnassus*. I had to suspend all activities, and so the news spread. The abundant sympathy I received only convinced me that I was soon to die. At last I had to face the urgent possibility, and I surprised myself by doing so to such good effect that I even slept peacefully that night.

The next morning Al Baruth came to go with me to the hospital for my first cobalt treatment. It was a beautiful spring day and we decided to walk across Central Park. As we were about to set out, the phone rang incessantly. My voicelessness and the burden of too much sympathy had induced me not to pick up the phone but to leave my answering service to deal with it. But the ringing persisted until in exasperation I asked Al to answer it. He did so and found that it was the answering service itself that was trying to speak to me. The doctor wanted me to see him instead of going to the hospital. When I saw the doctor he greeted me with "I'll never trust my eyes again." Apparently the biopsy had revealed that the canker was completely harmless. We still don't know what it was, but penicillin got rid of it within a week. The news of my reprieve spread rapidly and my voice returned miraculously, enabling me to enjoy a deluge of congratulations and one frighteningly cynical comment: "Aren't you lucky that the doctor didn't bury his mistake?"

acting, singing, and dancing. Other professional schools concentrated on acting, and students had to go elsewhere for the right kind of training in singing and dancing. He decided to start a musical theatre academy for the full-time training of actors, with special emphasis on the musical theatre, and persuaded some people that it could be a moneymaking venture. This was a near-fatal mistake, as the investors soon found out; to cut their losses, they never completed their promised investment, which caused crisis after crisis in the first two years of the school. It seems to me that no educational institution that does not compromise the quality of its training to make a financial profit can be self-supporting, much less profit-making. And Noel Behn did not compromise; he believed in his idea and that came first. He engaged three acknowledged leaders of the profession to head actively the three departments. I helped him to persuade his head of the acting department to return from a Hollywood studio, where, I suppose, he was the highest-paid teacher in the world. Then, too, he found and rented a remarkable old building at the junction of 23rd Street and 2nd Avenue. When I first saw it, I was reminded by its austere simplicity of a Welsh Noncomformist Chapel. It had been built in 1851 to house the Demilt Dispensary, a charitable organization which for seventy years had served the indigent sick. Behn induced a well-known theatrical designer to plan the adaptation of the building for the purposes of the school, and also agreed to pay a rent of $20,000 a year, which has since risen to $24,000. But soon the old building, old enough for fanciful people to have seen and heard ghosts in it, will be no more. It has been sold for demolition, to make way for some new institutional building.

In the fall of 1961, I was one of the many people Noel Behn talked to about his idea for the new school. I discussed the curriculum and staff with him, but made it clear, with an adamantine resolution, that I would not become personally involved with the school. It set out with promise but soon ran into rough seas. Behn and the three department heads came to see me and tried to persuade me to take the helm; despite the troubles, financial and organizational, it was already abundantly clear that the venture was worth saving. With great reluctance I agreed to accept the position of director for three months only, to help steer them into calmer waters. That was over six years ago, and I'm still there, though it is now a nonprofit institution with a new name, AMDA (American Musical and Dramatic Academy), and Behn and the three department heads have left. The school is now sailing smoothly on an even keel, and I expect that I too will soon be able to leave without disrupting the ship. But we have been through heavy storms together. I shall leave the AMDA ship with no sense of guilt because she has an excellent first officer in Joyce Worsley, a British-born American like me, whose wide experience both on- and offstage has brought her a richness of personality and humanity that in turn enriches the lives of the students.

During its first two years, while Noel Behn was still trying to run the school as a commercial venture, it ran deeper and deeper into financial trouble. That he managed to keep it going at all is a tribute to his financial wizardry and resilience of spirit. But the end was inevitable. In March 1964, he came to me and said that there was no more money in the bank account and no more to be got. What made the situation worse was that there was more than half a semester still to go, for which the students had already paid their fees. The dilemma was mine, because by this time the public thought of the school as mine. I was trapped. I had never wanted to be part of the school, and now I was presented with overwhelming reasons for closing it—indeed, I did not see how that could be avoided—and yet, although I was in no way responsible for the finances of the school, I could not face the experience of public failure. Then, too, I believed in the work of the school and loathed the prospect of putting teachers out of work. Not only did we have a staff of which I was proud, but they had been unbelievably loyal in difficult days; sometimes they had had to wait weeks for their pay to be made up. After sleepless nights I came to a decision, which brought no sleep. I told Noel Behn that the present operation should cease, a fact that should be made clear by his and his financial associates' never entering the building, and I would start a new school with a new name, without any break of continuity. I would establish a board of directors whose first task would be to apply for nonprofit status. The new venture was to start on April 1; All Fools' Day seemed the appropriate occasion for it. Noel Behn readily agreed to my plan and conditions, and left the school to embark upon a writing career; his first novel, *The Kremlin Letter*, immediately found its way into the best-seller list.

Aaron Frosch, my lawyer and friend, who looks after me with devotion and brilliance, was appealed to and readily came to the rescue, even though he would have preferred to see me freed from the school. Much faster than was believed possible, he secured our charitable status, and arranged that Richard's funds should be made available to meet the immediate financial crisis. To see the school through to the end of the term cost Richard $27,000. But I needed more money, much more, to get through the summer and start afresh in September, and I was determined that the school should not become an old man of the sea on Richard's back; the burden was mine, and I'm glad to say that it is now very much lighter.

Yet, although I was reluctant to accept more money from Richard, I was eager for his help. He was appearing in *Hamlet* on Broadway at the time, and I asked him if he would give a poetry reading for the benefit of AMDA. He agreed and suggested that I should ask his wife, Elizabeth Taylor, to appear with him. I did so, expecting the answer, 'Are you kidding?' But not a bit of it; she seemed eager to have a go. I was beyond measure delighted, and I marveled at her courage. She had never appeared in a public performance before. She is highly intelligent, deeply sensitive, and abrasively honest. She knew that many in the audience would come for the ghoulish joy of watching a high-wire artist working without a safety net. Beatrice Lillie summed up this element of the memorable evening by whispering to her neighbor during the performance: "If she doesn't get worse soon, they'll be leaving." The evening, indeed, was a triumph for her. Everybody expected that

Richard would be good—great poetry is his native element—but Elizabeth's radiant ease and mastery surprised even me, who had worked with her. But she is a lady of continual surprises. During our first work session together on the program, I had asked her if she had any particular poem she would like to do. Without hesitation she mentioned the poem that I would rate as about the most difficult in the English language to read aloud: Gerard Manley Hopkins' "The Leaden Echo and the Golden Echo." I was dumbfounded and embarrassed. What right had I to say "No" when it was all being done for the benefit of my school? From Richard she had learned to love the poem and was determined to attempt it. I stammered my hesitance and managed to postpone the decision for a few weeks, at the end of which time her reading completely persuaded me, as it was to persuade the packed and critical audience, which included many famous theatrical artists. The poem is a religious meditation on the evanescence of physical beauty, and when Beauty herself spoke the lines they were given a peculiarly poignant significance.

Richard had chosen a title for the evening, *World Enough and Time*, from Andrew Marvell's delightful poem "To His Coy Mistress." It was a great evening. Some even said that it was worth the hundred dollars many of them had had to pay. I introduced the poems and thus Richard and I shared a stage for only the second time in our lives. (The first had been for the Dylan Thomas Memorial in the Globe Theatre in London. Dylan Thomas was to bring us onstage together for yet a third time.) Not only was the evening a gloriously happy and exciting occasion, but it also succeeded handsomely in helping AMDA, which was enabled to start its new life in September 1964 without undue stress, although it seems to me that it will always need a certain amount of outside help.

Such help has to be elicited from the public, and pleas for it must compete with many others for worthy causes. "Benefit," which means some event held to raise money, has become a gruesome word to well-to-do New Yorkers. Week after week, during the season, and sometimes night after night, they are cajoled or dragged out, at inflated prices, to see films they don't want to see and plays they have no interest in, to honor people of whom they were previously unaware, to shuffle and jostle inch-by-inch with other victims on an overcrowded dance floor, to eat and drink at very late hours more than they want or ought, and all for some charity the very name of which many of them could not tell you. And yet without the benefit, many essential and deserving causes would languish, and to bring it about requires the enduring devotion and unremitting labor of dedicated people, chiefly women. It is true that they often have the help of a professional fund-raising organization, but even so their time and energies are consumed for months before the climactic night. For AMDA's first benefit, *World Enough and Time*, the volunteers did all the work alone. Indeed it was largely done by one lady, Liska March, as stage-struck as I am, with a knowledge of theatre, a critical judgment, and a business acumen which should have made her a name and fortune in the theatre, if she had not used her talents to help such theatrical institutions as the Actors' Studio and AMDA. Since that first "benefit," she has helped me to recruit a small nucleus of ladies who, year by year, have worked indefatigably to keep the doors of AMDA open. Two of them, Mrs. Mark Millard and Miss Dina Merrill, also give an annual scholarship to the school. Is it worth all the effort? Can people be taught to act? Isn't it a natural ability best learned by observation and practice in the theatre?

The whole question of the training of actors is a thorny one, and a particular source of controversy in the United States. One approach is that virtually anyone can be taught to act; mine is that acting is a special gift. All can speak, but there are few orators. I suppose most people can be taught to play the piano, but there are few pianists. All children, in playing school or shop or weddings or war, imitate the actions of adults in an imagined situation, and their skill varies with their powers of observation and imagination. This, indeed, shows that the crude basis for the actor's skill is universal, but it is interesting to note that most children become inhibited in their imagined re-creations of adult activities if they are watched by their elders. For me, this question of an audience is crucial. The test of any theatrical performance is not what an actor feels but what he causes his audience to feel. Complete absorption in a role is not enough; if it were, the best actors would be found in mental hospitals. Of course, unless an actor is able to present a truly imagined and felt character, he is unlikely to hold an audience, but there must always be a part of him instinctively sensitive to his effect on the audience and ready to spring into action when he feels he has lost or is losing them. Such action will be an instantaneous examination of his performance, and he may find that his concentration had slackened with a resulting loss of intensity, or it may be that he was so caught up by the reality of an intimate scene that he was just not talking loud enough.

Perhaps at this stage I should attempt a definition of an actor. He is one who finds his fullest self-realization by imaginatively assuming the being and actions of fictitious characters for the entertainment of audiences gathered in a theatre. Again I stress the theatre. There is a kind of theatrical training in this country that emphasizes the emotional release in acting to such an extent that audiences become almost an intrusion upon a private rite. To me, this self-indulgence is unhealthy.

This brings me inevitably to some discussion of the "Method," the hallowed word used to describe an approach to acting derived, often in distorted and unbalanced ways, from the work of Constantin Stanislavski, who made a stimulating examination of the processes involved in acting and built upon it a technique calculated to ensure an inner truth in a performance. But no one knew better than Stanislavski, or insisted more, that that inner truth has to be expressed through physical means, which must be at the instinctive service of the actor. A superbly controlled voice and body without an inner truth will result in a hollow performance that will never hold an audience, but an inadequate voice and an undisciplined body can irritate, embarrass, and even infuriate an audience. The correct training must amalgamate both processes.

There is a tendency in this country to ignore the physical, which requires hard and sustained effort, much of it boringly repetitive. Working on the inner technique is infinitely more pleasurable for most actors. An actor on the stage is seen and heard as well as felt. At any given moment his effect is total; every movement, every gesture, every sound he makes must be a full expression of what he is thinking and feeling. Too often I have seen truly felt performances in which the speech, the gestures, the movements were contradictions of the character being portrayed. It is wrong to suppose, as many actors do, that a true inner feeling will inevitably express itself in a true outward form. This will only happen when the voice, the speech, and the body have acquired by rigorous training and discipline a flexibility instinctively at the command of the inner truth, and no physical technique is of any use to an actor until it is so much an organic part of him that he is not really conscious of its employment. An actor who listens to his own voice and speech is lost. An actor in a musical play who is aware of his tones as he sings will never give us the illusion of truth in his character.

Some young actors, relying wholly on the emotional truth of their performance, have even acquired almost a contempt for a writer's words, thus ruling themselves out from all great drama. I have little patience with an actor, or a director for that matter, who uses a great play in a self-indulgent way. I believe his primary duty to be to interpret the author to the best of his ability.

When I first became the director of Noel Behn's school, the curriculum was established, and at first I was happily content to make that curriculum work without introducing any changes or extensions. The basic 64-week course contained instruction in acting, speech, individual singing, sight singing, musical theatre styles, Dalcroze eurythmics, and modern dance. For the information of those, who, like myself initially, have no idea what Dalcroze eurythmics are—or should it be "is"?—they (or it) are (or is) a method devised by a Swiss, Emile Jaques-Dalcroze, for the precise expression of musical rhythms in physical movement.

166

When the school became AMDA, I added some courses in the second year that I taught myself, because I was determined to give the students more practical acquaintance with what might be called literary plays, by which I mean plays in which the language is obviously the work of a creative writer and not merely that of a man with a keen ear and a good memory; in the latter kind of play, actors can improvise their way into the dialogue; they cannot do so with Shakespeare, or even with Shaw. I taught three courses, and still do. One is a lecture course in dramatic literature, in which I attempt to give students some appreciation, as actors, of great writers, from Shakespeare to Samuel Beckett. More and more the new regional theatres arising throughout the country are calling for actors who are at home in great plays, and while basic training in acting should always concentrate on the fundamentals of true human behavior at first expressed in their own language, the actor in training must be led on to express the same truth in language that transcends his own. I deplore the training of actors that stops at naturalistic work and never makes the leap to poetry, but I equally deplore training that starts with the Greek classics, and I have heard of such training both here and in Europe. The actor must be guided to climb the Everest of great writing gradually from the world he knows, not landed on its summit from a helicopter, and without an oxygen mask. For this purpose, he must first learn to love great words. To this end I give a course in rhetoric, by which I mean the art of persuasive speech, and a course in verse speaking.

I begin by proving to the students that spoken words alone will not convey meanings. Their first exercise is to read any editorial of their own choosing, an editorial rather than a news item because it has a point of view. I then question the class as to what they have gathered from the reading. Invariably it happens that some have gathered very little, some are unable to state the item of news that prompted the editorial, and some, when pressed for the point of view of the editorial, will express one the exact opposite of that of the writer. Then I turn my attention to the reader, now bereft of the editorial copy. I question him in detail to convey in his own words the substance of what he has read to the class. Very often it is disclosed that he had only a general idea of what the passage was about—he is not always right, even in that—and he left the details to the author's words, leaving them hopefully to do their own work without any real effort on his part. They learn from this basic exercise that only the reader's conscious thoughts, using the words of the writer, will convey thoughts. In a difficult disquisitionary play, where the dramatic excitement is in the thought, if the actor's concentration on the thought is dulled by constant repetition eight times a week his words alone will never stimulate an audience. In any case, to make an audience think is infinitely more difficult than to make them feel, which is why it is in some ways more difficult to play Shaw than Shakespeare.

After the editorial exercise, the students read passages of their own choosing, first involving physical descriptions and then the presentation of ideas. The first stretches their sensual imagination and the second their intelligence. I insist on their finding their own material, because it may, and often does, result in a joyous discovery for them, and also it means that something has pleased or excited them in the passage they have chosen. Thus they progress to the final exercise, prior to the application of what they are learning to dramatic parts, and that final exercise is the reading of a short story, a really short one, in which the emphasis is on atmosphere and character rather than on incident. I suggest Tchekov, Katherine Mansfield, D. H. Lawrence, and James Joyce as the kind of writer most suitable, but the choice is not at all restricted to these. The course ends with work on plays by Bernard Shaw and eighteenth-century and Restoration plays.

In rhetoric, the students soon learn that not even concentrated thought is enough to hold an audience; the listeners must be stimulated into continued attention. As in all acting, in which an inner truth must be fully expressed in an outward form, thoughts are expressed in sounds, which must be used in their richest variety to secure and hold attention, but again this flexibility of utterance must, by practice, become such an organic part of the actor's equipment that he uses it instinctively; studied effects will sound false. Art, like life, derives its interest from contrast. The chiaroscuro of life alone makes it bearable. Imagine a symphony with three slow movements. Similarly, the actor delivering a long Shavian speech must, like the effective orator or lecturer, have at his command all the resources of contrast in pitch, tempo, volume, and emphasis. But they must never be arbitrarily employed. The thoughts themselves must determine the shape of their utterance, but the urgent desire to communicate will inevitably seize upon the riches of variety, provided the speaker has those riches at his command.

Much of this discussion also applies to the speaking of verse, but there is more, much more. To begin with, actors trained in a naturalistic style of acting often find a deep confusion when trying to speak Shakespeare's lines. They seem to be saying, "How can I be true when the language I am speaking is unnatural?" First it has to be made quite clear that nobody, not even Shakespeare, spoke beautiful poetry, as his characters do for much of the time, and there must never be an attempt, by such overworn devices as false hesitancies, to make us believe that the real Richard II ever said:

> Let's talk of graves, of worms, and epitaphs;
> Make dust our paper and with rainy eyes
> Write sorrow on the bosom of the earth.

The point is that Richard felt like that, in the first realization of his own mortality and the possibility of his own imminent death, and the actor must feel it too. The inner truth is always the criterion of acting, but in Shakespeare it must be expressed by the consummate use of all that distinguishes poetry from prose. The actor needs the poetry adequately to reveal the height of exaltation and the depth of despair as they are experienced by the greatest characters of Shakespeare, but the actor must feel that the poetry is as necessary and natural for him as it was for Shake-speare. Not that all actors, even very good ones, will be at home in Shakespeare. There will be some who are always embarrassed by the lyricism of Romeo, and they should no more attempt it than a tone-deaf actor should try musical theatre. But I believe that there is a capacity for the natural speaking of poetry in most actors, although it may be dormant and require awaking from a long slumber; I must confess that in a few cases I have found it atro-phied beyond redemption, even though, when babies, the actors had probably reacted with gurgles and squiggles of joy when they heard a nursery rhyme before they could understand the words, thus reacting to sound and rhythm, two of the primitive and sen-suous qualities of verse.

Just as my course in rhetoric at AMDA is aimed at making the students at ease in prose masterpieces, the course in verse speak-ing is aimed at making them at home in Shakespeare. I begin with discussing the nature of poetry. There is no satisfactory definition. How can there be to magic? But I like the apparently silly one: "Poetry is what a poet writes." Given the poet, with his kind of vision and his skill with words, what he writes will be poetry, whatever its form; a bogus poet is a mere versifier. What is to me the finest poetry begins where prose leaves off. Prose is at its best when it is dealing clearly and interestingly with the rational; poetry is at its best when it is dealing with those experiences that transcend the rational, such as love and religion. When a poet deals with the inexplicable, he must reveal his experience by analogies; thus simile and metaphor are the heart of poetry, not decorations. This kind of preliminary discussion is essential for the majority of modern would-be actors who have no living acquaintance with poetry, and who often have a deep-seated feel-ing that poetry is a long-winded and deliberately obscure way of saying something that could be said much more clearly in prose. They must be led to react to the evocative excitement in imagery and to recognize in great poetry a universal expression of their own deepest experiences. They must feel that poetry is really the primitive language and prose the sophisticated; Homer is centuries older than Plato.

Their first exercise in verse speaking is to bring in a short lyric of their own choice. They must have pondered the experience that prompted the poem and then attempt to transmit that to the class by reading. There are differing approaches to the speaking of poetry. Most poets when they read poetry, unless they are actors by instinct like Dylan Thomas, will concentrate upon the form of the poem rather than its content, which is of little help in the training of an actor. He must master all the sensuous and imaginative devices of poetry—rhythm, sound, association—for the purpose of more powerfully conveying the truth of the experience. He must not act the poem, in the sense of imagining a character in some dramatic situation; that to me is vandalism, like using Mozart as background music in a B-film. Dramatic poetry is to be acted, lyric poetry to be spoken.

I ask that the first poem brought in should be one written approximately during the student's lifetime, so that the language will not in itself sound archaic to him. Then we start a journey—unfortunately it has always to be too rapid—back through the centuries, until we arrive at Shakespeare. Once there, we do not start with Hamlet or Lady Macbeth, but with the Chorus from *Henry V*, and all they have learned from their speaking of lyrical poetry becomes immediately relevant. There is no character to be created; it is the poet speaking directly to his audience.

That direct speech to an audience in itself constitutes a difficulty for many narrowly trained modern actors. I once knew an excellent and well-known actor, a member of my class for established professionals, completely fail at speaking a Chorus speech from *Henry V*, even after repeated attempts. In his training and his professional life he had used only one focus, that on other characters in a scene. He had learned and practiced that "action is reaction," that truth in acting comes from reacting truly to an impulse given by another actor, and that the actor must be, as far as possible, unaware of his audience. Now he was called upon to address them directly, and he found it to be a paralyzing experience. Then, too, there is the problem of the soliloquy, when the character is speaking aloud his unspoken thoughts. This question of focus is an important and neglected one. Sometimes an actor has to change focus instantaneously, as when he makes a quick aside to an audience. The most difficult focus of all occurs in musical theatre, in a love duet for instance, when the intimacy of the scene demands that the actors concentrate on each other to the exclusion of all else and yet the number has to be "sold" to the audience. The conventions of the old operetta are no longer acceptable, and are now a stock joke when guying the "good old days." Then, the lovers had no dilemma at all; when they sang they did so full-face to the audience, and only turned to their partner when silent.

The kind of speech taught at AMDA is what is known as "Standard Stage," which is equally acceptable on Broadway and in the West End, and, incidentally, offstage wherever English is spoken. Since speech is the medium of communication, my minimum requirement is that I should understand what is being said. This requires clearly distinguishable vowels and clearly articulated consonants. Cockney and Bronx accents are equally lacking in clarity. In the former case, when a man is talking about a "bad past," only the context could stop his listener from thinking about a "bed pest," and in the case of the Bronx, a "hot rock" becomes to my ears a "hat rack." And it is not only lower-class speech that indulges in this confusion. Nothing is worse than the slanderously named "Oxford accent," in which the words "fire," "fur," and "far" become lumped into an amorphous "fah."

Experience at AMDA has shown us that it takes the full sixty-four weeks for a student with a pronounced local accent to make standard speech part of his organic equipment, and if he has a "bad ear," or some subconscious fear that in losing his local speech he may be losing part of himself, or a disinclination for hard work, he will never lose it, thus crippling himself in his chosen profession. Of course, actors should so train their ears that they can assume several accents, acquiring them as linguists acquire languages. In this regard I find English actors generally much more versatile than American actors, who for the most part seem uninterested in the richness of variety of American speech.

I sympathize with the young actor who is reluctant permanently to change his speech pattern for fear that he is changing something fundamental in himself. There was the case of an AMDA girl student from the Midwest who lost her young man back home when he heard her new speech; he accused her of becoming "phony." But most students welcome the acquisition of "good speech," not only as a professional necessity but as a desirable part of growing up.

My own speech is not quite "standard." I am still recognizably from Great Britain. I made a conscious effort at an early age to escape from the restrictions of my Welsh accent, but to a prac-ticed ear the place of my birth is still apparent, and when I am emotionally worked up, which happens not infrequently, even an unpracticed hearer has been known to ask "Are you Irish?" which is usually the nearest he, or Hollywood, can get to Welsh.

I object to giving so much of my life to teaching, not because I don't enjoy it, but, perversely, because I enjoy it too much. It gives so much rein to the performer in me that I find it demand-ing and exhausting, and it drains me of the energy I should like to use in other activities. Any pedagogical desires I might possess find ample vent when I direct the kind of plays I am usually offered. I once inadvertently talked myself out of such a play; I was so eloquent about the star part that the actress who was to play it decided that it was beyond her; she withdrew and the venture died. But there are some satisfying rewards to presiding over AMDA and teaching there. The greatest is that rare moment when you see the sudden flowering of a superior talent. I don't know what percentage of the graduates from the school will make a satisfactory living from acting, but I firmly believe that the great majority of them will be the richer from having studied there, that they will have been made aware of the more abundant life of the spirit, the intelligence, the imagination.

It is not only in the classroom that I meet the students. I am their paterfamilias, and as such their court of appeal in time of trouble. I am not too readily available, but am accessible through channels. The interviews in my office run the gamut from tragic to farcical. It is much too glibly said that anybody who wants to be an actor must be sick—I think I could make out an even more convincing case for a would-be policeman; but it is undoubtedly true that the acting profession has its fair proportion of people with neurotic tendencies, an inevitable concomitant of a vivid imagination, which is the stock-in-trade of an actor. There was the case of the young man who, in improvisational exercises, took out his hostilities alarmingly, both on his partners and the building, until at last I had to send for his father, who was a psychoanalyst. He turned out to be a delightful man, who very soon made himself comfortable on my couch. He told me that, when his son had been very young, somebody had asked him what he wanted to be when he grew up. His answer was, "A patient." He had certainly fulfilled his wish.

But there was tragedy too. Twice I had to try to help young men who had attempted to commit suicide by taking what they had hoped was a fatal dose of sleeping pills. When they were made to realize that the sources of their despair were by no means unique, I think it helped. One of them was plagued by the guilty feeling that his being a difficult and rebellious son had caused the too-early death of his father; the other was desperate from loneliness and rejection in love. If it is true that there is a murderer in all of us, there is also a suicide.

For one brief period I was worried by the introduction of drugs into the school. I called all the students together and told them of the problem. I told them that AMDA had no guaranteed existence, as does an established college—at that time we were fighting for our financial survival—and that the surest way to close it

Errata

Early Doors by Philip Burton

The captions identifying Maximilian Schell
and Robert Drivas should be transposed.
(See third picture section between pages 174 and 175.)

John Gielgud in *The Importance of Being Earnest.*
(Theater Collection, New York Public Library, Astor, Lenox, Tilden Foundation)

John Gielgud and Carol Goodner in *Musical Chairs.*
(Theater Collection, New York Public Library, Astor, Lenox, Tilden Foundation)

Richard Burton's London *Hamlet,* 1953.

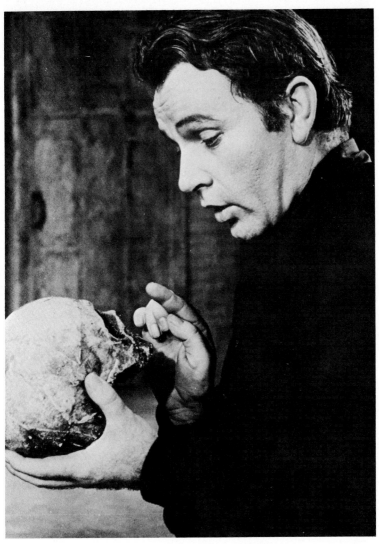

Richard Burton's New York *Hamlet*, 1964. *(The Bettmann Archive, Inc.)*

The Hamlet of Maximilian Schell.

The Hamlet of Robert Drivas. *(Charles Freedman)*

Philip Burton with Martha Greenhouse, a member of the company in Clinton.
(James A. Sasmor)

Philip Burton, Joyce Worsley, Sammy Davis, Michael Myerberg and Dina Merrill at an AMDA function. *(Alan Grossman)*

The lecturer in action in Modesto, California. *(Charles Rogers)*

quickly was to let the news spread, as it inevitably would, that students at the school used drugs on the premises. We had no further trouble. Over a year later a graduate asked to see me. He was a young man with some talent and I expected that he needed some advice on his career, but he surprised me by saying that he finally had come to confess that it had been he who had introduced the drugs into the school.

Poverty is a constant source of trouble for many of the students. I once was very irate with a student for missing a rehearsal. She was colored and lived in Harlem. My embarrassment and shame were profound when I discovered that she did not even have her subway fare. Most of the students have to work at some uncongenial job in the evenings and weekends in order to help to support themselves. Some of them even try to earn enough to support themselves and pay their fees, which I consider to be almost impossible. One student tried it, by working all night at the docks and coming to school by day. His talent was much above average too, but his school work inevitably suffered, and he had no option but to leave. Even parents who could easily support their children often do so only partially and reluctantly. Sometimes the son or daughter has gone to college under parental pressure, has stayed a year or two with deteriorating grades and has then left, against parental opposition, to embark upon the career he or she had always wanted; in such a case, the begrudged and only partial support of the parents is readily understandable.

Although AMDA absorbs most of my time and energy, a deal of it in finding the money for its continuance, I continue to live an active professional life outside, and I encourage other faculty members to do so too, for I consider it essential that teachers of an art or skill should continue to be practitioners, whenever a desirable opportunity occurs. Soon after I had been persuaded to join the original school, I escaped for a brief visit to Hollywood to take part in a fascinating but doomed-from-the-start project. Maximilian Schell had filmed an excellent *Hamlet* in German, primarily for European television, but with the hope that, if it were successful—and it undoubtedly was—it might be shown in cinemas. A Hollywood director, Edward Dmytryk, with whom Schell had worked on a film, decided to try to sell the *Hamlet* for distribution in America, and he and his partner, Samuel Weiler, in consultation with Max Schell, felt that its best chances would be in a dubbed version. I had maintained a pleasant friendship with Max since our meeting in *Interlock,* and we had spent many a stimulating half-hour discussing *Hamlet;* he knew the Schlegel translation as well as I knew the original. It was in consequence of this that he suggested I should be engaged for the dubbing: to choose the cast, rehearse them, and supervise the actual process.

The whole question of preparing a foreign film for a native market is a vexed and endlessly discussed one. To subtitle or to dub, that is the question. If, as I believe, the voice is as much a distinctive part of an actor as his face, the subtitle is the obvious answer, but it is a most unsatisfactory one. Sometimes the sub-titles are so long that you miss the picture, but they are often so short as to be absurd; I have known a lengthy tirade in the bawdy vernacular to be translated into a laconic "No!" At best, subtitling is a lame compromise, but the alternative can be infuriating; oc-casionally voices are so mismatched that the original actors should bring libel actions against the dubbers. Then there is the impossi-bility of the perfect synchronization of the new sounds with the original lips. Strangely enough, when the fit of one man's sounds to another man's lips is almost perfect, I find myself disturbed for another reason; I marvel at the cleverness of the accomplishment and am distracted from the content of the film.

The best solution of a problem incapable of a perfect solution is for the original actor to dub his own voice in the new language, and this was to happen in Max Schell's *Hamlet,* but only in the case of Hamlet himself. But with Shakespeare a new difficulty occurs. Good dubbing depends upon the manipulation of the translation until the sounds match the lip movements as nearly as possible. This you cannot do with Shakespeare; you cannot say: "To live or not to live; there you have my problem." The best you can hope for is no overlap; no sound from closed lips, or moving lips that are silent.

Maximilian Schell's English is excellent but still retains a German residue, so the other dubbers too had to be chosen from actors in Hollywood who still retained a German accent, of whom there seemed to be an abundance, and we soon assembled a good cast. Dmytryk and Weiler had hired the very latest dubbing equipment, which was miraculously flexible, and we all had a pleasant and apparently successful week. For me, the postscript to the experience happened in New York when the result of our work was shown to exhibitors. As soon as they saw that lip synchronization had not been achieved—they should have known without coming that it was impossible in the case of Shakespeare—they became scornful or irritated, and left. I still think there is an audience for this film in the big cities, perhaps without either dubbing or subtitling, which are equal disservices to Shakespeare.

About a year after I had become involved with the school, I made my first substantial contact with American television. (Previously I had acted on one show and been interviewed on several.) Two neophyte producers, Eric Blau and Ed Felder, both cultivated and endearing men, had had an idea for a new kind of hour-long television series. It was finally called, although not too happily in my opinion, *The Human Stage*. They engaged me for it in three capacities, as narrator, director, and discussion moderator. The subject of each program was to be a well-known play. I was to talk about the play briefly and introduce a climactic scene from it; this was to be followed by a discussion involving the actors and a couple of guests, including always a psychiatrist or psychologist. The program was to end with another scene from the play. The producers secured enough backing from WOR-TV, a New York station, to tape three shows, and they were all shown with some success, but they failed to get sufficient commercial sponsorship, and the series expired. The three subjects we dealt with were Ibsen's *Ghosts*, Strindberg's *The Father*, and Mary Shelley's *Frankenstein*. There was so little money available that camera rehearsals were woefully inadequate, but, even so, I was not ashamed of the results. In the first program we had Mildred Dunnock, in the second James Daly, and in the third Ed Carmel.

I should be very surprised if that third name were known to any of my readers. Ed Carmel makes his living by being "The Biggest Man in the World," and being exhibited in sideshows, where the rings from his fingers are sold as bracelets. Eric Blau, who knew him, wondered if I could get him to act Frankenstein's Monster. We were doing the show to rescue a remarkable work from its movie distortions, and because we knew it would provoke a stimulating discussion. The whole point of Mary Shelley's book is that the Monster has a Garden-of-Eden innocence. He has learned to speak and read; Milton and Plutarch have taught him about God and man. But his treatment at the hands of man has changed him from an angel of light to one of destruction. He says, in the moving confrontation with his creator, "Everywhere I see bliss, from which I alone am irrevocably excluded. I was benevolent and good; misery made me a fiend." When I first met Ed Carmel I was ashamed by my instinctive repulsion; he was huge beyond expectation. The poor fellow suffers from the disease of gigantism, for which there is now a cure, so he is probably the last of his grotesque kind in the world. After my hand had been lost in his in a handshake, I deliberately sat next to him to counter my first reaction. His voice accorded with his size; it was like a recording of a baritone played at too slow a speed. It was soon apparent that he was intelligent, imaginative, and sensitive. I asked him to read a passage from the script, which, being couched in early-nineteenth-century literary dialogue, would have been difficult for an accomplished actor to bring alive. He read it fluently. When I told him that he had the part, his gratitude was overwhelming. He had appeared in many movies, but all he had been thought capable of was inhuman growls and grunts. As I got to know him in the ensuing weeks I was humbled by his gentleness in face of the callous and frightened treatment his appearance caused him to suffer. Sustained physical effort was difficult for him; thus he could not walk far and yet taxi drivers usually refused to pick him up. He gave quite a good performance as the Monster, except that his memory failed toward the end of the strenuous taping session, but not disastrously. It was his contribution to the discussion which I shall never forget. He had sat silent during a heated discussion between a professor and the actor who had played Frankenstein. Finally I appealed to him directly to add his comments. His words made it clear that his identification with the Monster was complete, but his compassion was strong enough to understand people's reaction to him, and he remained unembittered.

I said earlier that Dylan Thomas had been responsible for my sharing a stage with Richard a third time. This time it was the stage of the Poetry Center in New York where Dylan himself had made memorable appearances, and where he had himself taken part in the first public reading of *Under Milk Wood*. But now he was dead, and we were there to honor his memory. There are as many people now who claim friendship with Dylan Thomas as there were pieces of the "True Cross" in Medieval Europe, but an undoubtedly authentic friend, and present help in time of trouble, was the sculptor David Slivka. He had made a death mask of Dylan, and from it had sculpted a full head in bronze. I later persuaded him to sell me one of the castings—there were only four or five—and I gave it as a wedding present to Richard and Elizabeth. It was installed in their apartment without Richard's knowledge, and when he returned from the theatre that night he was quite upset by the sudden shock of seeing it; there is a strange quality about it, a sort of life-in-death vividness. But to return to the memorial occasion. The artists of America, but largely Paul Jenkins, had decided to give one of the bronze heads to the National Museum of Wales. Richard was to receive the gift on behalf of the Museum, and I was to arrange the program and preside over it.

I am grateful to that occasion because it introduced me to Paul Jenkins, whom I now count a friend. He is an abstract artist of great distinction and distinctiveness. His work can be overwhelming in command of color and texture, power and flow. Each painting is for him an adventure, an act of discovery. What he says about his painting seems to me to have validity for all creative art: "Sometimes it seems as though I am keeping a storm door shut with one hand while I am painting with the other, in order to keep the known out so that the unknown may enter. To lean too heavily on metier could mean the end of discovery. On the other hand, to trust entirely to inspiration could lead to a hermetic art enclosed only in the arms of one beholder. I avoid considering the two separately, and work toward bringing them together." Paul is typecasting for "the artist," but a successful one. There is nothing bohemian about his appearance; he is handsome, with striking eyes and gray beard. When we meet, we usually talk theatre, for which he has a knowledgeable enthusiasm; indeed, he has an urge to write plays, and has started to do so, but they are going to be as individual and unconventional as his paintings. When I bought a house in Manhattan, he honored it and me with the generous gift of a large painting. To begin with, I found living with it like living with a person of tremendous personality —awesome, but difficult. But affection soon took over and now I miss it, for it is in storage; I sold the house and the ten-foot canvas will not fit into my present modern apartment. The picture brought me much incidental amusement, for visitors would often insist on using it as a kind of Rorschach test; the three favorite interpretations were the hull of a large ship bearing down on you, a praying rabbi, and a proud phallus.

In addition to Richard, Paul, and me, on the stage of the Poetry Center were David Slivka, Nancy Wickwire, who had taken part in that famous first reading of *Under Milk Wood*, and Malcolm Brinnin, who had been responsible for Dylan's appearances at the Poetry Center and had recounted the story with some anguish in his *Dylan Thomas in America*. There was another man whom I had invited to join us on the stage that Sunday afternoon, but he preferred to sit in the front row of the audience. It was Alec Guinness, who at that time was playing the wild Welsh poet in the

play *Dylan* on Broadway. For various reasons I had put off seeing the play until the day before the ceremony at the Poetry
Center. I was quite astonished by the performance of Alec Guinness; he himself had so little in common with the Dylan I knew
that the degree of identification he achieved with him was
astounding.

I have mentioned but a few of the multifarious outside things I
did and still do as President and Director of the American Musical
and Dramatic Academy. They are necessary to my sense of freedom, but nevertheless I have set a term to my work at the
academy and look forward to the day when I am completely free
again, not to retire—that has no attraction for me—but to undertake adventures that lie ahead, as yet unknown. But in 1964 I did
make one permanent determination for my future. I became an
American.

people who had lived happily in this country for fifty years, and yet had died British. But I ultimately came to regard this as an evasion. Some Americans seemed to suggest that I was selling my birthright for a mess of pottage. More than one said, "Nothing on earth would induce me to give up my American citizenship." And one dear old English lady, a schoolteacher who had been kind to me in my youth, died recently without forgiving me for what was to her an act of treachery. She was a product of the Empire days of Britain and must have agonized at their passing. I remember meeting her in Cardiff during the ominous days of the Blitz in 1940, when invasion was felt to be imminent; she had come to the city to buy bunting for the victory celebration, which was understandably at bargain prices just then. She could no more contemplate the possibility of defeat than a typical American can now.

My examination for citizenship was not without its amusing moments. Most of the would-be Americans waiting with me in the oppressively bureaucratic room of long benches were Oriental; I had visions of Formosa becoming the fifty-first state, a proposition with infinitely intriguing possibilities. Some of them were undergoing last-minute coaching in the Constitution of the United States, about which they would have to answer questions. The question most expected was "What are the three branches of the Government?" One aggressively confident young Chinese was arguing the answer with his coach, who insisted with pained repetition that the correct reply was "Executive, Legislative, and Judicial"; the nearly-a-new-American was certain that the three branches were "President, Senate, and House of Representatives."

My examiner was a courteous and well-educated young man who must have been rather new to his job. Apologetically he proffered me the card to read for my literacy test. Then came a question or two about the Government of the United States; one of them was indeed about the three branches. My mind jumped to the overconfident young Chinese; I doubted if his studied refusal to recognize the Supreme Court as an arm of Government would send him back to Formosa. Those preliminaries out of the way, my examiner studied my surprisingly large file and became embarrassed. Only a day or two before, a member of the House of Representatives had sought to prevent the entry into this country of Richard and his soon-to-be-wife, Elizabeth, on moral grounds. They were in Toronto, Canada, at the time, where he was appearing in *Hamlet* in preparation for Broadway. The immigration official had an uneasy feeling that the legislator's protest against Richard was a black mark against me, thus reversing the Biblical and classical law, and visiting the sins of the children upon the fathers. But he talked himself out of his own qualms and moved to a more certain objection. I had received a decoration from King George VI for my work with the Air Training Corps; there was apparently a rule which said I had to relinquish this, because it was a symbol of allegiance to another sovereignty. I was reluctant to give up the honor, and asked if a second opinion might be sought. The very obliging young man readily agreed to seek such an opinion, and left the room to do so. After some minutes he returned, and it was evident from his beaming face that I should be allowed to retain my M.B.E. (Military). There was precedent for such a procedure: General MacArthur had been allowed to retain his generalship in the Philippine Army. So I am indebted to that illustrious soldier for being still a Member of the British Empire, although an American citizen.

There yet remained the actual ceremony of becoming a citizen, at which publicly I would swear an oath of allegiance to the United States and forswear all foreign allegiances. Rather to my surprise this turned out to be an impressive function; I had expected that, with the daily processing of hundreds of new citizens, it would be perfunctory and mechanical. Perhaps I was lucky in the judge who presided that day. I did not learn his name, but I shall never forget him. Broadway would have cast him to play Oliver Wendell Holmes, father or son. He was tall, handsome, white of hair, and moustached, the epitome of all that is best in the New England tradition. He spoke to a few hundred of us drawn from many lands. As we awaited his appearance there was a low buzz of conversation in many tongues. I suppose most of those present would have been able to follow little of what the judge said, but they could not fail to be affected by his presence and the warmth of his utterance. The essence of his welcoming remarks was that we would best serve our new country by being true to the noblest traditions of our old country, that the United States of America owed its greatness to the richness of its diversity. As he was leaving the platform, he halted and gave us this benediction as an afterthought: "May this day bring you great blessings—and I don't mean material ones." It was thus that I became a citizen of the U.S.A. on March 2, 1964. If the judge who presided in New York on that day chances to read these words, I should like him to know my deep appreciation of the way in which he confirmed me in the rightness of a difficult decision.

That evening some friends gave a surprise party for me. It was a delightful and moving occasion. All the guests, carefully selected by the man who knew me best but several of whom he had not met personally, had to bring a verse they had written to mark the occasion and an appropriate gift costing not more than one dollar. I shall always treasure those mementos.

The party was held in my secretary's apartment. As I entered I was greeted by posters proclaiming "Philip Burton for President," a horrifying thought for both my new country and me, but a fate from which both of us had been protected by the wisdom of the Founding Fathers, who had decreed that only a native-born American could become President. My secretary, who was the hostess that evening, has since left me, at my instigation. Not that she wasn't a very good secretary, but she was an even better actress. I am convinced that those of my readers who are interested in the theater will get to know her name: Katherine Helmond. Just as I urged her to devote her life to the theatre, I dissuaded her husband from doing so, because he seemed to me to have unusual talent as an artist; he subsequently found that his greatest happiness was in sculpting. I have a hunch that his name will be known too; it is David Christian.

One of my chief motives in acquiring American citizenship was to gain the power to vote. It is some slight satisfaction to have a say, however faint and remote, in the disposition of the taxes that are squeezed out of one. As the November elections became imminent, I hastened to register as a voter. At that time I lived in the Chelsea district of New York City, and next to my house there was a large, new apartment house, all the residents in which seemed to have chosen to register on the morning I sought my voting card. I was at the end of a long line. Finally I got to the table, where I caused confusion. The ladies who presided at the table discovered who I was, and they knew that, only a few days before, Richard and his new wife had been at my house. Their reaction to the two celebrities was very different from that of the Representative in Washington. I finally managed to get back to the business of my voting card. A difficulty occurred. A new voter must pass a literacy test. I pointed out that I had already passed such a test when I became a citizen. A worried conference ensued between representatives from a few tables; they were joined by a sagacious-looking policeman whose sole contribution to the puzzled conversation was a continuous slow nodding of the head. I was becoming guilty about holding up the proceedings and I went over to the group and said I would willingly take another literacy test. They were overjoyed in their relief at this solution, and I was directed upstairs to the test room. There I found every desk occupied by Puerto Ricans, all of them in difficulties. A chic young lady was presiding, and I asked if I might be allowed to use my lap as a desk. This was unheard of, and the very suggestion seemed to cast aspersions on the seriousness with which I was taking the test. I had to wait for a proper desk. At last one of the Puerto Ricans gave up. The test was too much for him. He would not be allowed to vote. I took his place and was given my test paper. I understood why the disappointed man whose warmth I still felt on my chair had been defeated. The test was good and fair. It dealt with the statistical data of the Lincoln memorial, but all the many figures were given in words. It was an easy comprehension test for an English-speaking child but could have been difficult for a non-English-speaking adult, and to judge from the ruffled brows that surrounded me, it obviously was so. It was a much better test than the one I had been given to become a citizen, which leads me to the strange conclusion that it is easier to become a citizen than a voter.

When I first exercised my new privilege, I was aghast at the complexity of the machine with which I was closeted. Hitherto I had always voted by penciling a cross opposite my man's name on a piece of paper, folding the paper, and dropping it into a box. Only a blind party man can vote simply in an American election, and even he could have trouble with the multiple referenda with which the machine confronts him. An American voter really has to be literate and to have studied issues as well as men before the curtain of the booth closes behind him. It takes quite a time even to read the propositions about such things as bond issues, and not even a stool is provided. Then there is the complication that no official language can ever manage to be simple. At a subsequent election in which I voted, one of the issues in New York City was the continuance of the Police Review Board. One little man emerged from his booth, his face a big smile. He walked straight across to a nearby policeman to tell him proudly that he was against the Review Board and had voted "No." The poor man had really voted for the continuance of the Board, because the machine had asked him if he was in favor of its discontinuance.

In the same year that I became an American I also signed a contract to become part of a very American institution—the lecture circuit. W. Colston Leigh, the founder, owner, and active head of the largest lecture bureau in the country, and probably in the world, asked me to see him. I assumed it was yet another request to use my good offices in securing the services of Richard, a tiresomely repetitive motif in my life, and one to which I turn a politely deaf ear. But I was wrong. Mr. Leigh wanted to see me for myself. I was very impressed by his Fifth Avenue suite of offices. It was obvious that there was a lot of money in the lecture business, at least for him. He also had regional offices in Chicago and San Francisco. He was a well-built six-footer, slightly stooping, with gray close-cropped hair, his face usually creased into a twinkle. One could have mistaken him for a farmer, so successful that he had retired early. I did not take too kindly to him at that first meeting. Having ascertained that I might be interested in doing some cross-country lecturing, he went on to prove how difficult a job it would be for him to sell me; I began to wonder why he even bothered. He further mystified me by saying that under no circumstances did he want to hear me lecture because then he would not be able to sell me. I still don't understand that, but my attitude to "Bill," as he now is to me, has altered completely. It has changed from dislike to affection, and from an initial wariness to complete confidence. His excellent staff are models of friendly competence.

Even at that first meeting I was urged to suggest subjects and titles, and I came up with three acceptable ones, the format to be that of lecture-recitals rather than straight lectures. The three titles were: "The Miracle That Was Shakespeare" (I'm still frequently giving that one, four years later), "The Magic of Poetry," and "A Pageant of Kings." The last required the assistance of a young actor, and told the story of the dynastic struggle in England from 1399 to 1485 as shown in eight of Shakespeare's historical plays. Immediately one of the main hazards of the game became apparent; most engagements are booked six, nine, or twelve months ahead, and to mortgage the future in that way is limiting to one's activities. It became even more difficult for the young actor who accompanied me for the program "A Pageant of Kings." It was one thing to guarantee his appearance on a tour, but quite another for him to promise he would be free for an occasional engagement in a year's time.

A word about this young actor. His name is Christian Alderson. There must be a thing called the Pygmalion complex; if there is, I have it. It's a deep urge to fulfill myself as an actor or a writer through another person. Perhaps I should be unkinder to myself and call it a Svengali complex. It is not satisfied just by teaching a class; there must be a close personal identification with the pupil. My most notable subject was Richard, who became an integral part of my life, and to whom I owe as much as he owes to me. But there was one before him, Owen Jones, also a pupil of mine in Port Talbot Secondary School. He, too, came from a Welsh-speaking home. He brought me great satisfaction by winning the Leverhulme scholarship to the Royal Academy of Dramatic Art, and had embarked on a very promising career, which was cut short by an untimely death. There was a memorable day when I took his father and mother to London to see him play Laertes at the Old Vic to the uncut Hamlet of Laurence Olivier. Owen became an R.A.F. officer and died in the war, a victim not of the Luftwaffe but of bone cancer. There was another pupil, too, at that school in whom I saw great promise, but as a writer. While I was working for the B.B.C. in Wales he did some excellent scripts for me, but it was the private writing that never was published, including a full-length novel, that excited me most. When I left Wales, his writing petered out, and he devoted all his energies to schoolteaching, in which he found his highest satisfaction. It is some years since I have seen him, and recently his life has been complicated by marital problems, but even then a malaise of the soul was settling upon him that robbed him of all desire to write.

Christian Alderson is my latest protégé, and will undoubtedly be my last. It gave me an eerie shock when I discovered that his real name was Richard and that his father, like the other Richard's, was a coalminer. Christian had been a paratrooper, and, when he came out of the Army, he became a dancer with acrobatic overtones. He was so good that he was in continuous employment on Broadway. But dancing was not enough for him; he wanted to act, and in the summer of 1962 he came to the school of which I had just become the director. In that summer I did not teach him at all, but his gratitude to the school was so genuine that he insisted on doing work on the building to repay us. This brought him to my attention, and I discovered that he had an instinctive taste and a hunger for great literature. He longed to play Shakespeare, but, to start with, a West Virginian accent stood in the way. He was a mature man, and thus both the challenge and the difficulties were greater than they had been in Richard's case, for instance. I well remember the evening, many months later, when I knew that both our efforts were worthwhile; he brought one of Hamlet's soliloquies deeply alive. His first big test came when he played Oswald to Mildred Dunnock's Mrs. Alving in *The Human Stage* series; he did not disappoint. His latest activity is leading the Philip Burton Drama Quartet in engagements throughout the country. This group was my answer to a request by Colston Leigh. The Quartet presents a dramatic potpourri called *The Battle of the Sexes*, in which Christian surprised even me by the powerful intensity of his performance in a scene from Strindberg's *The Father*. I have high hopes for him.

I have now completed three seasons of lecture engagements and look forward to more. I don't very much enjoy the many thousands of miles of hectic traveling, particularly in the winter, the lecture season, but very rarely indeed have I regretted the journey. All the reassuring statistics of deaths in the air as contrasted with deaths on the road have never completely succeeded in stilling my fears of flying, but at least and at last I am inured to it sufficiently to enjoy meals aloft—there is always an added piquancy for me in meals served in places not intended for dining—and the earth seen from a plane never ceases to astonish me, in particular the very old and the very young; the Rockies seen from above seem ravaged survivals from the beginning of time and New York at night a glittering fairground that makes me awestruck and terrorstruck by the power and ingenuity of man. Whenever I return to New York, not the most engrossing book can keep my eyes from turning to the window and looking down. There is the world's most fascinating metropolis, and it is my home.

Despite the hazards of weather and those infuriating delays in landing at dangerously overcrowded airports, such as O'Hare in Chicago, when you go round and round and round and wish you had come by train, I have never once been late for an engagement, and only once has my luggage been mislaid. On one occasion I was certain I had missed a connection when my plane was an hour late in arriving, but the connecting plane was two hours late; a storm had slowed us, but a blizzard had slowed them.

My first lecture tour lasted five weeks and took me to the four corners of the country—San Diego, Seattle, northern Vermont, and Miami. The plane has shrunk the country but it has not affected the astonishing variations of weather; one day I was sweating in the sun in San Diego and the next day shivering in the snow in Idaho.

The audiences are as varied as the weather, although not in temperature; I have never experienced a chilly reception. There are two main types of engagements—colleges and clubs—although there are a few cities, for example Detroit and Sacramento, where a local impresario books lectures in much the same way that a theatre manager books traveling companies. The greatest variety of audiences occurs in the colleges; in some places you can depend on a packed and lively audience, and in others only a few hundred will be sprinkled throughout an auditorium built to contain thousands, and those few hundred comprising more townsfolk than students. Why is it that in some colleges the students seem avid for any expansion of their cultural experience, while in others the classroom is enough, indeed more than enough? There are some colleges where attendance is obligatory, and this I personally deplore, although I appreciate the argument in favor of it; after all, army conscripts have been known to learn something from their training. There was one experience of a conscripted audience that put me on my toes so much that I was poised to run away. It was at a university in a mountain state. I had been engaged to lecture on "The Magic of Poetry." I expected a specialized audience of English majors. Prior to the lecture I was taken on a proud tour of the campus, ending in the vast gymnasium, where members of the long-distance track team were noisily running their miles around the gallery. Only a quarter of an hour remained before I was due to begin, so I asked if I might be taken to the lecture room; I was told that this was it. I suggested that these acres of floor and miles of gallery were a little large for our purpose; both my lecture and I would be lost. The reply was that this was the only place that would seat all the students, and the place would be particularly full inasmuch as outsiders were coming too; poetry needed all its magic that morning, although it is true, of course, that a vast assembly has its own magic for the speaker also. The hush of a held silence shared by thousands is wonderfully satisfying to the man who has commanded it.

There is one kind of college that has never disappointed me in the quality of its audience, and that is a Mormon college. I find it difficult to lend any credence to the basic myth that resulted in the Book of Mormon, but in many ways the social results of the religion are admirable. I have often noticed how the devout adherents to what might be called the splinter religions of Christianity seem to excel in thrift, independence, and business acumen. The Quaker Rowntrees and the Cadburys of England are typical, and there was a branch of my mother's family that were Plymouth Brothers, a narrow sect particularly obnoxious to me in my teenage cynicism, who made much money from bakeries. Apparently it is true that if you seek first the Kingdom of God, or that particular and special corner of it that is the preserve of the select, all these things shall indeed be added unto you. But most of the sects that eschew liquor and tobacco, and in the case of the Mormons coffee, tend to be sworn enemies of the theatre as the Puritans have been from the days of Shakespeare. The Mormons are a notable exception; they love theatre. When I first visited Salt Lake City in 1939 I was impressed by many things, but one that I have remembered down the years was that Gilbert and Sullivan was taught as part of the high school curriculum. I have been both embarrassed and touched when my appearance before a Mormon audience has been prefaced by prayer, when God has been thanked for my presence, and this before I have uttered a word, but I have always enjoyed speaking and performing for them. I have also found the campuses markedly free from the student unrest that seems to plague other colleges.

My kindly feeling toward the Mormons would have appalled my mother. I have a vivid recollection from my childhood—and most of my childhood is oblivion—of my mother's secreting in a deep pocket of her skirt a frighteningly honed little knife, used chiefly to kill chickens for the table by pushing it through their necks while she held them fast between her sackclothed legs. This hidden knife accompanied her shopping expeditions for several weeks, for the rumor had spread that Mormons were in town for the nefarious purpose of kidnapping women. This distortion of the idealism of eager young Mormon missionaries is but another example of the terrifying results of the absurd fears that result from ignorance.

In most places, the hospitality I have received has been warm and tactful—occasionally it has been so overwhelming that I longed for a private half-hour—but that of the Mormons has been unfailingly perfect. There was one occasion in Utah when I had a heavy cold and had to leave early in the morning; the professor who insisted on driving me the fifty miles to the airport arrived a half-hour early with a complete breakfast prepared by his wife, including coffee. There was another occasion in Idaho when a faculty dinner was given in my honor. The Mormons eat meat much less frequently than other Americans, but because I was there we had meat. The professor on my right asked me how I liked the beef. Had my manners been as good as his, I should have hidden the truth, but I didn't. I told him the truth, of which he was completely unaware; it was pork.

Women's clubs have long been the target of American cartoonists and satirists. Always the members are big-hatted, big-bosomed and big-voiced, with small brains and large opinions. In my experience this is a canard. Generally speaking I have found my audiences in women's clubs to be intelligent, perceptive, and well-read. The derogatory epithet so often hurled at them, "culture hounds," they should take as a compliment. Already they are doing something to solve the problem that will face their menfolk in five hundred years, perhaps sooner. It seems to me that men are not making an adjustment to the one dominant sign of our time —the supersession of man by the machine. We still have the attitude of the primitive farmer who had to work from daybreak to nightfall in order to live, so that we still feel guilty when we do not work. But the time is coming when work to provide the necessities of living will take very little of our time, and education will be largely aimed at the enjoyment of leisure; instead of being taught to make a living, we will be taught to live. And women's clubs, with their serious and multifarious pursuits of culture, may be showing the way.

Of course, one cannot wholly escape the frivolous element in women's clubs, especially when the lecture is followed by a luncheon or tea at which questions are asked; but even here there are usually as many questions about Shakespeare as there are about Richard and Elizabeth, and now that the scandal has died down, Shakespeare leads the field.

Hospitality varies from the overwhelming to the nonexistent in the case of women's clubs. In the latter, but rare, category, you are left to find your own way to your hotel or motel, where there is a message awaiting you from the chairman, anxious to be assured of your safe arrival. You are told where and very precisely when to deliver yourself the next day. After the lecture you shake hands and depart, and that's that. The opposite of this reception is that you are met at the airport by a committee and a radio and television fanfare, and every moment of your stay is spent in a planned whirl of sightseeing and social engagements. Neither extreme makes me happy, but I do like being met and made to feel that I am with friends rather than employers.

The halls and rooms in which the lecture is given vary widely too. Gymnasia are the worst, but ballrooms are not much better. I don't particularly like vast cinemas either. Occasionally the hall is something quite unexpected; Christian Alderson and I once gave "A Pageant of Kings" in a large synagogue; the program involved our making the sign of the cross, which must have established a record of some kind. The best halls are the beautiful ones found in some women's clubs and the lovely theatres found on some campuses.

Some university theatres are among the best equipped in the country, but I am puzzled by the activities they house. Very rarely do I find any lively liaison between the English department and the drama department; particularly in the university, they should be part of the same educative process. Then again, there is an inevitable conflict in claims upon the students' time and energies between the academic and the dramatic, so that productions cannot be adequately rehearsed. My experience is that the physical aspects of the production far surpass the acting. How could it be otherwise? Young part-time amateur actors cannot be expected to excel in parts that would tax seasoned professionals, and they don't even give enough performances to learn by doing, because very rarely can they call upon audiences large enough to sustain a production for more than a week. In effect, they give a series of previews without ever arriving at an opening night. It is the usual experience of accomplished actors that they have to play a difficult role for at least three weeks before they can feel fully at home in it. What about the weekly change of bill in a resident summer theatre? That is such a shambles that it affords little artistic satisfaction to an actor, whose main emotion is one of relief that he managed to get through somehow, and this should certainly not be a criterion for a university actor.

It would seem that the solution to the problems of university theatre is that there should be a graduate school which would have close contact with the best in professional theatre. Indeed, this is happening in notable instances, such as Yale, for example.

When I arrive at a lecture hall, I am usually provided with a microphoned lectern, often misnamed a podium, but I prefer to function without this barrier between the audience and me. Of course, the speeches from plays I give are learned in advance, but the lecture itself I try to keep as flexible as possible. I have never read a lecture in my life. I usually know my opening sentence, but after that I become a part of my audience, and my ears are often surprised by my mouth. At least it keeps me from getting bored. I have learned to assess an audience very quickly, and to gear my remarks to my sense of their knowledge, intelligence, and sophistication.

I derive a great satisfaction from lecturing, and particularly from giving lecture recitals, but even they are poor substitutes for what working in the theatre gives me, so I was easily persuaded to direct a season of six plays in the summer of 1965, and to act in two of them. Each of the productions was to play for two weeks. Thus, the extreme horrors of the one-week run were to be avoided; for the actor, a two-week run is much more than twice as good as a one-week run. One of the producers was a friend of mine, and he had lofty and exciting ambitions. He had that combination of artistic sensitivity and business know-how that makes a good producer, but unfortunately the place he chose for his operation did not have enough people to sustain it. The audiences were good, sometimes excellent, in quality, but too small in quantity. The place was a charming and civically proud little community in New Jersey. Its name was Clinton, and it contained a delightful little theatre, which the town leaders had restored to its old excellence. Backstage there were still posters of silent films, faded by fifty years. We gathered a good company; some of the senior members had worked with me in my professional classes, and most of the junior members had newly graduated from my school.

The community greeted us warily. Would we pay our bills? Would we offend local morals? But this soon changed to a warm acceptance, and out of our season was born a desire to establish a Clinton Arts Festival. I agreed to become its artistic adviser, and there were dreams of year-round activities sufficiently attractive to draw patrons from New York City, of which Clinton was to be put in easy access by a new highway. But meetings, discussions, plans, and dreams all came to naught for lack of money. Indeed, the only practical result of the season was that I, in common with several Clintonians, was called upon to pay a share of a guarantee made to the local bank for a loan negotiated by the producers to enable them to complete the season. Yet I regarded it as money well lost, because I had had a good summer.

Our first play was Tennessee Williams' *Cat on a Hot Tin Roof*, and we opened with a fanfare. The Mayor gave a reception on the lawn of his house and invited all the mayors for many miles around. Most of them came, and we all proceeded in motorcade to the first night of our first production. Rich food can upset plain stomachs, and our first offering was too rich for some of the audience. Many sophisticated New Yorkers spend their summers near Clinton and we had counted on their patronage, but this we discovered was sparse, and we had to give our energies to building up a truly local audience. We succeeded to an exciting extent, but the community was just not large enough, and as in all other communities, even the large cities, a sizable proportion of the population was impenetrably apathetic to theatre; some were actually hostile. On the Sunday morning after the opening, I was crossing the beautiful bridge of which Clinton is justly proud, when I was stopped by an irately pious lady who told me that I and the company were doing the work of the Devil and we should be ashamed of ourselves. I have often wondered what I should have said in reply, but I was given no opportunity, because she stalked away in smug triumph.

Much discussion had gone into the planning of the season. The producers and I had agreed that we would avoid the ordinary Broadway comedy fare, but we knew that we dare not become too esoteric. I even reluctantly agreed that we should do one surefire, popular comedy, as box office insurance. We chose *The Man Who Came to Dinner*, which did indeed do much the best business of the season. The play had the additional advantage of needing the recruitment of several local amateurs. But to counterbalance this play we decided to end the season with an avant-garde play requir-

ing a small cast, so that the main body of the company would no
longer be on the payroll. We chose Pinter's *The Caretaker*,
largely, I suppose, because there was some interest in seeing my
playing of the old man in it, a role which I thoroughly enjoyed;
but I was only beginning to be at home in it when we closed. It is
one of my hopes for the future that I shall be given an opportunity
to play the part again. Strangely enough, that puzzling play ran
second at the box office to *The Man Who Came to Dinner*, and
stimulated a lot of discussion. One night the audience was invited
to stay for such a discussion after the performance, and nearly two
hundred did so and stayed for some hours. On the stage to open
the discussion there were, in addition to myself, a Catholic priest,
a nonconformist minister, and a psychiatrist. The play is so rich in
its implications that all our different insights provided fruitful
speculation.

I, as director and actor, was chiefly concerned with realizing the
characters fully. In Aston, the elder brother, I saw something of
Dostoevski's "Idiot," Prince Muishkin. Both have that innocence
and simplicity that trouble the world's conscience and that land
both of them in mental institutions. It is significant that Aston's
most precious possession is a statue of the Buddha, and it is
equally significant that the younger brother, Mick, smashes the
figure, for it is a symbol of that in his brother with which he
cannot cope. Mick is an ambitious young workman who is decent
enough to feel and accept responsibility for his brother, and
ordinary enough to resent the burden. The resulting conflict in him
finds violent expression, but never against Aston himself. The old
derelict, Davies, whom Aston shelters, is the butt of Mick's
sadistic violence. I feel that Davies is but one in a series of old
men whom Aston has befriended, only to be cheated each time. I
suppose Mick always hopes that the right one will turn up some
day and relieve him of some of the burden of looking after Aston,
and thus he submits the old man to cruelly amusing tests. Davies
himself plays a lone and crafty hand against a hostile world bent

on robbing him of his independence, privacy, and identity. The interactions of the three characters provide one of the most stimulating plays I have ever worked on.

To stimulate interest in another play, Bernard Shaw's *Mrs. Warren's Profession*, which contains one of the greatest confrontation scenes between mother and daughter ever written, I gave an afternoon lecture, which attracted more people than I expected. The other two plays we did, Eugene O'Neill's charming piece of nostalgia, *Ah, Wilderness!* and Arthur Miller's powerful melodrama, *All My Sons*, needed no help for acceptance by the community. Sophisticated audiences now find both plays dated, the one by its sentimentality and the other by its theatrical contrivance, but our audiences brought to the plays a freshness of reception that was rewarding.

For the actors in the company, the summer was a great enrichment of their professional experience. It is essential that actors be given an opportunity to play a wide variety of parts, and this is almost impossible in the more lucrative fields of Broadway, movies, and television; one success there, and you are in danger of being cast in similar parts for the rest of your career. Fortunately, more and more resident companies are arising throughout the country, and this is going to fulfill an artistic need for actors, particularly for the younger ones. I tell the students at AMDA who are about to graduate that the worst thing that could happen to them is to get trapped in a long-running Broadway success, particularly in the small parts they are likely to be given.

Directors, too, tend to be typed. The names of certain directors spring to the minds of producers as they seek one to stage their projected show, and those names are determined by the project itself, whether it be a musical, a light comedy, a classical revival, a psychological drama, or an avant-garde play, and yet the directors are often as anxious to try their hand at something new as are the actors. It has been said, with some justification, that the actor is predominant in England and the director in America. Personally I think the playwrights have increasingly come to dominate the theatre in both countries. This development is wholly desirable, but the director is certainly more important in America than he is in England. There are Broadway practitioners who have suffered their way into cynicism who would say that the critic's is the greatest power in the theatre, and that singular possessive is neither a mistake of grammar nor a misprint.

The evolution of the director is interesting, but somewhat obscure. It is probable that, until the appearance of the separate functionary known as the director in America and the producer in England—the cinema is unifying the nomenclature—his work was done by either the author or the leading actor, with a stage manager keeping a record of the decisions made during the rehearsals. It is sometimes said that in the good old days there was no such thing as a director in the theatre. This is arrant nonsense. There must always have been someone to extract some shape from the chaos that would have resulted from the conflicting egos of actors who by their very natures are concerned, and rightly so, with making the most of their parts and standing centerstage as often as possible. (I have heard of an old actor-manager who used to begin rehearsals by having a semicircle marked out centerstage and proclaiming that only he and his leading lady were ever to stand within that sacred area.) I can conceive much more readily of a symphony getting itself played without the help of a conductor than I can of a play getting itself produced without somebody taking charge of it; that somebody we now call the director. His function is to interpret the play, guide and coordinate the physical circumstances of its staging (the setting, lighting, costumes), cast it, usually in consultation with the author and producer, and conduct rehearsals with the object of getting the best possible performances from his actors, and such as will contribute to his interpretation of the play. In the case of a new play, he will probably have worked with the author on the script long before the first rehearsal, and will probably work with him again on improving the script after it has been submitted to the test of audiences. In the case of musicals, of course, he must have some knowledge of music. It is obvious from all this that a director must have the encyclopedic knowledge of a Bernard Shaw, the artistry of a Picasso, the insight of a Freud, the analytical skill of an Aristotle, and the inspiring leadership of a John F. Kennedy. I also think it essential for him to have had some experience as an actor, and desirable for him to have done some writing. Clearly this superman is so rare as to be virtually nonexistent, and even successful directors have weaknesses in some fields; thus several of them are at the mercy of the designers of sets, costumes, and lighting, and others are of very little help to their authors. One skill is indispensable to a director; he must be able to deal with actors, and to help them to give of their best. Those two functions are not the same.

Dealing with actors is a very personal relationship, and no two can be treated in the same way. Actors are notoriously sensitive, and during rehearsal, particularly as the opening night approaches, they are as fretful as thoroughbreds at the starting gate. Their nervous insecurity betrays itself in divers ways; the director becomes a father figure, who, by his very being, is loved by some and hated by others, and often loved and hated by the same person at the same time. He must build up the confidence of some and puncture the cocky and limiting self-assurance of others. He must have a word for everybody; I soon learned that if you say nothing to an actor, he immediately assumes that you are dissatisfied with him. The company is a tightly knit family engaged on the same adventure, and it experiences all the joys and tribulations of family life, the director being the father. The loneliness of the director on opening night is sad to behold, and sadder to experience. For better or for worse his work is finished; the family is on its own, independent of him. Although he will visit it again to see how it is getting along, he will only be a visitor, sometimes welcome, sometimes unwelcome; he may even cause trouble if he is no longer proud of what the family is doing, but the erring children will not be too upset, because tomorrow Papa will have gone again.

The director's skill in dealing with his actors as people is an adjunct to his dealing with them as artists, and here there is a wide disparity of techniques. Some directors come to the first rehearsal with a clear and fixed idea of how every moment of the play should look and sound and feel, and they impose their detailed conception upon the cast; it is left to the actor to make it all come alive for himself. There is an oft-quoted dialogue between such a director and an actor to whom the mechanical was death: "Move to the fireplace on that line." "Why?" "Because I told you to." In the sharpest contradistinction to that approach is that of the director who comes to the rehearsals with a very fluid conception of the play, and acts as a sort of chairman of the group, which by tentative trial and error brings the play to life. My position is that the performances must be elicited, not imposed, but because, as I have previously said, I believe the prime duty of the director to be to the author, he must have clear and unshakable convictions about the author's intentions and see to it that the production conveys those. At the same time he must be fluid enough to adapt his ideas of the characters to the strengths and weaknesses of his actors. As for how he elicits what he wants from his actors, it again depends upon the actor, because no two work in precisely the same way. Apart from the different training that they may have had, they are different in their intelligence, knowledge, and experience; a word to the wise may be enough, but something very different may be necessary for the unwise, who yet may be the better actor. "He gives line readings" expresses the ultimate contempt of an actor for a director, and it is deserved if the director insists that the actor imitate his reading of a line of dialogue, but if an actor has difficulty in understanding what the director wants from a certain line, and logical analysis has failed to convey the idea because he is the kind of actor who works by instinct rather than intelligence, very often a line reading will enable him to grasp the required impact of the moment, but the director must be very careful to use his reading as an illustration, not a pattern.

It is a puzzling irony that I, who am associated in the minds of actors with Shakespeare, had to wait for thirteen years in this country before I was invited to direct a full-scale production of a Shakespearean play. It was *Hamlet*, which I directed in the open air in the Sylvan Theatre in Washington, D.C., in the summer of 1967. The Shakespeare Festival had been established some years before by Ellie Chamberlain, who, in the face of great difficulties, had worked it up to the point of considerable public acceptance and some official help from the Parks Department. Ellie had been one of the most loyal members of the audience in New York, some ten years before, when I gave my twenty lectures on "The Actor's Shakespeare." By 1967, she had recruited an energetic and enthusiastic board of directors, and they felt that the time had come to take a big step forward. They engaged Dickie Moore to help them; he had grown from a famous child film star into the head of a public relations firm. They secured the Washington premiere of the film of *The Taming of the Shrew*, which starred Richard and Elizabeth, to help them in their drive for funds. Dickie Moore talked me into going to Washington with him to have my photograph taken with Secretary of the Interior Stewart Udall, in the make-believe act of receiving from him my ticket for the premiere. Or was he receiving it from me? The photograph, which was the object of the occasion, is as ambiguous as my memory. Even the ticket was make-believe, and I did not attend the premiere. But there was no make-believe about Secretary Udall's interest in the Shakespeare Festival. I had expected him to regard the posing for a photograph as yet another irksome duty of office, that we would be ushered in—click!—and ushered out, but he surprised me by becoming genuinely interested in our conversation, which lengthened into a very pleasant half-hour. I myself became so enthusiastic about the festival that when Dickie Moore suggested, during our return flight to New York, that I could help them still further by directing the 1967 play, I readily agreed, provided I could choose the play. I wanted to do *Hamlet*, because I had found in my professional class a potentially exciting Hamlet: Robert Drivas. Dickie Moore told Ellie Chamberlain of our conversation, and, while she welcomed my participation, she was very doubtful about the choice of play. The festival had never done a tragedy, and she was dubious about its acceptance. But for me it was *Hamlet* or nothing, and so it was *Hamlet*.

The conditions for the production were, from my point of view, far from perfect. To begin with, I am not enthusiastic about open-air theatre. First, there are the hazards of weather, and we had a phenomenally wet summer, which caused several performances during the six-week run to be canceled and others to be abandoned; the threat of rain that did not come still kept cautious people away. But it is the distractions of the open air that chiefly disturbed me, and we had one overwhelming distraction to contend with; airplanes landing at and leaving from the National Airport often flew right over the stage, and always near it; when the ceiling was low, so were the planes. It was extraordinary how the company and the audience managed to keep their concentration on the play during the roar of jets. There are two other large airports to serve Washington, but, despite protests of residents, the more conveniently placed National Airport continues to carry the bulk of the traffic; Congress will obviously be reluctant to do anything about it, because its members like to have their constituencies as accessible as possible.

The site of the theatre is exciting; it is at the foot of a slope on the top of which is the Washington Monument. It is thrilling to stand on that stage at night and command the attention of four thousand people and be dimly aware of the floodlit monument at the top of the hill. The stage itself is surrounded by trees and bushes, which can be used as an effective enrichment of the action. Thus, at one moment in *Hamlet* we saw the mad Ophelia in the distance picking the flowers she would use in her fantasy on stage.

Apart from my objections to staging the production in the open air, I was also disturbed to find that of the thirty-five actors I needed for the production, only nine would be fully professional, but here I need not have been apprehensive, for some of the local actors were good, and the loyalty and dedication of the "spear carriers" was admirable. I had complete confidence in the nine players I took with me from New York because they had all been members at some time of my professional class. I knew their work well, and, what is equally important, they knew me well.

Before I started work on the production, I had some misgivings about the set and costumes, because both the designers were local people engaged in other occupations, but it turned out that they were very gifted men who performed miracles. Bob Troll is a designer for the Parks Department, but his hobby is stage design, and he gave me a superb set, which he not only designed but constructed and painted. Construction and paint had to withstand the onslaughts of wind and rain, a fact which my previous experience had not allowed for. The only other open-air production I had directed had been the Margam Abbey Pageant thirty years before, in which the setting was natural, battered into beauty by eight hundred years of Welsh wind and rain. Apart from the practical necessities I demanded of the set for *Hamlet*, which required a multiplicity of levels and entrances, I gave the designer as a theme Hamlet's line, "Denmark's a prison." The set was a large one, seventy-two feet long and twenty feet high, and its imitation stonework had to have sufficient credibility by day because it would still be daylight when the play began; on lucky nights, daylight would dissolve into the magic of moonlight. It was essential that the painted canvas should have the appearance of rough-cut stone, an easy effect to accomplish on an indoor stage, but I had not allowed for the rain, which would tend to strip any application off the canvas. (The modern solution of the problem is to mold the walls of plastic, but this we could not afford.) Bob Troll experimented by immersing various applications in water for twenty-four hours, and thus he arrived at a durable solution of the problem.

I was equally fortunate in the dress designer, John Peter Halford, an Englishman who, like myself, had fallen in love with America and become a part of it. For us Caesar's dictum was altered to "I came, I saw, I was conquered." John had been a costume designer in England for one of the television companies. He is now designer for a large store in Washington, but his heart is still in the theatre; the Shakespeare Festival gives him an opportunity to do the work he chiefly loves. Not only did he give us costumes that were both beautiful and practical and that created brilliant patterns of color in the ensemble scenes, but he did it with very little money; I think I am right in saying that one of the costumes worn by Julie Andrews in the Broadway production of *Camelot* cost more than all forty costumes used in our *Hamlet*.

There was one personal worry I had about Washington in the summer; I cannot stand heat. The mere thought of sweltering in the Washington sun for hours on end made me feel faint. When I sit in the shade I still turn boiled-lobster-red, and then peel, and then turn red again. I once went for a boat ride off the coast of Maine, sitting carefully under cover, but leaving my bare arm out in the cooling breeze; the sun caught that arm and it swelled to twice its size. Fortunately this torment was not to be mine in Washington. During the afternoon we rehearsed in an air-conditioned college theatre, the splendid stage of which was large enough to accommodate the ground plan of our set. Only in the evening did we venture to work in the westering sun, and only on a few evenings of that wet summer did that become onerous. Even so, Queen Gertrude thoughtfully provided me with a straw hat of noble proportions, like those worn by Sir Winston Churchill when he painted on the Riviera.

The audiences were a constant delight. The theatre is free, but, to help meet the expenses, about one thousand seats are sold for one and two dollars. Yet the free patrons far outnumber the paying ones, and free theatre presents the same challenge as free television; if the spectator's attention is not caught and held, he will wander off as readily as he switches off at home. In many cases, he has only wandered in anyway, to sit on the grass slope and watch for a while. It was for this reason that Ellie Chamberlain had doubted the holding power of a tragedy, but she need have had no doubts. The variety in the audience was astonishing, ranging from Shakespearean scholars to those who did not know who was going to win the fight in the end, Hamlet or Laertes; from those who took pleasure in collecting their twentieth Hamlet to those who gasped audibly when the Queen drank from the poisoned cup. The sophisticated were titillated by unusual and unexpected touches, the uninitiated were absorbed by the plot; it takes fresh eyes and ears to remind us how brilliant a storyteller Shakespeare is.

I was much exercised by having to cut the play. I had been given a categorical injunction that the performance had to finish by 11:15 P.M. at the very latest. That left two and one-half hours of playing time for a play that takes half as long again for its complete performance. I spent painful hours in hacking the text, only to become more and more exasperated. Then I remembered that, when Richard had played Hamlet on Broadway, among the many presents he had received was a contemporary copy of the text used in a very famous production of the play which had taken place in the Lyceum Theatre in London in 1897, exactly seventy years before mine in the Sylvan Theatre in Washington. That *Hamlet* had been Sir Johnston Forbes Robertson's but the theatre had been Sir Henry Irving's, whose badly mauled versions of Shakespeare's plays had so infuriated Bernard Shaw that he took the occasion of the new *Hamlet* further to castigate Irving, who led the fashion of cutting the texts so much that he virtually presented extracts from the plays displayed in elaborate trappings. Shaw had said: "The Forbes Robertson *Hamlet* at the Lyceum is, very unexpectedly at that address, really not at all unlike Shakespeare's play of the same name. . . . The story of the play was perfectly intelligible, and quite took the attention of the audience off the principal actor at moments. What is the Lyceum coming to? . . . The effect of this success . . . makes it almost probable that we shall presently find managers vying with each other in offering the public as much of the original Shakespearean stuff as possible, instead of, as heretofore, doing their utmost to reassure us that everything that the most modern resources can do to relieve the irreducible minimum of tedium inseparable from even the most heavily cut acting version will be lavished on their revivals." I eagerly studied the Forbes Robertson text and decided to use it. Much though I regretted many omissions, for me at least, and possibly for other Shakespearean enthusiasts, it had an antiquarian interest, for several old theatregoers had told me without hesitation that Sir Johnston Forbes Robertson's *Hamlet* had been their greatest theatrical experience.

I so much enjoyed directing *Hamlet* in Washington and the success of the production was such that I was well disposed to returning to do another production in the summer of 1968. When it was suggested that I should both direct *King Lear* and play him, I too readily agreed. I had essayed the part many years before, when I was much too young to play it and too innocent to know that I couldn't. I longed to try again before I became too weak from age to carry Cordelia in for the final scene. But slowly counsels of caution prevailed. Suppose it turned out to be a really hot Washington summer? I wilt, even sitting in the shade. What would happen to me, playing such a strenuous part on an open stage? But I continued to toy with the idea until I broached it to Richard in Rome three months later; he was so amazed by my idiocy in even contemplating the possibility that I dropped it forthwith. Then I had no great desire to return to Washington, and yet I felt guilty because Ellie Chamberlain and her board of directors had been led to expect me back. Finally I came up with an idea that would put the onus on them, because they might easily conclude that it was too dangerous an idea. It was to do *Romeo and Juliet*, making the Capulets colored and the Montagues white. I am strongly opposed to gimmicky Shakespeare, by which I mean productions given startling forms in setting or purpose merely to catch the attention by being different. To be fair, I must state that Alfred Baruth described my idea for *Romeo and Juliet* as "contemptible," thus hoisting me with my own petard. But to me it makes the story more immediate and vivid, because it springs from the unreasoning hatred of two houses. Furthermore, I believe the lesson of the tragic result of such hatred is a salutary one for the times. Never were Benvolio's words more pertinent: "These hot days is the mad blood stirring." I wanted further to emphasize the difference between the two houses by dressing all the Capulets in shades of red and all the Montagues in shades of blue. Tybalt, who would be a sort of Black Power advocate, was to be in vivid red.

Somewhat to my surprise, my idea was warmly welcomed by the festival people in Washington, and I became excited about it, especially after I had preliminary conferences with the designers, Bob Troll and John Peter Halford, who were very stimulated by the idea. Originally I meant the production to be timeless and somewhat abstract in setting, but it is the most romantic of all tales and calls for color and warmth. Finally, it was decided to give it a setting reminiscent of New Orleans in the first half of the nineteenth century, although it was not to be a slavish reproduction of that place and period; the procession to the masked ball would have a feeling of Mardi Gras. It was essential to Shakespeare's play that both families should be "alike in dignity"; consequently, our production could have no relevance to the economic plight of so many American Negroes today. There would be forty-two people in the cast and, quite without design, half would be colored and half white. Washington is predominantly a Negro city, and I hoped this *Romeo and Juliet* would bring them out to see it in great numbers; very few of them came to see the *Hamlet*, although both the King and the Ghost were Negroes.

While we were still planning the production of *Romeo and Juliet*, the world was shocked by the assassination of Martin Luther King. Would the spilling of the blood of that peace-loving martyr cause more blood to be spilled, or would his sacrifice achieve more quickly those things for which he died? Of one thing I am sure: had he lived, he would have approved of the black-and-white *Romeo and Juliet*, and would probably have honored it with his presence. For a time we wondered if his murder would cause the abandonment of our project, but the production did take place.

Activities associated with Resurrection City and the Poor People's March caused us some slight inconvenience during rehearsals, by pre-empting the theatre for a few days. For three more days the police advised us not to use the theatre, but the cast unanimously decided, although with some trepidation, to ignore the warning, and we suffered no harassment of any kind. Our greatest difficulty was in finding enough local Negroes willing and able to fill the subsidiary parts, but this was finally and happily solved; the resulting company was one of the most congenial with which I have ever worked. We had, perhaps, more than the usual quota of crises. Thus, Romeo was taken to hospital on the second day of rehearsal with viral meningitis, and during a performance of the final scene Paris was wounded by a dagger that punctured his lung. Both eventually returned to the cast.

As I expected, the production was a very beautiful one, and I was proud of its total effect. It is thrilling to think that, weather willing, more people are likely to see it than will see any other summer production of Shakespeare anywhere in the world, for it will be the sole production of the festival and will play for six weeks to sometimes as many as five thousand people at a performance. From my point of view, the black-and-white casting of the hostile houses worked admirably, because several spectators made the same comment to me: "After the first half-hour we forgot the color difference, and just saw the people." A half-hour in the theatre; how long outside?

Chapter Ten

Shakespeare

This final chapter is both a footnote and a climax to the other nine. In my teens I discovered Shakespeare for myself. I sometimes think that self-education is the best and most abiding education; I certainly have forgotten most of what I was taught in school and college. When I became an untaught teacher of English in the high school in Port Talbot, I tried to show my pupils some of the riches I had found in Shakespeare, and avoided as far as possible consideration of textual, verbal, and grammatical quibbles. I pointed out to them that sometimes their ear was a surer guide to the truth than the scholarly footnote; for instance, in this passage from the Chorus of *Henry V*,

> Now entertain conjecture of a time
> When creeping murmur and the poring dark
> Fills the wide vessel of the universe,

every footnote I have ever read on the word "poring" says that it means peering through the dark, yet it is quite clear that the complete metaphor implies that darkness is pouring into the vessel of the universe; the very scholars who warn you to pay little attention to Elizabethan spelling—Shakespeare's own name in contemporary documents is spelled half-a-dozen different ways —have been themselves caught by "poring" over a word instead of listening to a poet.

The more I studied Shakespeare the more I realized what a superb master of the theatre he was, and when I ceased to be a schoolmaster, I found great joy in discussing his characters with actors and passing on to them such insights as I had gained. Shakespeare belongs to the theatre and only becomes fully alive there. His text is no more his play than the score of a symphony is a symphony, and no less. The fact that the text and the score often get maltreated and misinterpreted in performance does not mean that they do not rely on performance for their full life. Thus I have no patience with that kind of academic criticism that regards the characters as personified abstractions with no life beyond their words. They were written by an actor to be played by actors, and to be brought by them to a full and vibrant life on the stage.

I settled in America at a time when there was a revival of interest in Shakespeare in the theatre, and I found that actors were ill at ease with him. There was a feeling that he belonged to the English, as though the many notable American players of Shakespeare had never lived. He belongs to all English-speaking peoples, and much American speech is nearer to his own than most of what is heard in England. It was to overcome the American resistance to Shakespeare that, without meaning to, I found myself increasingly engaged in talking about his plays to actors, in holding classes in which I tried to teach them to understand and revel in him. And now I find myself talking about him to audiences all over the country. It seems that the reluctant teacher is destined to be an apostle of Shakespeare for the rest of his life. In that sense this chapter is the climax of this book.

But what to say in it? The subject requires several books, not one chapter. For my present purpose, I shall content myself with some examples of my approach to Shakespeare for actors, in the hope that others than actors may find some stimulation in them.

First, I beg my students to become thoroughly grounded in the text of a play before reading critical studies of it; very few such studies are going to help them anyway. Next, they must learn to trust the text; Shakespeare means what he says. Thus in *Othello* Iago tells us that he is "four times seven years"—the arithmetical sum that we automatically do when we hear those words will help to fix the age in our minds—whereas Othello tells us that he is somewhat "declined into the vale of years," and yet I have seen a production of the play in which the Iago was not only much older than the Othello, but was obviously so. Shakespeare is rarely specific about ages; when he is, we should do well to pay attention to it. Why, for instance, does he stress the fact that Juliet is not yet fourteen, whereas she is sixteen in the story he used as his source? Nothing gives a clearer indication of Shakespeare's intentions in a play than the changes he deliberately makes in the stories upon which they are based.

It seems to me that Juliet's age is crucial to our understanding of the play; it stresses her sexual innocence. She is not ignorant about the game of love and the acts of sex, for she has been suckled and reared by that most lovably earthy character, the Nurse. She knows all about the rules of dalliance, that, even though she loves him, the lady must appear to shun the advances of the lord, but in the balcony scene all rules melt in the ardor of an overwhelming love; and she breaks the cardinal rule of the game by being the first to mention marriage, and urging an immediate one. "Fain would I dwell on form," she says, and she is well schooled in the required behavior, but she cannot so dwell.

Romeo, on the other hand, seems to me to be a sophisticate. He was probably written to be played originally by Richard Burbage, who was born in 1567. Conjectural dates for the writing of the play vary from 1591 to 1596, but the most commonly accepted date is 1595, by which time Burbage would have been twenty-eight. In an era when the expectation of life was much shorter than ours, boys became men at a much younger age than they do now; thus it is reasonable to assume that Burbage's Romeo was a mature man; the actor had already played Richard III. We get a good indication of Romeo's character by considering that of Mercutio, that delightfully bawdy and exuberant cynic. Why does Shakespeare make him the kind of witty man-about-town he is? His function in the plot is to get killed by Tybalt, and any amiable friend of Romeo would serve that purpose—Benvolio for instance. But Mercutio's bright sophistication reflects that of Romeo, for in their battle of wits it is Mercutio who cries quits. At the beginning of the play Romeo is mooning about his lady, Rosaline; he is playing the game of love, enjoying the sorrowful delights of rejection, for Rosaline is also playing her set part in the patterned game. Romeo is in love with love, as is Orsino in *Twelfth Night*, but the game is forgotten in the overwhelming experience of true love. When the mature Romeo meets the tremulous beauty of innocence, who offers herself to him in all her honest fragility, but with clear intelligence and full knowledge, he undergoes something of a spiritual experience. It is not for nothing that their first dialogue is cast in the form of a sonnet, a sort of liturgy of love, and that it is based upon religious figures of speech, albeit set in a light bantering tone.

I am not suggesting that *Romeo and Juliet* is a Lolita story, nor that Juliet must be played by a fourteen-year-old girl, but that the encounter of sophistication with innocence is at the heart of it, and that it is with these qualities that the parts should be played.

This poetic use of age is characteristic of Shakespeare. How old is Hamlet? There is only one clear indication, and that is in the graveyard scene, after his return from England, when we learn by implication that he is thirty years old. But he is a student in the university at the beginning of the play, and in Elizabethan days students usually left the university at the age at which they now enter; we are to think of him as a very young man. The action of the play occupies but a few months and yet in that time Hamlet has aged ten years. This, I think, is precisely what Shakespeare intends; the Hamlet who returns from England is a much more mature man than the one who left Denmark.

What of King Lear's "four score and upward"? This precision is Shakespeare's; Holinshed, his source for the story, mentions only Lear's "great yeres," and that he reigned "fortie yeeres." But Holinshed does set the story in ancient biblical times, "in the year of the world 3105, at what time Joas reigned in Juda," and Shakespeare takes the hint. Antiquarianism is a comparatively recent study—neither Shakespeare nor his audience found anything amiss in having in ancient Rome clocks that struck the hour—but he does strive to set King Lear in pre-Christian and pagan Britain; thus he carefully avoids the use of the word "God" in favor of "the gods." Eighty was a phenomenal age to the Elizabethans, and they would regard it as a mythical longevity, in much the same way as we regard Methuselah's nine hundred years. Lear is not a doddering old man; minutes before his death he carries onstage a fully grown woman, and sets her down gently, which most actors find more difficult than carrying her on. He is a gigantic Job, except that he brings his sufferings upon himself; in his madness he achieves true wisdom and acquires the stature of an Old Testament prophet. What is to me the theme of the play, purification through suffering, is also biblical. Incidentally, Lear's madness and his tragic fate are entirely Shakespeare's invention, and it is these which change a sad tale with a happy ending to a great tragedy of cosmic significance.

To such considerations are we led by contemplating those rare instances in which Shakespeare gives a specific age to his characters. From the foregoing it is abundantly clear that I attach much importance to comparing the story he took from other writers with the one he made his own, always from the standpoint of helping the actor to be true to Shakespeare's intention. A notable example occurs in the case of *Measure for Measure,* in which we are given a brilliant and timeless study of the lustful Puritan Angelo, who is so highly sexed that, like the alcoholic who must completely forswear liquor, he must deny his desires, because to indulge them would foil his drive to political power. However, when he achieves that power, he cruelly punishes in others the gratification of the lust he denies in himself. It is Shakespeare's intention in Isabella that is most clearly revealed by comparing her with her counterpart in the original story. In both stories her brother, Claudio, is the first victim of an old law that Angelo revives, making adultery punishable by death. In both stories she pleads with Angelo to show mercy to Claudio, and in both stories Angelo is so overwhelmed by desire for Isabella that he promises to spare her brother if she will sleep with him. But now occurs the deeply significant difference: In the original, Isabella does sleep with Angelo, who nevertheless fails to keep his promise to her; in *Measure for Measure* she does not sleep with him—a substitute for his bed is somewhat clumsily contrived —and to make the point clearer, Shakespeare makes Isabella a novice, a deeply religious woman whose destiny seems to be that she will become a nun. The actress must make us believe her when she says, "More than our brother is our Chastity." This is no pious resignation to imposed moral standards, but a fiery assertion of spiritual values. Isabella is deeply and angrily shocked when she finds that Claudio, who also professes them, loses them in his fear of death. She had expected

> That, had he twenty heads to render down
> On twenty bloody blocks, he'd yield them up
> Before his sister should her body stoop
> To such abhorred pollution.

It was G. K. Chesterton who pointed out that white is not an absence of color, but a very positive one, that goodness is not merely an absence of evil, but a strong assertion of the contrary principle. Isabella really believes that death is but the gateway to eternity, believes it with her whole being, not merely with the usual acquiescence to an inherited belief, and this puts the death of her brother into what is to many people an unreal perspective. However much the actress playing Isabella feels that, in refusing to sleep with Angelo, she is making an undue fuss about very little, she must imaginatively assume the values Shakespeare intended Isabella to have, or she cannot play her. She must have no reservations about her angry outburst to Claudio when he begs her to accede to Angelo's condition in order to save his life:

> Die, perish! Might but my bending down
> Reprieve thee from thy fate, it should proceed.
> I'll pray a thousand prayers for thy death,
> No word to save thee.

The actress who is embarrassed by that speech should avoid Isabella, as, when she gets old enough to play her, she should avoid Lorca's Yerma, that study of a peasant woman who felt that motherhood was her welcome destiny, only to be frustrated by the impotence of her husband. Why didn't she divorce him and marry a man who could give her a child? Divorce was as impossible to Yerma as adultery was to Isabella.

All dramatists share the ability to create characters that come alive on the stage, but, granted this common talent, there are two main impulses that separate them. There are those like Arthur Miller and Ben Jonson, whose main preoccupation is with man in relation to society, and those like Tennessee Williams and William Shakespeare, whose main preoccupation is with man in relation to himself and God. This latter is the abiding problem binding Samuel Beckett to Sophocles. The social dramatists tend to have a shorter span of significance than the personal ones, who endure and speak to men of all ages when their voice is great enough to have universality. But there is one play of Shakespeare in which his voice has become distorted by the experience of mankind since his day, and that is *The Merchant of Venice*. Buchenwald and Belsen make us see Shylock as a mistreated Jew and not the villainous moneylender Shakespeare saw, although his godlike compassion made him see the human being in the conventional villain. That stock character is well known in Indian literature dealing with village life, where the moneylender is a blight upon the village economy. So much has Shylock become the center of interest in the play that one New York critic wrote of "Morris Carnovsky in the title role," although it is clear that that honor belongs to Antonio, a much neglected part. In the trial scene Portia says, "Which is the merchant here, and which the Jew?" If it really were a play about Shylock, it would be a bad one, because he does not appear in the fifth act. Henry Irving remedied this error of Shakespeare by cutting out the fifth act and tying the plot up very quickly at the end of the trial scene. Why does Shakespeare give the title of the play to a second-string character? Because he embodies the ideal of the play, which is about money and the love of it, and Antonio is the man to whom it means nothing, while Shylock is the man to whom it means everything.

Seen from this point of view, Bassanio is the man who is converted from his love of money by his love of a woman. He starts out as a blatant fortune hunter in pursuit of Portia. His first description of her is that she is "richly left," and many Jasons come in quest of her golden fleece. He relies on winning her to repay his debts, but then really falls in love with her and must be overwhelmed with guilt at his original mercenary motives. It is for this reason, surely, that he chooses lead in preference to gold and silver, as a sign that his values have changed. To me it is an infuriating debasement of the theme when the director makes Portia signal the right casket to Bassanio by stressing the rhyme with "lead" in the song, "Tell me where is fancy bred." Portia is one of Shakespeare's most brilliant heroines—her opening description of her suitors is a dazzling display of insight and wit—and she must know what is happening to Bassanio; thus, the speech in which she gives him everything has a beautiful poignancy, because it is the complete proof of her absolute trust in his now unsullied love.

Many an actress has had trouble with Portia's famous plea to

Shylock to show mercy, because it appears that the clever lawyer is cruelly playing a cat-and-mouse game with the Jew until she finally robs him of his revenge with the "Shed thou no blood" ploy, which she carefully conceals until the lethal moment. But this is to miss the essence of the play. The object of the "quality of mercy" speech is to try to deliver Shylock from his own obsession, which can only be achieved by an act of compassion on his part. It is not for Antonio's life that Portia is pleading—that is already assured by the legal loophole she has discovered—but for Shylock's salvation, for his deliverance from his devil.

Time, too, has made our full acceptance of Jessica difficult. No longer do we sympathize, as we are meant to, with her running away from a home that she describes as "hell." Now we tend to regard her escape as the desertion of a lonely and ostracized old man. And the final decision of the court, that as part of his penalty "he presently become a Christian," is to us both cruel and absurd. To sum up, I really think it is impossible fully to reveal to modern audiences the intentions of Shakespeare in *The Merchant of Venice*; history has turned the villain into the victim.

Shakespeare is very careful to engage our sympathies as his stories need, and takes pains to restore the balance if they are in danger of tipping to the wrong side. Malvolio, in *Twelfth Night*, is an interesting example. Never should we forget the meaning of his name: Ill-Wisher. Even Olivia, who says that she would not have him miscarry for half her dowry, says to him in his first scene, "O, you are sick of self-love, Malvolio, and taste with a distempered appetite." Shakespeare is very conscious of the importance of first entrances, and so should actors be; first impressions on the stage are as potent as they are in life. Malvolio has to suffer some belittling and even harsh indignities during the play, and Shakespeare prefaces each of them with a reminder that he deserves some measure of punishment. Just before he is to be trapped by the device of the fake letter, we meet a new character in the play, Fabian, another member of Olivia's household, and an amiable fellow, whom Malvolio has tried to bring out of favor with her by carrying tales about his going to a bear-baiting. And again, just before the whole plot against Malvolio is to be revealed at the end of the play, we are once more reminded of his apparently motiveless malice; the admirable sea captain, who helped Viola in her distress after the shipwreck, we suddenly learn is in prison "at Malvolio's suit." Fabian tries to put the treatment of Malvolio in proper perspective:

> How with a sportful malice it was followed
> May rather pluck on laughter than revenge,
> If that the injuries be justly weighed
> That have on both sides passed.

But Malvolio, true to the end to his sick self, goes out angrily, saying, "I'll be revenged on the whole pack of you."

There are innumerable engaging little detective puzzles throughout Shakespeare, and Fabian is one of them. When one compares today the script of a new play as it goes into rehearsal with the script of the play as it opens on Broadway, the remarkable thing about Shakespeare's text is not that there are so many difficulties but there are so few. Changes must have occurred in rehearsal, and probably still more in subsequent revivals of a play, and in those days script copies were very few and jealously guarded; rival companies would be happy to get their hands on the script of a successful play, for there was no copyright law to prevent them from performing it. The first printed copy of *Twelfth Night* is in the First Folio, thus appearing more than twenty years after its first performance, and seven years after Shakespeare's death. It amuses me to think that the unexplained appearance of Fabian may have been the result, in some production of the play, of a theatrical crisis of the kind that seems an inevitable part of theatre, and must always have been so. Maria tells Sir Toby and Sir Andrew, "I will plant you two, and let the fool make a third, where he shall find the letter"; but when we get to the scene, the fool is absent, without any explanation, and in his place we find

Fabian, of whom Shakespeare makes the use I have already noted. It could be that this incident is tied up with an apparent contradiction in the play. Viola, in adopting the disguise of Cesario in order to enter the Duke's service, says,

> I can sing
> And speak to him in many sorts of music.

It seems to me clear that the boy who originally played the part —possibly Shakespeare's own young brother, Edmund, younger than the poet by sixteen years—sang the beautiful song "Come away, come away, death," but that by the time of a revival a year or two later, incipient manhood had claimed his dulcet soprano tones; yet they wanted to keep him in the part as long as possible, so the actor who played Feste was prevailed upon to sing it. (That throws another light upon the character too, for his secret moonlighting emphasizes his professional and mercenary nature; he will sing for whoever pays him, if he can get away with it, although he is under exclusive contract to another management.) My conjecture is that the actor agreed, with the stipulation that he should be excused from the garden scene, which was Malvolio's anyway, and in which Feste would be reduced to being one of three hidden heads, just bobbing up for an occasional comment; thus was Fabian born, to take his place.

Perhaps the most brilliant instance of Shakespeare's control of our sympathies is in the character of Richard II. In the beginning of the play we are led to despise him for his weakness and his malicious cruelty. When he is sent for to visit his sick uncle, John of Gaunt, that epitome of selfless patriotism, he says:

> Now put it, God, in the physician's mind
> To help him to his grave immediately!
>
> .   .   .   .
>
> Pray God we may make haste, and come too late!

And his last words to the dying old man are,

> And let them die that age and sullens have,
> For both hast thou, and both become the grave.

By the end of the play this same man commands our total respect and admiration. How is this wonder accomplished? First, he takes him off to Ireland and out of our sight for four scenes, during which we meet his sorrowing Queen, who is consumed by love and concern for her "sweet Richard"; also we learn that the opposition to him is growing to fatal proportions, but he is blissfully unaware of it; sympathy for the all-unknowing underdog is aroused in us. Then when we do see him again, he is made slowly aware of his imminent and inevitable downfall, and he begins to grow in stature as his delight in the panoply of kingship is transmuted into love of England. His realization of his common humanity is revealed in deeply moving words:

> I live with bread like you, feel want,
> Taste grief, need friends. Subjected thus,
> How can you say to me I am a king?

From this point on, his descent to defeat, deposition, and death takes on a spiritual quality, so much so that we feel no hint of presumption or blasphemy when he says,

> Yet I well remember
> The favors of these men. Were they not mine?
> Did they not sometime cry "All hail!" to me?
> So Judas did to Christ. But He in twelve
> Found truth in all but one; I in twelve thousand,
> None.

Richard makes his new sense of values explicit in his final scene with the Queen: "Our holy lives must win a new world's crown." Our last view of him sets the seal on our admiration, for he surprises us by fighting manfully and hopelessly against heavy odds. His murderer pays him a final tribute: "As full of valor as of royal blood." *Richard II* is Shakespeare's first treatment of the theme of purification through suffering, which was to achieve its supreme expression in *King Lear*.

There is an aspect of Shakespeare, suggested by *Richard II*, that much intrigues me; it is the connection between the lyrical poet and the dramatist. There was a time when the dramatist had some difficulty in keeping the poet in check. Having just written the very successful long poems *Venus and Adonis* and *The Rape of Lucrece*, and working now on the sonnets, the poet strained at the restrictions of dramatic necessity, and the result was the three most lyrical plays: *Richard II*, in which there is not one line of prose, *Romeo and Juliet*, and *A Midsummer Night's Dream*. All these plays contain passages of the most exquisite lyricism, and therefore are the most difficult plays for actors whose tongues are not completely attuned to poetry. From the point of view of the language, Henry V is an easier role than Richard II, Hamlet than Romeo, Olivia than Titania. But the dramatist never really lost control, and a most wonderful association evolved between him and the poet. The dramatist used his lyrical gifts in much the same way as music is used in a well-constructed modern musical play; when words are no longer enough to express the feeling of the situation, be it love or hate, ecstasy or anger, a heady happiness or a deep despair, music steals in and serves to unburden the heart. In much the same way the lyrical temperature will rise in a Shakespearean play. It is for this, probably subconscious, reason that in *Romeo and Juliet*, a play suffused with lyricism, the dialogue becomes a formal sonnet to heighten the pitch of the first meeting between the two lovers.

One further example in which the heightened poetry serves a purely dramatic purpose must suffice. It is from *Twelfth Night*. Here Shakespeare achieves, as he often did, what would be dismissed as impossible if it were given as an exercise in a playwriting class. Briefly the situation is that a great lady has been told that a young messenger boy, from a noble lord who is in love with her and refuses to take no for an answer, has been impudent to the head of her large body of household servants. The messenger is standing at the gate of her lodge and refuses to go away until he has seen her. In a mixture of amusement, curiosity, and annoyance, she decides to see him; it will relieve the tedium of the day and serve to put him in his place. Within five minutes she has fallen desperately in love with the young boy, and, through Shakespeare's wizardry, we believe it. How has he accomplished this impossible feat? It happens that the boy is a disguised girl, herself in love with the lord whose messenger she is. It would take a line-by-line analysis to show how the emotional tone of the scene subtly changes as the girl expresses her true feelings under the cover of her disguise. This ambivalence is shown by the gradual intrusion of verse upon the prose with which the scene opens, like music beneath the dialogue in a musical play that is working up to a song, until at last the beautiful melody bursts forth. More and more intrigued by the mystery of the messenger, the lady is led to ask what he would do if he, like his master, were hopelessly in love. This gives the girl the chance to express and yet keep secret her own hidden love. In answer to the lady's question, she says:

> Make me a willow cabin at your gate,
> And call upon my soul within the house;
> Write loyal cantons of contemned love
> And sing them loud even in the dead of night;
> Halloo your name to the reverberate hills,
> And make the babbling gossip of the air
> Cry out "Olivia!" Oh, you should not rest
> Between the elements of air and earth,
> But you should pity me!

Small wonder that, after a brief silence and half to herself, the lady says, "You might do much," and follows this with the inquiry, the eagerness of which she finds difficulty in hiding, "What is your parentage?" She obviously hopes that it is Prince Charming in disguise.

I often give the "willow cabin" speech to my students as a test of whether they are deeply sensitive to poetry, for it owes its magic to all that distinguishes it from prose; indeed, if the lines were reduced to their prosaic meaning, the result would be arrant nonsense: The desperate lover would spend his life at the gate leading to his beloved's mansion, and there he would build a cabin of a most unsuitable timber, and spend his days in writing love songs and his nights in singing them. But, of course, that isn't what it means at all. It is the perfect expression of a love doomed to die unsatisfied. The willow is not a timber, but the symbol of a beautiful sorrow. "Soul" is the magical word in the next line. If the word "heart" or "love" is substituted, the echo of the word "call" is lost. The third line is a triumphant expression of the bitterness of frustration. If it is changed to "Write loyal verses of despised love," the actress is robbed of the sounds of Viola's misery. Incidentally, that word "cantons" was made up by Shakespeare for the occasion, as a substitute for "cantos," and it is its sole use in literature. But how much stronger on the tongue it is than the usual word! Just as Shakespeare felt the need for the sound, so must the actress. I have often wondered if Shakespeare had derived the feeling for that line from his Stratford schoolmaster, Thomas Jenkins, or from some other Welshman, for it is closely akin to the essential Welsh verse form of cynghanedd, which is based upon the balancing of sounds within a line. To judge from his plays, Shakespeare delighted in the Welsh; he gave us Glendower, Fluellen (his English attempt at the unique consonantal sound with which the Welsh name "Llewellyn" begins), and Sir Hugh Evans; his Lady Mortimer speaks and sings only in Welsh, and has to be interpreted by her father.

What actors most need from me is help in the understanding and interpretation of their characters, and perhaps it may be of interest if I illustrate my approach by discussing two characters whom I think to be consistently misinterpreted: Polonius and Lady Macbeth.

Most actors base their characterization of Polonius on Hamlet's remark ending a scene in which he has been baiting the old man under cover of his pretended madness. In his exasperation at being treated warily as though he indeed were the madman he has led Polonius to think him to be, Hamlet vents his annoyance with the phrase, "These tedious old fools!" To accept this as the whole truth is as misleading as to believe that Cassius says the whole truth about Caesar when he denigrates him, for his own purposes, to Brutus. Hamlet has much reason to be furious with Polonius, and to be deeply suspicious of him. He has transferred his loyalty to the new King, as indeed he should, but to Hamlet it is yet another proof of the frailty of vows. Then again, Ophelia has suddenly been denied to Hamlet, and he must suspect the interfering hand of her father. It is probable that there is something in Polonius of Lord Burghley, Queen Elizabeth's devoted, but crafty, counselor for forty years, who was the bitter enemy of the Earl of Essex, of whom it is equally probable Shakespeare was an admirer. It has been argued that there is something of Essex in Hamlet. Essex's attitude to Burghley is certainly mirrored in that of Hamlet to Polonius. By the time Shakespeare wrote *Hamlet*, Burghley had been safely dead a few years, and Essex so recently that he must have been much in Shakespeare's thoughts. Polonius is often tedious and is certainly old, but he is no fool. Although he is proud of his long record of successful service to the throne, he is willing to acknowledge that he was wrong about Hamlet's regard for Ophelia.

> I am sorry that with better heed and judgment
> I had not quoted him. I feared he did but trifle
> And meant to wreck thee, but beshrew my jealousy!
> By Heaven, it is as proper to our age
> To cast beyond ourselves in our opinions
> As it is common for the younger sort
> To lack discretion.

There is considerable evidence in the text that Polonius in his youth had been a gay blade; he obviously doesn't disapprove of the kind of life he expects Laertes to be living in Paris, for it will

be but an echo of his own youth. It is his own remembered propensities that make him fear Hamlet's designs on his beloved
daughter; a lecher is cynical about a lover. Hamlet refers to these
values of Polonius when he says "He's for a jig or a tale of
bawdry, or he sleeps." A distrust of people is a fundamental part
of the nature of Polonius, and, like Lord Burghley, he depends
upon spies and informers. It is the only way he knows of working,
and he employs it in his family. He gives detailed instructions to
Reynaldo on how to spy upon Laertes in Paris; he uses his own
daughter as a decoy for Hamlet; he meets his death by spying on a
meeting he has arranged between Hamlet and his mother. But this
worldly old man is full of pragmatic wisdom. His famous speech
to his son is full of excellent advice; what is more, it is directed to
a particular person, and therefore, by implication, gives us some
insight into the character of Laertes, for his father knows him to
need this particular advice. We already know that he shares his
father's values about love and sex, for he too has warned Ophelia
to "be wary" of Hamlet, and to keep "out of the shot and danger
of desire." We gather from his father's admonitions that Laertes
tends to be free of tongue, too ready to make friends, somewhat
ostentatious in his dress, and, in money matters, generous when
his purse is full and quick to borrow when it isn't. Like his father,
too, he becomes a pawn of the King, and like his father, dies a
victim of his own dishonorable act.

The indications of Laertes' character seen in his father's advice
to him are an illustration of one of the ways in which an actor can
find the signposts to his part. Another occurs in Hamlet's praise
of Horatio. It is usual to value most highly in our friends those
qualities that we lack. Hamlet says:

> . . . thou hast been
> As one in suffering all that suffers nothing
> . . . Give me that man
> That is not passion's slave, and I will wear him
> In my heart's core . . .

Hamlet betrays his suffering to the world; more, he parades it, by ostentatiously wearing black in a court that is celebrating a wedding. And most certainly he is "passion's slave"; impetuosity that o'er-leaps the bounds of reason is characteristic of him.

I always warn my students against dismissing too readily some passages that seem to have little dramatic relevance. Thus, for example, when Hamlet denounces the new King's revival of a practice which had been "more honored in the breach than the observance" during his brother's reign, we learn much about father, brother, and son. The old Viking practice was that during a royal party at night, trumpet and kettledrum sounded whenever the king took a deep draught of wine. Hamlet uses very derogatory terms in talking of this custom:

> The King doth wake tonight and takes his rouse,
> Keeps wassail and the swaggering upspring reels.
> And as he drinks his draughts of Rhenish down,
> The kettledrum and trumpet thus bray out
> The triumph of his pledge.

Hamlet's further comments contain the words, "heavy-headed revel," "drunkards," "swinish." From all this I gather that his father had been somewhat austere and puritanical, and that, by contrast, Claudius was uninhibited and sensual, "Hyperion to a satyr"; they reflect the Stoic-Epicurean contrast as shown in Brutus and Antony, and in the clash between the City and the Court, a basic fact of Shakespeare's theatrical life and which ultimately was to result in the beheading of a king, Charles I. Claudius is sexually very attractive to Gertrude, who probably found her first husband more admirable than enjoyable. Hamlet inherits his father's values; time and again he denounces sexual license, and when he feels his pure Ophelia is tainted by the values of her father, her brother, and the court, he abuses her in terms of sexual degradation. The appearance of chastity as a mask for lust he sums up in his punning use of the word "nunnery," which was a nickname in Elizabethan times for a brothel, and a part of the sarcastic legacy of the Reformation in England. How different all this is from Hamlet's charmingly innocent love letter, which Polonius has obtained from Ophelia and reads to the King; to the master-of-spies, Polonius, the intimate letter is but a captured document. I find that consideration of Hamlet, Shakespeare's most fascinating character, is beginning to creep into these pages, despite my determination to deal only with Polonius and merely to illustrate my approach to the text. I must desist forthwith, lest he take over chapter, book, and me.

I said some chapters back that my whole personal exploration of Shakespeare really began as a result of seeing a production of *Macbeth*, in which the leading players were Henry Ainley and Sybil Thorndike. I felt something was wrong; Burbage could never have been dominated by a boy player as Ainley was by Thorndike. The Sarah Siddons tradition is at fault. Hazlitt says of her Lady Macbeth: "We can conceive of nothing grander. It was something above nature. It seemed almost as if a being of a superior order had dropped from a higher sphere to awe the world with the majesty of her presence. Power was seated on her brow, passion emanated from her breast as from a shrine; she was tragedy personified." Such a description, it seems to me, would have been more appropriately accorded to a performance of Macbeth. Advocates and portrayers of this powerful Lady Macbeth find difficulty with her fainting, and are reduced to assuming that she pretended to faint to distract attention from her husband. But I feel sure that, if this had been Shakespeare's intention, he would have left us in no doubt about it. The Lady Macbeth I see in the text would have fainted. To me she is completely a woman, not partly a monster. She is a woman who really needs the help of the infernal powers to "unsex" her. Some actresses I have seen play the part need the help of no such prayer.

The truth about Lady Macbeth is revealed in the sleepwalking scene, in which she relives the murder as she actually felt it. Now there is no mask of callousness, which she had assumed to help her husband to go through with the plan. Then she had said, "A little water clears us of this deed," but that only covered the truth, now revealed in sleep: "What, will these hands ne'er be clean? . . . all the perfumes of Arabia will not sweeten this little hand." She had said to him, "What's done is done." That is now subtly and revealingly changed to "What's done cannot be undone." She, much less than he, is unable to follow her own advice, and eschew

> . . . those thoughts which should indeed have died
> With them they think on.

The doctor says of her, "Her heart is sorely charged." It most certainly is, and she is finally driven to commit suicide. In sharp contrast, Macbeth died fighting a hopeless fight.

Macbeth and his lady are very different in temperament. Shakespeare often thinks in terms of dramatic contrasts, even in physical terms—tall and short, fat and thin, old and young—and in the Macbeths he seems to be dealing with a particular difference of temperaments: the overimaginative and the underimaginative. To Macbeth, "Present fears are less than horrible imaginings," and this he tells us in his first soliloquy, which gives it a primary significance. He has no difficulty in committing the deed of murder, only in contemplating it. Once the deed is done, he can describe it in gory detail. Lady Macbeth, on the other hand, can face the thought, but not the fact. Once she has seen the bloody corpse of Duncan, she can never forget it. It is with her in her sleep: "Yet who would have thought the old man to have had so much blood in him?" When Macbeth brazenly describes the corpse he has himself made, "his silver skin laced with his golden blood," she faints, because she has seen it. She knows her weakness, and in her invocation to the powers of evil, she prays that the night be so dark, "that my keen knife see not the wound it makes." Unlike Macbeth, she sees no visions of bloody daggers and ghosts with "gory locks." She sarcastically dismisses both as "the very painting of your fear." Where he sees a ghost, she sees an empty stool. But she can never forget the bloody daggers and the gory corpse that she has seen.

I always stress the fact to actors that even the greatest figures of tragedy are different from us only in degree, and in seeking to play them they must find that seed of identification that will grow into a performance of truth, and hopefully of stature. The Macbeths have their diminished equivalents in many an ambitious bourgeois couple. Husband and wife are as one in achieving their ambition; he needed all her help in rationalizing the expedient, in quelling those scruples she actually shared but pretended not to, so that she would not have to live with a disappointed and frustrated man. But once the position is achieved, he no longer needs her, and no longer even tells her the secrets of the intrigue in his professional life. "Be innocent of the knowledge, dearest chuck, till thou applaud the deed." Often these days it results in a divorce in middle age; in the case of the Macbeths, it led her to a lonely suicide.

I do not mean to suggest that Lady Macbeth does not share the ambition of her lord, but she does not use him merely to satisfy her own ambition. He it is who first mentions "murder," and this in his first soliloquy; and she reminds him that it was he who first broached the subject to her. He complains, "I have no spur to prick the sides of my intent," but he has; it is his wife; that is her function in the marriage.

The old question of whether the Macbeths have children again implies, as in the case of Hamlet's apparently contradictory ages, the criterion of statistics rather than that of Shakespeare's poetic necessity. When Lady Macbeth needs to use a supreme argument to accuse Macbeth of weakness of will, she says:

> I have given suck, and know
> How tender 'tis to love the babe that milks me.
> I would, while it was smiling in my face,
> Have plucked my nipple from his boneless gums
> And dashed the brains out, had I so sworn as you
> Have done to this.

But later Macduff says of Macbeth, "He has no children." Some commentators, to resolve the contradiction, have suggested that Macduff is speaking of Malcolm, but this interpretation sacrifices the essence of Macduff's feeling, which is that full revenge for the murder of his children is impossible because Macbeth has none. Surely the truth is an artistic one; in the first instance, Shakespeare needed Lady Macbeth to have had a child, so that she could use it as an argument, and in the second instance, it was an equally dramatic necessity that they had no children. If the actress is worried by the contradiction, it will do no harm for her to assume that the child died, and that this commonplace event in Shakespeare's time made it possible to talk of the child without referring to its death. I have invented many such solutions for actors to problems that don't worry me at all, as I'm sure they didn't worry Shakespeare, and which don't worry the audiences that see the plays, unless they have studied them carefully.

Some Shakespearean scholars may be surprised, puzzled, and even infuriated by some of the things I have said; especially those scholars who resolutely ignore the fact that plays are meant to be played, and who tend to regard the texts as the esoteric domain of the learned, which are somehow tainted and diminished by being spoken by unlearned actors. But there is another kind of scholar to whom all actors of Shakespeare owe much: those who have illuminated his world and his theatre; they have enabled us to understand his plays better now than at any time since he lived. And there are a few critics like Granville-Barker whose theatrical knowledge and instincts have helped actors to bring Shakespeare to life on the stage. For my part, in my classes I am a man of the theatre talking to men and women of the theatre about the greatest man of the theatre, and such insights as I have gained are aimed solely at enabling my students to play him better, that they, in turn, may excite me in performance, for since no two men are the same, no two actors are, and so every performance is unique and capable of bringing new light to well-known characters speaking well-known words. I always advise an actor never to approach a part by working out in what ways he can be different; he should work on the truth of the character, confident that it will be different because he himself is unique. To strive to be different betrays an insecurity, and a confident egotism is necessary to survival for an actor.

Since I came to America, Shakespeare has increasingly filled my life. It is appropriate that he should have the last word.

Grateful for the past, I am eager for the future. Shakespeare's Dauphin speaks for me:

> The day shall not be up so soon as I,
> To try the fair adventure of tomorrow.

Postscript

"The fair adventure of tomorrow"? Is the man deaf and blind? Doesn't he watch his television, listen to his radio, read his newspapers and magazines? Isn't he aware of napalm in Vietnam, violence and rioting in America, hypocrisy and lying in high places, and the bomb that can reduce the live world to a dead moon? Yes, he is aware of all these horrors, but he still finds it thrilling to be alive. It is just because every tomorrow is so infinite in its exciting possibilities that the destructive forces must be kept in check at whatever cost. If life were really not worth living, there would be little point in striving to stop the bomb from falling. Love and comradeship and generosity and sacrifice can flourish in the darkest places; blind parents can give birth to seeing children.

I have little patience with husbands and wives who find the future so bleak that they decide to have no children because it is not a fit world in which to bring them up; that is a judgment of presumptuous arrogance. I have more patience when the decision to have no children is a selfish one; that I can understand because it springs from human weakness. Whatever the future may be, we should remember that people have found moments of transcendent happiness in the bleakest hours. If the bomb does fall, it will

237

catch people making love. Life is to be measured by its intensity, not its duration.

Some important modern playwrights are obsessed by the apparent pointlessness of life, in contrast to my own feeling about it, and yet I welcome them and am exhilarated by their questioning. Samuel Beckett's *Waiting for Godot* I consider a truly great play. It may be that he sees life as a mere waiting for an answer that does not come, but the compassionate humor itself with which he depicts those who wait is for me evidence of a quality that makes life worthwhile.

My life has had its share of difficulties and disappointments and sorrows, and I'm sure there are more to come, but it has been, and I know it will continue to be, wonderful to be alive. I love life.